AFTERTHOUGHTS

AFTERTHOUGHTS

By the Right Hon.

GEORGE W. E. RUSSELL

"Epimetheus, the after-thoughted, receiveth access of vigour in looking backward, and groweth reversely from age to youth."

Bayard Taylor.

Essay Index Reprint Series

BOOKS FOR LIBRARIES PRESS
FREEPORT, NEW YORK

First Published 1912
Reprinted 1968

LIBRARY OF CONGRESS CATALOG CARD NUMBER:
68-16975

PRINTED IN THE UNITED STATES OF AMERICA

TO

CHARLES ROBERT

EARL CARRINGTON & KNIGHT OF THE GARTER

WITH AFFECTIONATE REMEMBRANCE

OF OLD DAYS AND DOINGS

IN

"THE COUNTY OF STATESMEN"

CONTENTS

I

LADY DE ROTHSCHILD

LOUISA, LADY DE ROTHSCHILD, died on Thursday, the 22nd of September 1910, at Aston Clinton, near Tring. She was in her ninetieth year, and had been in good health until 10th June, when she had a fall going downstairs. Since then she had been unable to walk, but on 3rd August she was taken to her country house, and had been able to go out in her bath-chair and even in her carriage. But quite recently her general health began to fail, and the end came painlessly.

The Sephardin, or Jews of Spain and Portugal, are the aristocracy of Judaism ; and among the Sephardin there was no more honourable family than that of Montefiore. In the fifteenth century the Montefiores migrated from Spain to Italy. They were established at Ancona in 1630, and subsequently at Leghorn, whence, in the eighteenth century, Moses Vita Montefiore moved to London. This Moses Vita was grandfather of the celebrated philanthropist, Sir Moses Montefiore, and also of Abraham Montefiore, who married Henrietta de Rothschild, of Frankfort, and had, with other children, a daughter, Louisa, born on the 28th of May 1821. Abraham Montefiore died early, and his family were brought up by their mother, who spent several years in Italy and Germany. Her English home was a villa at Stamford Hill, which is now an Industrial Home for Jewish Girls ; and thence she moved to Great Stanhope Street, Mayfair. It was from there that her daughter, Louisa Montefiore, was married in 1840 to Anthony de Rothschild, who was created a baronet in 1847.

Sir Anthony and Lady de Rothschild acquired the estate of Aston Clinton, and built themselves a London house—now 19 Grosvenor Place—on the site of an abolished hospital. The house was remarkable, in an age when Victorian ugliness reigned supreme, for its artistic scheme of decoration (still preserved), as well as for the treasures of painting and bric-à-brac which it contained. Both there and at Aston Clinton, Sir Anthony and Lady de Rothschild exercised a varied and brilliant hospitality, in which what was merely fashionable was agreeably relieved by the presence of such men as Disraeli and Bishop Wilberforce, Thackeray, Charles Villiers, Bernal-Osborne, Robert Lowe, Delane, and Matthew Arnold. The mention of Thackeray's name suggests a pleasant reminiscence of that really kind-hearted man. Lady de Rothschild once remonstrated with him on the contemptuous tone which in his writings he adopted towards the Jewish race. He promptly made amends by inserting the following paragraph in the second chapter of " Pendennis ":

" I saw a Jewish lady only yesterday, with a child

at her knee, and from whose face towards the child there shone a sweetness so angelical that it seemed to form a sort of glory round both."

That child was Constance de Rothschild, afterwards Lady Battersea.

Sir Anthony died in 1876, and Lady de Rothschild disappeared from general society, of which she had never been very fond ; but she continued to receive, both at Aston Clinton and at Grosvenor Place, the friends (and they were neither few nor insignificant) to whom she was most warmly attached. There were no visits which gave her greater pleasure than those of Mr and Mrs Gladstone. Blest, beyond most people, with " the ornament of a meek and quiet spirit," and detesting all forms of self-assertion and display, Lady de Rothschild had gifts of character and intellect which made her society uniquely delightful. Though her life was prolonged, she had none of the infirmities of age. Her memory was singularly retentive, and her accounts of the scenes, events, and personages of her earlier life had a peculiar freshness and piquancy. Not many years before her death she paid a visit to Lord Beaconsfield's grave at Hughenden, and petrified the custodian of the churchyard by telling him that she not only had known Mr Disraeli, but remembered him and Mrs Wyndham Lewis dining at her mother's house before their impending marriage was announced to the world. That was a recollection which linked her to the thirties of the last century; but her interest in the doings and personalities of to-day was as keen as a girl's. She was not in the least degree old-fashioned; she was wholly free from social prejudice, and had an open mind for new views and new customs. She had always been an insatiable reader, and, as the principal languages of the Continent were as familiar to her as her own, her range in literature was very wide. Her conversation was, like her person, exquisitely gentle and refined; but she had a keen eye for absurdities and comicalities, and in matters of serious importance her convictions were clear and resolute. She was gentle in speech and firm in action. She was a lifelong and enthusiastic Liberal, a staunch Free-Trader, and an ardent supporter of all movements which favoured National Temperance. It was obvious to all who had the advantage of intimate conversation with her that none of her opinions were taken at second-hand, but all rested on a strong foundation of careful study and clear thought. Matthew Arnold, after describing the mental gifts of another member of the Rothschild family, added—"but my unapproached favourite is, and will always be, Lady de Rothschild of Aston Clinton"; and, after a sermon by a popular but flowery preacher, he wrote to his mother—"Some of the thinking, or pretended thinking, of the sermon was sophistical and hollow beyond belief; and I was interested in finding how instinctively Lady de Rothschild had seized on this."

But Lady de Rothschild's intellectual gifts, rare and admirable as they were, are less worthy of commemoration than the moral influence which she brought to bear on all who came in contact with her. "Evil speaking, lying, and slandering," vulgar gossip, and malicious tittle-tattle could not live in her presence. She enthroned in the shrine of her inmost heart the highest ideal of life and duty, and that ideal seemed, insensibly and unspokenly, to purify the surrounding air, and to elevate the world in which she lived. Perhaps her most enduring memorial will be found in the quiet village which for fifty-seven years was her home. Aided by her husband and her daughters, and reinforced by the zeal of others whom she had inspired, she converted it into a Poor Man's Paradise.

(Reprinted from *The Times.*)

II

NOT FAMOUS BUT FAITHFUL

According to a heathen poet, that life has not been badly lived which, from first to last, has eluded the observation of the world. Christian poets, or at least poets who lived in Christian times, have not always seen so clearly, or felt so soundly. Success, fame, publicity, triumphs which the world applauds, achievements which leave "footprints on the sands of time"—these, according to our modern singers, are the elements of the truly admirable and satisfying life. A friend of my own, who versified, and often very prettily, for schoolboys, expressed this sentiment with engaging simplicity. He imagined the boys of a Public School answering, one by one, to the roll-call of their names:

> "One by one—and, as they name us,
> Forth we go from boyhood's rule,
> Sworn to be renown'd and famous,
> For the honour of the School."[1]

Of course, much must be conceded to the exigencies of rhyme, and "name us" may have required "famous" for its answering dissyllable; but it was an unlucky combination. Sworn to be renowned, sworn to be famous—these, methinks, are instances of very vain and unprofitable swearing. Whether a man will, or will not, attain renown, whether he will, or will not, "be famous," are issues which lie quite outside the scope of even the most heroic resolve. "Owen Meredith" realized this bitter but salutary truth when he wrote the "Last words of a sensitive second-rate poet":

> "Comfort me not; for, if aught be worse than failure from overstress
> Of a life's prime purpose, it is to sit down with a little success.
> Talk not of Genius baffled. Genius is master of man.
> Genius does what it must, and Talent does what it can."

Genius, I presume, does not lay down plans of life, nor "swear to be renowned" or anything else. It cleaves its unforeseen way through the Empyrean, and commands, even without desiring, certainly without seeking, the admiring regard of the world. Talent, conscious and perhaps over-conscious of itself, sits down and looks ahead, and calculates and resolves; but, not being Genius, it is not "master of man," or superior to adverse fate; and, though it may "swear" with all its heart to be "renowned and famous," it finds too often that it has miscalculated its power.

But, even supposing that renown and fame were objects which lay within the scope of man's resolve, I would submit that the heathen poet taught a sounder philosophy. A life entirely unrenowned, a life which leaves no trace of fame behind it, or a life of utter obscurity and insignificance, may be, and every day is seen to be, an infinitely nobler thing than a career which has filled the world with awe and wonder, has altered the map of Europe, or opened a new era in thought or speculation. The faithful who were not famous are the true benefactors of the race. "The growing good of the world is mainly dependent on unhistoric acts; and that things are not so ill with you and me as they might have been is half owing to the number who lived faithfully a hidden life, and rest in unvisited tombs."

Such thoughts as these were lately forced upon the mind by a Memorial Service held in Westminster Abbey. Such a service in such a place is indeed a signal honour, and in this case it has been censured as excessive and inappropriate. But, in granting it the Dean of Westminster showed a sense for what is really great, which his critics rather conspicuously lacked. Following in his wake, I am moved, before the incident is forgotten, to offer my tribute to the memory of Mr John Talbot.[1]

There are in England some five or six families—scarcely more—which even the most exacting genealogists of Foreign Courts recognize as historically noble. One of these is the House of Talbot, which enjoys the Premier Earldom of England, and held its lands when Domesday Book was compiled. The twentieth Earl of Shrewsbury may "ruffle it," as our forefathers said, with the Esterhazys and the

[1] The Rt. Hon. J. G. Talbot, born Feb, 24, 1835; died Feb. 1, 1911.

Dorias, and bear himself with unabashed front among the Grandees of Spain. A younger son of this great family was father of John Gilbert Talbot, who inherited, together with his historic name, an ample fortune and a charming estate in Kent. He married young, and most happily; soon became M.P. for his county, and, without effort or self-seeking, attained a position in his party and in the House which, in a man of a different mould, might have inspired the resolve to be "renowned and famous." If such desires had ever found a lodgment in John Talbot's bosom, the great event of his mid-career must have stirred them into activity. In May 1878 Mr Gathorne Hardy, who had sate for the University of Oxford since he ousted Mr Gladstone in 1865, was made Lord Cranbrook. It was the most critical moment of the Eastern Question, and feeling on both sides ran furiously high. The representation of the University of Oxford was the most coveted prize of public life. Gladstone himself had said of it that he "desired it with an almost passionate fondness." The Liberals, by a strange perversity of choice, brought forward Professor Henry Smith, a mathematical genius of the highest rank, but so half-hearted a politician that E. A. Freeman said he was better qualified to sit as Member for Laodicea in the Parliament of Asia Minor. The Conservative party in the University asked Mr John Talbot to forsake his seat for West Kent, and to become their representative. It was an extraordinary tribute to his

quiet and dignified character, and a proof of the absolute confidence which everyone felt in his rectitude and straightforwardness. He had no gifts of brilliant speech or writing to attract intellectual admiration, and the fact that he was cousin to Lord Salisbury, then Chancellor of the University, could scarcely have affected more than a very limited section of the voters. The plain truth is that he was invited to accept the most desirable of all places in the House of Commons, simply because he was, and was known to be, a Christian gentleman wholly free from vanity and ambition, and holding with strong conviction those theories of religion and politics from which the University of Oxford will never emancipate itself. So John Talbot ceased to be M.P. for Kent, and entered the lists at Oxford against Henry Smith. Liddon, then a resident in Oxford, wrote thus about the difficulties which beset the issue :—
"To vote for Talbot was to vote for Lord Beaconsfield and his Eastern policy. To vote for Smith was to vote for that variety of Liberals which is too academical to care about questions of right and wrong." But the country clergy, who determine the result of all contests for the Universities, saw in Talbot a man after their own heart, and he was returned by some fifteen hundred votes. For the remainder of his life this quiet, unshowy, unassuming gentleman was installed in the safest of all Parliamentary seats, and, had his inclinations led him that way, it cannot be doubted that some of the great

rewards of political service would have fallen to his lot. He did, indeed, accept a minor office under Lord Beaconsfield, and he held it for two years; but, after the General Election of 1880, he never again was a candidate for office. He felt that his appointed work in life lay elsewhere. If one could connect the idea of passion with a man of such calm and self-controlled temperament, one might say that the Church of England was the passion of John Talbot's life. He loved her with the restrained fervour of the Tractarian school. In Parliament he was the most vigilant defender of her legal rights; and in his daily life, alike in London and at his home in Kent, he was her most strenuous yet most unobtrusive servant. He had learnt from his earliest youth to serve God in serving men, and time would fail to enumerate all the various forms in which he laboured for the spiritual and material benefit of his fellow-creatures. As a diligent Member of Parliament, member of a County Council, Chairman of Quarter Sessions, and in half-a-dozen more places of public duty, he toiled at the secular part of social service; and to more distinctly spiritual works, such particularly as Rescue and Reclamation, he gave a personal devotion which ended only with his life. Such men are the very salt of society. They live their lives in the unrewarded, and almost unrecognized, discharge of self-imposed duty; and by their daily practice show, though they would never dream of saying, that they hold everything they possess—

birth, affluence, leisure, social station—as a stewardship for which an account must one day be rendered.

I knew John Talbot for just on thirty years; and, though I shared none of his political opinions, and perhaps not all his religious ones, I rejoice to lay this most unworthy tribute on his honoured tomb.

III

THE GOLDEN MEAN

Is " the mean " ever entitled to the honorific epithet which philosophers have attached to it ? The question appeals rather to temperament than to reason, and will be answered accordingly. But, if we concede that " the mean " is, or can ever be, " golden," then it is seen at its best in the character and career of Lord Goschen.

Mr Elliot's book[1] begins, as all biographies should begin, with a pedigree, and this pedigree traces the family of Goschen to a Lutheran pastor in Saxony who was living in the year 1609, and was called Joachimus Gosenius. But human ancestry is not limited to three centuries, and the question at once arises whether the Goschens were originally Jews. In the present day, when prejudice against the Ancient People scarcely survives except in the breast of Mr Belloc, it is curious that Lord Goschen always repudiated the suggestion of Jewish descent with something like indignation. Once in debate Mr T. M. Healy referred to Mr Goschen as being an

[1] " The Life of George Joachim Goschen, First Viscount Goschen, 1831-1907." By the Hon. Arthur D. Elliot.

eminent authority on the Christian religion, and Mr Goschen angrily interrupted with the question—"What does the hon. member mean?" To which Mr Healy blandly replied that he meant what he said, and passed on. The illustrations of this book certainly suggest that, if Goschen was not of Semitic descent, Nature does not always write a legible hand; and all the qualities of his mind and character—his industry, his perseverance, his financial genius, his adroitness and adaptability, his devotion to public order, and his love of domestic life—are qualities eminently Semitic. If we decide that Joachimus Gosenius was a Gentile, we yet may trace the Semitic strain in George Joachim Goschen through his mother, Henrietta Ohman. Or yet again—and this perhaps is the wisest course—we may dismiss all speculations about ancestry, and confine ourselves to the facts that the elder George Göschen was Goethe's publisher; that his son, William Henry Göschen, settled in England and founded the mercantile firm of Frühling & Göschen; and that William Henry had a son, George Joachim, who was born in 1831. At eleven years of age little George Joachim was sent to a school in Saxe-Meiningen, and three years later was transferred to Rugby, where Dr Tait was then Head Master. There is something that touches the heart in the picture of this German boy of Oriental appearance, short-sighted and unathletic, with "a solid foundation of mental material," "revelling in books," "writing several languages," but "ill-equipped for classical work," pitchforked into a crowd of Tom Browns and Harry Easts—let alone the Flashmans. As was to be expected, he was unpopular and unhappy; but, with the tenacity which marked him throughout his life, he persevered through all discouragements, made his way to the top of the school, and left it covered with glory. "Public-spirited, authoritative, courageous, good company at all times"—that is the verdict of a contemporary. He had undergone, and overcome.

In October 1850 Goschen went up to Oxford as a Commoner of Oriel College, of which he subsequently became an Exhibitioner. Pure scholarship was not his strong point, but by force of work he obtained a First in Classical Moderations. As his favourite studies were "Aristotle, Plato, philosophy, logic, and history," it is not surprising that he secured a First in the Final Schools. He was "the best First in, and an uncommonly good one," though "all but plucked for Divinity." Meanwhile he had made a considerable mark as a speaker at the Union, of which he was President in 1853. One of his speeches deserves remembrance, for it curiously bodies forth the principle which guided his whole political life. "He who joins a party, as a party, at the first commits a fatal error which it will be difficult to retrace. He who procures the dependence of others has sold his own independency of will; he who has fettered his actions by joining a party . . .

has committed a crime against his country, and done himself an injury of which he must reap the fruits."

Goschen quitted Oxford at Christmas 1853, and in 1854 he joined the firm of Frühling & Göschen. Even while he was still an undergraduate, his father had been corresponding with him about Russian Loans and Foreign Exchanges and similar mysteries of finance, and he was so apt a pupil that before long the proud parent was able to say—" They call George the ornamental partner in our firm. *I* call him the driving wheel of the machine." But, though a financier, Goschen was in his way a romancist, almost a troubadour. He had lost his heart and recovered it more than once before (at twenty-two) he determined on a marriage which his father, on prudential considerations, disapproved. Here again was a trial of endurance, and Goschen's quiet persistency again emerged victorious. His father packed him off to South America, there to represent the firm and extend its operations. But new scenes, new surroundings, new occupations were powerless to effect a disenchantment, and George Goschen returned from his two years' exile to marry the lady of his choice. It was, if ever there was, a marriage of affection, and it was as happy as it deserved to be.

For the next few years Goschen devoted himself with whole-hearted assiduity to the business of his firm. His success was commensurate with his abilities. At the early age of twenty-seven he was made a director of the Bank of England, and in City circles he came to be known as "the Fortunate Youth." In 1861 he greatly increased his fame by publishing a treatise on "The Theory of the Foreign Exchanges," which was translated into all the European languages, ran through repeated editions, and is still regarded as authoritative. The young financier had, as it were, codified "the laws which govern our money-markets and our foreign commerce," and in doing so he had, half-unwittingly, laid the foundations of his political success. At the General Election of 1859 the City of London had returned four Liberals unopposed, and in May 1863 one of these four seats was vacated by death. Forty years later Goschen wrote :

"At this distance of time I can still vividly recall my unbounded astonishment when two friends came to my office with the suggestion that I should stand for the City of London. Though from early days Westminster had been the goal of my hopes, I had never dreamt that the opening would come so soon or in so brilliant a form."

Some attempt was made by the Conservatives to create prejudice against the Liberal candidate on account of his foreign name (which he still spelt Göschen) ; but it was met by a triumphant reference to the names of Rothschild, Baring, Lefevre, Disraeli, and Ricardo, and to "the country of the lately deceased Prince Consort." Goschen was elected without opposition, pledging himself in his Address to "Parliamentary Reform, the Ballot, the abolition of Church Rates, and the removal of religious disabilities." On this last part of his programme Goschen felt very strongly, and from his entrance into Parliament he fought boldly and persistently for the abolition of Tests in the Universities. He spoke also on financial and economic subjects, on which he was already a recognized authority; and, in seconding the Address at the opening of the Session of 1864, he uttered an emphatic protest against the doctrine of Non-intervention in Foreign Politics. "Those professing to desire peace at any price seem often unwilling to pay the heavy price which might be asked for it—and that is war itself." The Parliament of 1859 was dissolved in July 1865. There were six candidates for the four seats in the City, and Goschen was at the head of the poll. Lord Palmerston, who had been Premier for six years, died in October, and was succeeded by Lord Russell, with Gladstone as Chancellor of the Exchequer and Leader of the House of Commons. Russell desired to make his administration rather more decidedly Liberal than Palmerston's had been, and, with a view to that end, he asked Goschen to join him in the now abolished office of Vice-President of the Board of Trade. Three months later he admitted him to the Cabinet as Chancellor of the Duchy of Lancaster; and this he did without even mentioning the subject to Gladstone, who, as Leader of the House, thought that he had some right to be consulted. It took Lord Morley exactly three years of Parliamentary life to secure admission to the Cabinet; Goschen accomplished the same feat in two years and nine months. The ministry was not long-lived. The painfully moderate Reform Bill perished unwept in June 1866, and Goschen, with his chief and his colleagues, retired into Opposition.

The Session of 1867, in which the Tories created Household Suffrage, Mr Elliot dismisses in a sentence; and we may do the same. In 1868 Gladstone, leading the Opposition in the House of Commons, declared war against the Irish Church Establishment, and Goschen was heartily on his side. A General Election was now impending, and Goschen, in his address to the City, declared himself in favour first of Irish Disestablishment, and then of reduction of expenditure, national education, the nationalization of the Universities, the revision of local rating, and the more business-like administration of the public departments. He was again returned at the head of the poll, this time with six candidates below him. A month later he entered Gladstone's first Cabinet as President of the Poor Law Board, and soon began to display all the administrative and legislative vigour which had been expected of him. His principal achievement was to bring order and system into the chaos of local administration, with all its overlapping areas and conflicting jurisdictions; and he crowned the work by expanding the Poor Law Board into a much larger and more powerful department, which he called "the Local Government Board." In 1871 Goschen was promoted to the First Lordship of the Admiralty, where, by resisting what he thought excessive demands for further retrenchment, he annoyed Gladstone and "steadily won the confidence of the Navy and of men acquainted with naval requirements"; but unfortunately the Government of which he was a member was rapidly losing popular favour, and of course he had his share in its declining fortunes. Gladstone dissolved Parliament in January 1874, and was soundly beaten at the General Election. Goschen was again returned for the City, but with three Conservatives above him. Disraeli, soon to become Lord Beaconsfield, formed a strong Government, and Goschen found himself again in Opposition.

In 1875 Gladstone's retirement, imagined to be final, from the Liberal leadership threw the Liberal party into dire confusion. Cohesion was relaxed; every man went his own way; and the triumphant Tories beheld with natural complacency the distracted counsels of their defeated rivals. It was a situation exactly suited to Goschen's idiosyncrasy, and he soon found the opportunity of putting into practice that doctrine of Party which he had enounced in the Union at Oxford. The immediate occasion of the severance from his former colleagues was the proposal to extend the Suffrage to the agricultural labourers. To that proposal Goschen was, by conviction, and even passionately, opposed. In this sense he declared himself in 1877, and, as the extension became an accepted part of the Liberal policy, he found himself separated on a vital and immediate issue from the Liberal party. Nor was this all. The Eastern Question was now at its height. Lord Beaconsfield was doing his best to drag us into war on behalf of Turkey; Gladstone was opposing him with supernatural vigour; the advanced part of the Liberal party was supporting Gladstone, and the moderate men were either opposing him or standing aloof. Goschen joined the anti-Gladstonian faction, and thereby more completely severed himself from the militant and democratic Liberalism. In January 1878 a newly constituted Liberal Club at Oxford (strangely called the Palmerston) held its Inaugural Dinner. There was a brilliant array of speakers, headed by Gladstone and including Goschen. Towards the end of the proceedings a toast was proposed by a young Fellow of New College, who had the courage—perhaps the audacity—to make a Jingo speech at a vehemently anti-Jingo gathering. Goschen saw a man after his own heart, asked to be introduced to him, and founded that same evening both a lifelong friendship and a political career. For the Jingo orator was Alfred Milner, and Goschen's influence made the career of the Lord Milner whom we know.

As the General Election of 1880 drew near, Goschen's alienation from his party became all but complete. He seemed likely to be defeated in the City; so he announced his retirement from that great constituency, and took refuge in the tiny borough of Ripon, since disfranchised, where the Liberals were complaisant enough to elect a man who had almost renounced Liberalism, though he criticized Lord Beaconsfield. When the election was over and Gladstone formed his second Cabinet, Goschen's hostility to the agricultural franchise debarred him from a seat in it; but Gladstone offered him the Vice-Royalty of India and the Embassy at Constantinople. Both were declined; but he accepted a temporary mission to Turkey as Special Ambassador; and then, returning to his place in Parliament, became one of the most unsparing and effective critics of ministerial blunders, especially in the East, during the disastrous years—1883, 1884, 1885.

The extension of the Suffrage to the labourers was now accomplished, and redistribution followed. Ripon was absorbed in a division of Yorkshire, and Goschen became Liberal candidate for East Edinburgh. He was returned by a large majority at the General Election of 1885, and the most important stage of his public life began. In December 1885 it became known that Mr Gladstone had been converted to Home Rule. One of the most obvious and most important results of this discovery was that it gave discontented and half-hearted Liberals a convenient excuse for "ratting." For this they had long been yearning. They were thoroughly out of sympathy with Gladstone's policy, and still more so with the Radicalism which they saw looming ahead. Yet a wholesome fear of the constituencies, which still were loyal to "the Grand Old Man," restrained them from open rebellion. They believed that, on the whole, Gladstone's policy was popular, and they were afraid to put themselves in public opposition to it. Home Rule gave them exactly what they wanted. Gladstone had now adopted a policy which, whatever else it was, certainly was not popular; and, in making it the occasion of their severance from him, they felt that they were assured of widespread sympathy. Yet they wanted leadership—someone to rally and combine them, a voice to express what they felt and a brain to organize the campaign. All this they found, ready to their hand, in Goschen. During the anxious months of January-June 1886, no one played a more active or a more effective part. In the House he was, as an Irish critic remarked, "as busy as the Devil in a storm," and outside it he contrived to diffuse himself even more widely than Mr Chamberlain, and to stimulate panic in a fashion which Lord Hartington never attempted. The battle for and against Home Rule was the supreme moment of his life, and it elicited the fulness of his powers. By far the greatest speech he ever made was delivered at the meeting in the Opera House on the 14th of April 1886, which announced to the world a "Unionist Party," where Liberals could join with Tories to resist Home Rule.

In passing, be it said that Goschen, though an accomplished, was not a pleasing speaker. His voice was harsh and raucous; his gestures were ungraceful; his utterance suggested a perennial cold in the head. His language was elaborately prepared, and occasionally contained a phrase which struck home at the time and was remembered afterwards; but its rhetorical ornaments were tawdry, and the sarcasm savoured (to quote Disraeli) of Sadler's Wells. All these qualities were present in the oration at the Opera House, and yet the intensity of the speaker's feeling, the vehemence of his tone, and the skill with which he appealed to passion and panic, made it a rhetorical success of the first class.

"Some people talk about our houses being set on fire. If so, Captain Shaw will have to put them out. Others say that the dagger may again be brought into use. If so, we shall make our wills and do our duty."

At the "Home Rule Election" of June 1886, Goschen lost his seat at Edinburgh. In the following December he joined Lord Salisbury's Government as Chancellor of the Exchequer, and was returned as a Conservative for St George's, Hanover Square, which he represented till he accepted a peerage in 1900.

Here, really, the interesting part of Goschen's career comes to an end. His six Budgets we need not here discuss, nor yet his second term of office at the Admiralty. He had been absorbed in the Conservative party, and his thoughts and words and acts were the commonplaces of Conservatism. Yet once again before the end he was forced to reconsider his political attachments and to manifest, as of yore, his independence of Party. Mr Chamberlain's desperate attempt to involve the country in the calamities of Protection stung Lord Goschen into hostile activity, and his indignant refusal to have part or lot in " a gamble in the food of the people " was one of the most creditable incidents in his long and prosperous career. His physical and mental powers remained unabated to the last, and he died quite suddenly in his seventy-sixth year. Other statesmen may have been more widely popular, but none had more devoted friends; and that is an epitaph which any man might envy.

V

CHARLES KINGSLEY

My title to write about Kingsley is twofold. I knew him personally; and one of his books had a very definite influence on the formation of my opinions. Though he has been dead for seven-and-thirty years, my mental vision of him is perfectly clear. He was not, I suppose, above the middle height, but his extreme attenuation made him look taller. There was not a superfluous ounce of flesh on his bones, and he seemed to be compact of wire and whipcord. His features were strongly marked, trenchant nose and prominent chin; his eyes bright and penetrating; his skin furrowed and weather-beaten; his abundant hair and bushy whiskers, originally dark but tinged with grey. In all his movements, actions and gestures he was nervous and restless. It seemed impossible for him to sit still, and, except when he was asleep, his life was an incessant activity. Much of his restlessness was, I imagine, due to his stammer. He loved talking, had an enormous deal to say on every conceivable subject, and longed to say it. But his stammer was always checking him. He gurgled, and gasped, and made faces, and would sometimes break off in a conversation or a meal, rush out into the open air, and liberate his suppressed emotions by rapid exercise or physical exertion. Yet, as has often been observed in similar cases, when he had to preach, the stammer subsided, and, though there was some facial contortion, the flow of the discourse was never interrupted. He said to his friend Tom Hughes : " I could be as great a talker as any man in England but for my stammering. When I am speaking for God in the pulpit, or praying by bedsides, I never stammer. My stammer is a blessed thing for me. It keeps me from talking in company, and from going out as much as I should do but for it."

One of Kingsley's peculiarities was that, except on Sundays, when he wore a black coat and a white neckcloth, he always dressed like a layman ; and in his grey breeches and gaiters, thick shooting-boots, and parti-coloured tie, he might have passed for a farmer, a gamekeeper, or a country gentleman. In his nature and habits he combined some of the attributes of all three characters, if, indeed, they are not really one. He was descended from a family of Kingsleys who once owned land at Vale Royal in Cheshire, but had, as the phrase is, come down in the world. Charles Kingsley the elder, after spending what was left of his fortune, took Holy Orders, and was successively a curate in Devonshire, a " Warming-pan " in Cambridgeshire, and Rector of Chelsea. All these experiences in greater or less degree coloured the life and writings of Charles Kingsley the younger, who was born in 1819, and educated at Magdalene College, Cambridge.

As regards Charles Kingsley's first year at Cambridge, we have his own frank confession: "I was very idle, and very sinful." The rougher elements of his nature got the upper hand. He gave up religion. He neglected his work. He frequented low company. He sought distraction in every form of sport—boating, hunting, driving, fencing, boxing, duck-shooting in the Fens. He had some vague thoughts of quitting Cambridge and going out to the Far West as a prairie-hunter. In a word, he had drifted from his old moorings (for his training had been rigidly Evangelical), and had not yet found that "Anchor of the Soul" which was to steady his life. The discovery, however, was not long delayed.

During the Long Vacation of 1839 Kingsley was at a garden-party in Oxfordshire, and there he met Miss Fanny Grenfell, whom he eventually married. In after-life he said,—"The 6th of July 1839 was my real wedding day." Miss Grenfell (who is drawn as Argemone in "Yeast") was ardently religious in the Tractarian way; and under her influence Kingsley soon reverted to a more orderly and scrupulous mode of life. He did not become a Tractarian, but he resumed his habits of prayer and Bible-reading, and "opened his heart to the Light, if the Light would only come." He resolved to obtain a good degree, and, with that end in view, he gave up hunting and shooting, and made "a solemn vow against cards." He read from seven to eight hours a day, and, under the steadying influence of appointed work dutifully done, he began to emerge from doubts and uncertainties. Carlyle's "French Revolution"—surely the least theological of books—had a notable effect on his mind, "establishing and intensifying his belief in God's righteous government of the world." After he had renounced the wild dreams of his reckless youth, he had chosen the Bar as his profession, and had entered himself as a law-student at Lincoln's Inn. But his views of life were changing, and in 1841 he determined to seek Holy Orders. He thus wrote about himself to his bride-elect: "*Saved*—saved from the wild pride and darkling tempests of scepticism, and from the sensuality and dissipation into which my own rashness and vanity had hurried me before I knew you. Saved from a hunter's life on the Prairies, from becoming a savage, and perhaps worse. Saved from all this, and restored to my country and my God, and *able to believe*."

Throughout his life, whatever Kingsley's hand found to do he did it with his might; and, when he determined to distinguish himself at the University, he worked extremely hard—hard enough, indeed, to injure his health. By these violent exertions he secured a very good degree—a First Class in the Classical Tripos, and a Second in the Mathematical Tripos. His tutor wrote: "It was nothing compared to what might have been attained by a man of his powers"; but considering how he had misused his first and second years at Cambridge, it was marvellous that he accomplished so much in his third.

All this time his innermost thoughts were bent on marriage; but Miss Grenfell's friends were strongly opposed to the alliance, and resisted it by all means in their power. This was in his mind when he wrote a friend: "I have been toiling much harder than my health would allow for the last six months, not because I felt distinction here an object, but because, having a battle to fight with the world—a bride to win as a penniless adventurer from rich relations,—I found it necessary to attack Mammon with weapons which he could feel and appreciate; and the first weapon thrown in my way was the tangible proof of talent and application, and claim to attention, implied in a good degree."

He had now clearly marked out his line in life. On the 10th of July 1842 he was ordained Deacon by Bishop Sumner of Winchester, and on the morning of the ordination he wrote as follows:—"God's mercies are new every morning. Here I am waiting to be admitted in a few hours to His holy ministry, and take refuge for ever in His Temple. . . . Oh! my soul, my body, my intellect, my very love, I dedicate you all to God."

And now, at the age of twenty-three, he settled down to a curacy in Eversley, on the borders of

Hampshire—a pretty place which was destined, though he little guessed it, to be his home during the remainder of his life. Except for his separation from her whom he loved better than his own soul, he was now extremely happy. He had "found himself," and was in his element. "He could fling a flail with the threshers in the barn, turn his scythe with the mowers in the meadow, pitch hay with the hay-makers in the pasture. Knowing every fox-earth on the moors, the 'reedy hover' of the pike, the still hole where the chub lay, he had always a word in sympathy for the huntsman, the keeper, or even the poacher. With the farmer he discussed the rotation of crops, and with the labourer the science of hedging and ditching." There were kennels in the parish, at Bramshill House, where Sir John Cope was Master of the Hounds afterwards known as Mr Garth's; and there Kingsley's knowledge of horse-flesh and fondness for sport (though he seldom indulged it) made him so popular that, when he first announced a Confirmation and invited those who required it to come to him for instruction, the whips and stablemen sent a message to say that they had all been confirmed once, but that, if Mr Kingsley wished it, they would all be happy to come again. He was ordained Priest at the end of a year's diaconate. "Wonderful Grace of God, that I should now be God's priest and servant! I often read 1 Cor. xv. 8, 9, with tears. . . . I am getting very strong, and have been threshing wheat a good deal these last two wet days, which is splendid exercise." Thus passed the years of his apprenticeship. In 1844 the rectory of Eversley fell vacant; Kingsley was appointed to it, and, before he had actually taken possession of it, he was married. The self-effacing devotion of five years was at length, and abundantly, rewarded.

Thus far, we have only brought Kingsley to the threshold of his life's work. That work, so far as it was peculiar to himself and outside the ordinary lines of clerical activity, began with the year of revolution—1848. There had been a time of disheartenment and disillusion. The Reform Act of 1832, concerning which such glorious things had been prophesied, did not produce the Millennium. The working people found that political power, wrenched from the aristocracy, had passed into the hands of the mercantile and trading classes, and that Labour had derived no advantage from the transfer. The political leaders of the Democracy, untaught by experience, still believed that merely political reforms could cure the evils under which the poor suffered, and clamoured for a new Reform Act. The five objects for which they agitated were: Universal Suffrage, Ballot, Payment of Members, Electoral Districts, and the Abolition of the Property Qualification for Parliament. These points constituted what was called "The People's Charter," and "Chartism" became a recognized, and dreaded, element in national life. To political unrest was added the stimulus of physical suffering. The winter of 1847-1848 was marked by widespread distress, and the poor, in town and country alike, were seeking angrily for deliverance from intolerable evils. The spring of 1848 brought this disturbance to a climax. Thrones went down with a crash all over Europe, and it seemed not unlikely that the political convulsion would spread to England. There were dangerous riots in London, Edinburgh, Glasgow, and Liverpool; men's hearts failing them for fear and for looking after those things that were coming on the earth.

Kingsley, whose pen could never be idle when his feelings were stirred, uttered his soul in "Yeast." It is a curious, disorderly, miscellaneous book, beginning as a novel (with an admirable account of fox-hunting) and ending in a kind of phantasmagoria; but valuable because wrought out of the author's experiences as a country parson in a district where moral and sanitary reforms were equally disregarded, and where the flagrant iniquity of the Game Laws incited, only too successfully, to murder. "Yeast" is, in short, Kingsley's plea for the Agricultural Poor; and, before the ink was dry on the last page, he had flung himself into the cause of the Poor in London. The Rev. F. D. Maurice, then Reader at Lincoln's Inn, had gathered round him a little band of ardent reformers, who realized, as the politicians did not, that political reform is related to social reform only as the means to the end; and who, because they avowedly based their public actions on the principles of the Gospel, acquired the nickname of "Christian Socialists." To these men, of whom I hope to speak more fully in another chapter, Kingsley joined himself, and threw all his energy into the service of the People's cause. The 10th of April 1848 had been appointed as the day of a great Chartist Demonstration on Kennington Common, and timid Londoners worked themselves into an indescribable panic. They firmly believed that their shops were to be looted and their dwellings burnt down; and that there were to be concerted attacks on the Bank, the Tower, the Government Offices, and the Houses of Parliament. The defence of London against its visionary foes was entrusted to the Duke of Wellington, who, by the simple expedient of barricading the bridges, produced an absolute calm. Heavy rain drenched the oratory on Kennington Common. The police arrested a few ring-leaders, and the Monster Petition in favour of the Charter was taken to the House of Commons in a four-wheeled cab. Panic gave place to laughter. Then, of course, there ensued a reaction. The respectable classes, who had been the most sorely frightened, were now the most offensively brave; and it became the cant of the moment to say, not only that Chartism was a spent force, but also that poverty and misery and oppression were the dreams of crack-brained sentimentalists, and that the poor, whether in town or country, had nothing to complain of. This reaction from abject terror to comfortable callousness gave Kingsley his opportunity. In concert with the other Christian Socialists, he set to work, with the object of showing that, though the good sense and good temper of the people had averted a disaster, still the poor were labouring under intolerable, undeserved, and remediable wrongs. A series of articles on "London Labour and the London Poor," published in *The Morning Chronicle,* showed such as were willing to learn that there was really a great mass of misery at the base of a boastful civilization; and the Christian Socialists, in order to show the best ways of remedying it, began to issue a series of tracts called "Politics for the People." In the first of these Kingsley declared himself in favour of the Charter, but complained that it did not go far enough. It stopped with a reconstruction of political machinery, but said nothing of the social reform which that machinery, if it was to be worth anything, must produce. In the second, borrowing a name from the Chartist literature of the time, he announced that there was a true "Reformer's Guide"—even the Bible, which contained "the voice of God against tyrants, idlers, and humbugs." In subsequent numbers he extolled "A Fair Day's Work for a Fair Day's Wages"; protested against the "Devil's Gospel of Unrestricted Competition"; and poured scorn on the Malthusian doctrine that the resources of the earth were inadequate for the lives which God might plant on it. He also contributed some admirable papers on the National Gallery and the British Museum, intended to interest the workers in their own property, and several of the most stirring ballads which he subsequently wove into his novels. Under the pressure of all this exciting work, added to his ordinary duties as a Parish Priest, his health temporarily broke down. He had to quit Eversley for a space, and, while he was recuperating at the seaside, he wrote "Alton Locke, Tailor and Poet." This book was intended to be a protest on behalf of the poor in London, urging their claims on the same grounds as those on which, in "Yeast," he had pleaded for the agricultural labourers. In choosing a tailor for his hero he directed attention to the disgusting abuses of the tailoring trade, which he had already exposed in a famous tract called "Cheap Clothes and Nasty." Of course it is not to be conceived that a man of Kingsley's fiery temperament, writing as the passion of the moment whirled him along, could escape unjust, or even just, criticism. Of unjust criticism he had more than enough, perverting his doctrine and exhibiting him as a teacher of heresy and profligacy. Of juster criticism, touching rather style than substance, a specimen is afforded by the gentle author of "Rab and his Friends," who wrote thus of "Alton Locke":—"A book which is my especial horror, as being of the 'tremendous' school of literature, everything at highest pitch—words, sentiments, politics, religion, character (if it deserves the name), conversation."

Another, and a striking, incident of Kingsley's career as a social reformer remains to be told. The "Great Exhibition" of 1851, following in happy contrast on the tumults and revolutions of 1848, seemed to be, as someone said, an International Sacrament of Social Peace and Goodwill. Immense crowds of strangers were drawn to London, and for their benefit many of the clergy threw open their churches and organized courses of sermons on the great topic of the day. At the request of the Incumbent of St John's, Fitzroy Square, Kingsley undertook to preach one of these sermons, choosing for his subject (at Maurice's suggestion) "The Message of the Church to Labouring Men." The text was: "The Spirit of the Lord is upon me, because He hath anointed me to preach the gospel to the poor." What, the preacher asked, is the Gospel? It is Freedom, Equality, and Brotherhood. Freedom, where a man is free to do, not what he likes, but what he ought; Equality, where each man has equal opportunity to educate and use his faculties; Brotherhood, where a man believes that all men are his brothers, not by the will of the flesh, but by the will of God. The Bible proclaims Freedom from external tyranny and internal passion; Baptism proclaims Equality, as the rain that falls alike on the evil and on the good; the Eucharist proclaims Brotherhood, by the one Bread which unites all who receive it into one Body. The preacher concluded thus :

"God is my witness that I speak the truth when I tell you that these thoughts are not matters of doctrine but of experience. There is one man at least in this church now who has been awakened from the selfish, luxurious dreams of his youth, by that message of the Bible and of the Sacraments, to see the dignity of the People's cause—to feel it at once the most peremptory of duties and the most glorious of privileges to proclaim, in the name of Jesus of Nazareth, the message of the Church of Christ—that the will of God is, good news to the poor, deliverance to the captives, healing to the broken-hearted, light to the ignorant, liberty to the crushed ; and, to the degraded masses, "*the acceptable year of the Lord*"—a share and a stake, for them and for their children after them, in the soil, the wealth, the civilization, and the government of this English land."

As to what ensued, let us hear Mr Thomas Hughes, who was present :—"At the end of his sermon the Incumbent got up at the altar and declared his belief that great part of the doctrine of the sermon was untrue, and that he had expected a sermon of an entirely different kind. To a man of the preacher's vehement temperament it must have required a great effort not to reply at the moment. The congregation was keenly excited, and evidently expected him to do so. He only bowed his head, pronounced the blessing, and came down from the pulpit." He passed straight through the crowd of working men that thronged him with outstretched hands and an eager "God bless you, sir," on their lips, and went into the vestry, where his friends gathered round him to express their sympathy, and to take the sermon from him that it might be printed exactly as it was written. This was done, and a stained and tattered copy lies before me as I write.

IV

THE CHRISTIAN SOCIALISTS

IN beginning this chapter, I must complete my account of Charles Kingsley. We have already seen that the most vivid and romantic part of his life was the period in which he worked with the Christian Socialists. The remainder of his career was perhaps more decorous, but certainly less interesting. He became in turn a Cambridge Professor, a Court Chaplain, and a Cathedral dignitary. Though he had a fanatical horror of Romanism, he had always been a staunch believer in the Church, the Priesthood, and the Sacraments. In his later days he astonished those who had only known him superficially by coming forward as one of the boldest champions of the Athanasian Creed, and an insistent teacher of the truth of the Intermediate State. He was still in the fulness of bodily and mental activity when he died of neglected pneumonia in his fifty-sixth year. I purpose now to give some fuller account of the Christian Socialists, among whom, in his earlier days, he had played so conspicuous a part; and high above all that company towers the figure of Frederick Denison Maurice, whose splendid but mysterious genius occupies a place in English theology similar to that which is occupied by Turner in English art.

Later on, I will tell the story of his life, and seek to expound his theology. Now, I am speaking of him only as the prophet of Christian Socialism. He was Reader of Lincoln's Inn ; and this post gave him a special opportunity of influence. His audience in the chapel on Sundays contained a number of eager and impressible young men, reading for the Bar or recently called to it, on whose ears the awful beauty of his eloquence fell with the solemnity of a new Apocalypse. By degrees he began to gather round him a group of disciples, who met every Monday evening at his house, for social and religious discussion. The disciples brought their friends ; and among them, or soon added to them, were Tom Hughes, bubbling over with the enthusiasms of Rugby and Oxford ; Edward Vansittart Neale, a Berkshire squire who was said to have squandered three fortunes in the People's cause ; John Malcolm Ludlow,[1] who has only just now left us, and was then a young barrister just returned from some exciting experiences in revolutionary Paris ; Septimus Hansard, afterwards so well known as the devoted rector of Bethnal Green ; Lord Goderich, long loved and honoured as the first Marquess of Ripon ; and Charles Kingsley, with his boundless energy and ever-ready pen.

The social and political state of England in those "Hungry Forties" was black with misery and

[1] Mr Ludlow died October 17, 1911.

seething with discontent. Friedrich Engels, in his "Condition of the Working Class in England," held up to an astonished Europe the vision of the cellar-dwellers of Manchester and the intolerable life of the British artisan, as a kind of warning lest its peoples should come also into this place of torment. All the hopes of the people gathered round the Charter, which came to be a symbol, to some, of the Good Time Coming; to others, of an impending revolution in which the scenes of Paris in the Terror might be re-enacted in the streets of London. On all these strange and awful phenomena the little band which had gathered round Maurice looked with very different eyes. All alike were passionately eager to deliver the poor from misery and oppression; but their notions of ways and methods differed widely. Some (like the "Young Englanders" whom I shall presently describe) believed in the Crown and the Aristocracy, as benignant powers which ought to be quickened into beneficent action. Some were Whigs, or Liberals, or Radicals of the recognised types; some were Republicans; and some had dreams of Communism. In a happy moment, someone discovered or invented a title which all could adopt. For thirty years Robert Owen had been preaching, and enforcing by splendid self-sacrifice, a new creed which he called "Socialism"; but he taught it in defiance of what he conceived to be the Christian religion. Maurice's disciples were essentially and profoundly Christian. They welcomed Owen's scheme for setting up a kingdom of peace and goodwill and brotherhood on earth, and they saw that it was in the strictest harmony with the Christian religion as taught by Maurice in "The Kingdom of Christ." In two words, they were "Christian Socialists," and as such their names still live in our religious and political history. The task of holding all these diverse elements together, softening differences, and welding all into one for a common purpose, would for most men have been an impossibility; but the prophetic genius of Maurice, and the profound reverence in which all sections held him, surmounted the difficulty. He never aimed at playing a leader's part. He was one of those men who are leaders in spite of themselves, and his effect on the movement was that of a restraining and curbing force. His object was to Christianize Socialism; and he used all his power to check extravagance and ferocity; to stifle evil-speaking and recrimination; and to purge the movement of anything which might bring dishonour on the Christian name.

In sketching the story of Kingsley's life, I described the shaking of the nations in the spring of 1848; the ignominious collapse of the 10th of April; and the insolence of the reaction which followed that collapse. Now was the moment for the Christian Socialists to act. Kingsley had rushed up from his parsonage to place himself under Maurice's command; Maurice had sent him on to Ludlow, and the work began. On the 6th of May the first number of

"Politics for the People" was issued. It made its direct appeal first to the working classes, and then to all who were seeking to deliver their brethren fast bound in misery and iron. The characteristic which distinguished this appeal from the common literature of Democracy and Chartism was that it founded itself on religion. It freely acknowledged the shortcomings of the Church and her rulers in the cause of social service, and it sought to infuse a new spirit into ancient forms. "We have used the Bible as if it were a mere Special Constable's Handbook, or an opium-dose for keeping beasts of burden patient while they were being overloaded." Henceforward it was to be put to very different uses. Mosaic legislation was quoted in the interests of the labourers. The fire of the prophets was borrowed for the destruction of Mammon and his strongholds. The sanction of the Divine Workman of Nazareth was invoked for the social service of humanity; and the Church, as being the society which He founded, was to be the Great Mutual Benefit Society for the overworked and underfed. Perhaps it is not very odd that a newspaper conducted on these lines came to an end with its seventeenth number; but the Christian Socialists were not the men to be disheartened by a failure. Before long they set out with a fresh venture, and this time "the defiant flag was nailed to the mast." The new serial was named "The Christian Socialist." In so naming it Maurice was inspired by the resolution to commit himself and his comrades "at once to the conflict we must engage in sooner or later with the Unsocial Christians and the Un-Christian Socialists." "I seriously believe," he said in the first number, "that Christianity is the only foundation of Socialism, and that a true Socialism is the necessary result of a sound Christianity." His colleague, John Ludlow, pursued the same theme. "The new idea has gone abroad into the world that Socialism and Christianity are in their nature not hostile, but akin to each other; or rather that the one is but the development, the outgrowth, the manifestation of the other."

Thus the later as well as the earlier journal was founded on the rock of the Christian confession; but the activities of the two were different. "Politics for the People" had been, as the name implies, political in the widest sense. "The Christian Socialist" (which later changed its name to "The Journal of Association") was mainly economic. Ludlow had returned from Paris full of enthusiasm for the *associations ouvrières*, and resolved to imitate them here. Maurice denounced with fiery energy the misnamed gospel of unrestricted competition, which "expected universal selfishness to do the work of universal love." Kingsley thundered against "the Manchester School" as the "embodiment of competitive selfishness." All agreed in pressing the idea of Association as the law of the Christian Kingdom, and therefore as the way of salvation for workmen, as for all human kind. Maurice taught, and the others echoed, that "the workmen, by uniting themselves into Co-operative Producing Associations, could eliminate the profits of dead capital, and abrogate the ferocity of the competitive struggle." It is difficult in these later days, when Co-operation and Co-operative Societies have became synonymous with all that is orderly and respectable, to realize the panic-stricken hubbub which these first attempts evoked ; nor have I space here to trace the history of the movement. In 1852 an "Industrial and Provident Partnership Bill," legalizing Associations, became law, and the storm abated. Free Trade, so hardly won in 1846, was beginning to fulfil its promise. Times were better. Discontent died down. The political crisis had passed. The Christian Socialists never disavowed their creed, and never formally dissociated themselves from one another ; but, with the same grand end of Social Salvation in view, they more and more tended to pursue it by different paths. Some, like Vansittart Neale and Ludlow, clung firmly to Co-operation. Some, like Lord Goderich and Tom Hughes, betook themselves to politics, endeavouring to infuse the spirit of Social Reform into the dry bones of commercial Radicalism. Kingsley more and more applied his genius to the cause of Sanitary Reform as affecting Public Health, and preached it through his novels. Maurice came to feel that the best way of helping the workmen was to give them the kind of knowledge which, by quickening their interest in the past, might guide the present and illuminate the future. The combination of the ideas of Studentship and Fellowship—a brotherly and non-competitive pursuit of knowledge—was the aim which he set before himself. It was realized in the foundation of the Working Men's College in Great Ormond Street, which by many is regarded as his most enduring memorial. And then, just when the skies were brightening, there fell upon England the shadow of a colossal crime. The Crimean War, like all similar adventures, distracted the national mind from all the enterprises of righteousness and mercy, and amid the cruel and clamorous jealousies of the nation the tender plant of Christian Socialism was trampled underfoot.

Social historians have sometimes tried to draw a comparison between Christian Socialism and the contemporary movement which was nicknamed "Young England."[1] Both had the same object—the Social Regeneration of England—and yet they differed very widely. That difference was not merely a difference of worldly station, for the Christian Socialists had among them men of rank and wealth. Nor was it a merely political difference, for Maurice believed as firmly as Lord John Manners in the sacred power of the Crown, and Kingsley was a worshipper of the House of Lords. Nor, yet again, was the difference religious, for the Christian Socialists were at least as loyal to the Creeds and the Sacraments as Disraeli

[1] See p. 354.

and George Smythe. No, the difference was this: "'Young England' believed that salvation could be effected by the romantic and kindly philanthropy of the wealthy and the deferential gratitude of the poor." The Christian Socialists believed that "the Church must apply herself to the task of raising the poor into men," and that "the business for which God sends a Christian priest to a Christian nation is to preach and practise Freedom, Equality, and Brotherhood, in the fullest, deepest, widest meaning of those three great words."

Even the briefest account of Christian Socialism would be glaringly incomplete, if it omitted a sketch of John Frederick Denison Maurice. If Maurice had dropped his second and third names and called himself by the name of that "Son of Thunder" who was also the Apostle of Love, his character would have been exactly expressed in his appellation. But, by a curious choice, he dropped the "John," and became known to the Church and the world as Frederick Denison Maurice. He was born in 1805 of Welsh and Nonconformist ancestry; his father was a Unitarian minister. Though he was born and brought up in villages—one near Lowestoft and the other near Bristol—he seems never to have had the slightest touch with nature. "I never knew the note of a single bird," he said. "The treasures of the earth and sky are not for me." He read no novels, played no games, took no exercise beyond solitary walks;

and, even in those walks, his mind was occupied with social and theological speculation. It was, in brief, a thoroughly unnatural boyhood, but the atmosphere of the home was quite enough to account for it. The Unitarian father thought of nothing but his chapel, his politics, and his private pupils. The mother renounced Unitarianism, and accepted Calvinism of the most repellent type. One of the daughters joined the Church of England; another became a Baptist; and amidst this hurly-burly of theological strife the shy, sensitive, thoughtful boy grew up to a melancholy manhood.

In 1823 Frederick Maurice entered Trinity College, Cambridge, with all the painful shyness and awkwardness natural to a youth who had been reared unbrokenly in such an extraordinary home. His tutor, Julius Hare, soon recognized his mental gifts, and before long he began to gather round him some serious-minded friends. He now was turning his thoughts towards the Bar, and with that view he transferred himself to Trinity Hall, then a specially legal college. But straight ahead a formidable barrier crossed his path. According to the unhappy system then prevailing at the Universities, he could not take his degree without declaring himself a member of the Church of England. "A Fellowship, and probably a distinguished Academic career, awaited him if he were to make the declaration. The very fact that worldly advancement seemed bound up with such a pronouncement made him distrust the arguments which would lead him to accept it. So he slipped quietly away from Cambridge without his degree."

From Cambridge Maurice came to London and plunged into journalism, in which his career was brilliant—he was an editor before he was twenty-five—but unprofitable. All the while his innermost mind was bent on religious speculation, and his opinions were growing into a definite form. Mainly under the influence of Coleridge's teaching, he had broken with the Unitarianism of his youth, and now he openly joined himself to the Church of England and was baptized. In view of what subsequently occurred it should here be said that he never was a "Broad Churchman." He passed from Unitarianism to a kind of Liberal Catholicism which held him to the end. "There rose up before me," he said, "the idea of a Church Universal, not built on human inventions or human faith, but on the very nature of God Himself, and upon the union which He has formed with His creatures." Throughout life he maintained what would have been to lesser men an impossible position of aloofness from the "Broad Church," the "High Church," and the "Low Church" parties. The Church, the Creeds, the Sacraments, and the Ministry were the corner-stones of his theology. He interpreted these things in a fashion which was all his own; but his interpretation has affected, to an extent not always realized, the teaching of the Church of England in the present day. Maurice now resolved to seek Holy Orders, but he did not return to Cambridge.

Early in 1830 he entered Exeter College, Oxford, and having taken his degree was ordained Deacon in 1834. For two years he served a country parish, and in 1836 he returned to London as Chaplain of Guy's Hospital. He subsequently became Reader at Lincoln's Inn, Professor of English History and also of Theology at King's College, Principal of the Working Men's College, Professor of Moral Philosophy at Cambridge, Incumbent of St Peter's, Vere Street, London, and Vicar of St Edward's, Cambridge. He died in 1872.

This is the barest outline of Maurice's life, and the space at my command will only suffice to give some very short account of his character and teaching. In the character there was that curious mixture of dissimilar qualities which I tried to convey when I referred to St John as at once "A Son of Thunder" and the Apostle of Love. Maurice was the gentlest, humblest, and tenderest of human beings; but, when confronted by cruelty, tyranny, baseness, or intellectual dishonesty, he was the most furious and passionate of combatants. "I cannot," he said, "be always meek and gentle with the butchers of God's words and Church"; and with these "butchers," or men whom he esteemed such, it was his lot to be brought into almost lifelong conflict. His three most important battles—no gentler word is applicable—I shall now try to describe.

I. The first began in 1837 with the publication of "The Kingdom of Christ, or Hints on the Principles, Constitution, and Ordinances of the Catholic Church."

This book appeared originally in the form of "Letters to a Member of the Society of Friends." Maurice started with the attempt of the Quakers to establish a Kingdom of Christ on earth, and his object was to show that such a Kingdom already existed in the Catholic or Universal Church. Its Sacraments, its ordinances, its ministerial succession linked it indissolubly to the first ages of Christianity, and it united people who were separated by every imaginable difference of race, colour, and geographical position. It was, in short, continuous and world-wide, whereas Quakerism began in the seventeenth century, and had never extended beyond England and America. This was a sufficiently bold challenge, and brought the replies which might be expected. But Maurice did not content himself with challenging one particular sect. He went through all the divisions of Christendom one by one, and had his appropriate rebuke for each, and for every subdivision of each. Romanism seemed to him as vulnerable as Zwinglianism, and Puseyism no better than Lutheranism. The upshot of his whole contention was that all "isms" and schisms are sins against the Unity of the One Church, which rests upon the Confession of the Threefold Name; to which men are admitted by Baptism, and in which they are united by the Eucharist. He finds this unity best represented, and least marred by wilful perversions, in the Church of England, and boldly affirms of that Church that it is the outward and visible Kingdom of Christ in this land.

Naturally, the publication of this book brought down on its author a heavy fire from opposite quarters. Dissenters attacked an ex-Unitarian who had quitted Dissent for Establishment. Romanists assailed an Anglican who insisted that the Catholic Church was a thing infinitely larger and more ancient than the Roman obedience. Tractarians smelt heresy in a doctrine of Baptism which differed from Dr Pusey's; and the Low Churchmen could make no terms with a theology so steeped in Sacramentalism. But, in spite of all this complicated hostility, "The Kingdom of Christ" lived and worked, and its influence may still be traced in the writings of such men as the Bishop of Oxford and Dr Scott Holland.

II. In 1853 Maurice published a volume of "Theological Essays." Of these essays he said: "They express the deepest thoughts that are in me." "I believe," he cried, "that I was to write this book and could not honestly have put it off." The book was intended to reaffirm the truth of historic Christianity, and to clear away a cloud of misrepresentations which had gathered round it. This is not the place in which to trace the sequence of Maurice's great argument, but the results which ensued from the publication of the book must be briefly narrated. It should be borne in mind that Maurice was, what few theologians are but all ought to be—a philosopher. He knew, as few of his contemporaries knew it, the history of human thought. He dwelt in habitual communion with those elect minds which in every age have tried to pierce the ultimate mysteries of being. In truth he was a spiritual descendant of Plato, who "dreamt God." The metaphysical faculty, so strongly developed, was bound to affect his theology. He could not confine his speculations within the written limits of Bible, or Fathers, or Formularies. All these had their properties and functions, but they must be interpreted in the light of the Absolute Truth. If this necessity applied to documents which bore the most authoritative sanction of the Church, it applied still more forcibly to the misconceptions and inexactitudes of popular religion. True theology was at one with true philosophy, and whatever contradicted the one contradicted the other. This conviction impelled Maurice, in the last of his "Theological Essays," to denounce the popular notions of Eternal Life and Eternal Death. In popular thinking, eternity meant an endless extension of time. To Maurice it meant rather a condition of Timelessness. "The things which are seen are temporal; but the things which are not seen are eternal." The true antithesis is not between a short time and a long time, but between the things of sense and the things of spirit. Eternal Life and Eternal Death do not mean unending life and unending death. Eternal Life is the life of the soul in God, and Eternal Death the loss of that life. "I do not pronounce what are the possibilities of resistance in a human will to the loving Will of God."

The result of this utterance was exactly what Maurice foresaw, and even desired. Never was there a more chivalrous, a more quixotic spirit. He had felt himself bound in conscience to challenge the prevalent Puritanism of the time on a point where it was peculiarly sensitive, and he faced the resulting fury with a buoyant heart. The Council of King's College, where he was a Professor, called him to account. He would not explain, or withdraw, or qualify, or resign. He demanded from the authorities of the College, "not any personal favour, but justice." They replied by dismissing him from his professorships, without even condescending to formulate the charges of false doctrine on which they professed to act.

III. The third and last great controversy in which Maurice was engaged is even more difficult to treat in cursory fashion than the earlier ones. In 1858 the Rev. H. L. Mansel, afterwards Dean of St Paul's, preached before the University of Oxford a course of Bampton Lectures on "The Limits of Religious Thought." His doctrine was hotly challenged by Maurice, and, amid the blinding storm of sermons, pamphlets, and reviews which the controversy provoked, it is difficult to see quite clearly the ground which each protagonist took. Perhaps, however, the following account will not be very far from the mark:—

It was a time of religious unrest. The "Broad Church" party (these labels, though odious, are necessary), following a lead from Germany, had begun to question the moral rightness of certain events in the Old Testament, and to affirm that they were inconsistent with the Moral Perfection of God.

To this Mansel replied that the creature had no apparatus for criticizing the Creator, the finite for judging the Infinite. We only knew right from wrong by revelation. If, therefore, we found in the Bible (which he regarded as synonymous with revelation) that certain acts had been done apparently with Divine sanction, then those acts must have been right. The difficulty of reconciling them with moral perfection was insuperable in the limited state of human faculties. All we had to do was to believe that the acts were right because God sanctioned them. Then we must jog along, and wait for the solution in another stage of being. All this was the direct opposite of what Maurice believed. To the age-long question, "Canst thou by searching find out God?" his answer had always been an impassioned "Yes." God had revealed Himself to such as chose to seek Him in Conscience, in History, in the Church—above all, in Him who was the Light of the World. It had been the privilege of man, by striving and searching and suffering, to discover that moral beauty which is synonymous with the character of God, and to learn that "in knowledge of Him standeth our eternal life." This gradual apprehension of the Divine Character had been the religious history of the human race; and when men, in days of darkness or partial illumination, had acted cruelly or deceitfully, they had acted in ignorance of that perfect morality which the Founder of Christianity finally revealed.

"Maurice is in the tradition of those who 'at least' were 'very sure of God.' He was a seer, a mystic, a prophet; charged with thoughts sometimes too great for human utterance, and occupied with a Vision beyond the boundaries of time.

"Developments of newer knowledge and a civilization increasing in complexity, are sweeping modern Society into new interests, to which the age in which Maurice lived seems remote and far away. The nineteenth century, in its simplicities and ardours and austerities, already stands apart as something removed from the energies of its successor. Is the Vision also destined to vanish, in which these men thought was included all the hope of the world? Even in such a case their work will not be forgotten. If in the generations to come the quest has been abandoned, and mankind has learnt to abide in contentment in the plain, heedless of the challenge of the distant hills; there will still be honour for the memory of those who set forth so bravely, upon an adventure which thus proved in the end all hopeless and barren. But if the old tradition remains, and amid the noise of the busy streets some will always hear the calling of an adventure beyond temporal attainment; it is to the memory of such as this man that these will turn, for the record of the travellers who once toiled up the hazardous way, towards the peaks which lose their summits in the cloud.[1]"

[1] C. F. G. Masterman.

VI

A PRIESTESS OF FREEDOM

THE "high midsummer pomps" of 1911 forced other events into the background. The 14th of June was the centenary of the birth of Mrs Beecher-Stowe, and, in a normal summer, I should have made a point of commenting on it. But that summer was abnormal; and, in our vivid drama of sovereignty and militarism and ecclesiastical pomp, there was no appropriate place for the "little bit of a woman, thin and dry as a pinch of snuff," who emerged from a Calvinistic manse and a New England girls' school to strike the resounding blow under which American Slavery reeled to its fall.

To-day let me make tardy amends for an enforced omission, and recall to the memory of my readers the main features of an extraordinary career. Harriet Beecher was born in Connecticut, and came, on both sides, of stock at once intellectual and devout. The character of the home may be reasonably inferred from the fact that at the age of twelve Harriet composed an essay on the question whether the Immortality of the Soul can be proved by the Light of Nature. It was inevitable that a girl whose relaxations took this severe form should become a teacher; and Harriet taught in a school which her eldest sister had founded, devoting her leisure to literary composition. At twenty-four she married a professor—one Calvin Stowe;—became the mother of a numerous family; proved herself a remarkably capable housewife, and by the profits of her pen helped to keep the pot boiling. At forty she began to write "Uncle Tom's Cabin," and before the year was out she was famous.

The "Peculiar Institution"—to use the patriotic synonym for Slavery—lent itself readily to the purposes of painful fiction. Twenty years before "Uncle Tom" appeared, Mrs Trollope, a most vigorous though now forgotten writer, drew, in a book strangely named "Jonathan Jefferson Whitelaw," a picture of domestic life in the American Slave States, which, just because it is less lurid, is even more impressive than "Uncle Tom." But "Jonathan Jefferson Whitelaw" was a book for English consumption. Probably Mrs Stowe never heard of it; certainly she copied nothing from it. Her thoughts were turned to the horrors of Slavery by what she saw on a visit to Kentucky; and, when once she had chosen her subject, material for her book poured in upon her in terrible abundance. The Abolitionist press teemed, week by week, with reports of unimaginable brutalities; and the pursuit of a fugitive slave whom some of her own relations had sheltered from his pursuers brought the accursed thing to her own door.

"Uncle Tom's Cabin" appeared serially in *The National Era* of Washington. Its force, fluency, passionate earnestness; its complete mastery over all the moods of pathos and even of disgust; its piled-up agony; and, strangely harmonized with all this, its unlooked-for humour, took the world by storm. As soon as the story appeared in book form it sold like wildfire. One hundred and twenty editions appeared in America, and forty in England. It was translated into every civilized language. It was dramatized again and again, and has not even yet lost its popularity in music-halls and provincial theatres. "It made the crack of the slave-driver's whip and the cries of the tortured blacks ring in every household in the land, till human hearts could endure it no longer." The slave-owning interest attacked the writer with incredible ferocity, and decried her facts as the creations of a diseased imagination. Her reply was "The Key to Uncle Tom's Cabin," in which she published authenticated instances of horrors even more loathsome than those which she had depicted. Some precisians thought—perhaps quite rightly—that the painful subject handled in the episode of Cassy and Legree made unsuitable reading for young people. So they produced a bowdlerized version called "A Peep into Uncle Tom's Cabin," which brought the pathos and the sensationalism, though not the ethics, of the original story into English nurseries and schoolrooms. It may be questioned whether any work of fiction ever produced so tangible an effect as the impetus which "Uncle Tom's Cabin" gave to the destruction of American Slavery. The author's account of the matter was characteristically simple: "I did not write it; God wrote it."

In 1853 Mrs Beecher-Stowe made her first visit to Europe. In England she was welcomed with a popular enthusiasm which down to that time had never been bestowed upon a foreigner. Society, from Queen Victoria downwards, received her with open arms. Harriet Duchess of Sutherland, in every sense the noblest of the great ladies who surrounded the Throne, received her with royal honours at Stafford House, which acquired for the nonce the nickname of "Aunt Harriet's Cabin." Lord Shaftesbury wrote in his diary: "It was a singular and most useful gathering. We had every rank of life, every form of opinion, political and religious—Bishops, Dissenting Ministers, Tradespeople, Peers, Quakers, and the wives of all. The homage was general; and everyone seemed delighted with the soft, earnest simplicity of her manner and language." Bishop Wilberforce wrote: "She spoke to me with interest. 'There was a time when your father's work for Emancipation seemed as hard as ours does now. Yet he succeeded.'" Money, quite unsolicited, poured in upon her from people whose hearts had been stirred by her appeal, and who made her their almoner for the general purposes of her crusade or for the service of individual cases.

The visit to England was the triumph of her life, and it heralded the triumph, twelve years later, of her cause.

At every stage of her struggle against the greatest of human abominations Mrs Stowe was nobly backed by her brother, Henry Ward Beecher. In 1856 the great preacher gave in his church at Plymouth an object-lesson in Slavery, not soon forgotten by those who witnessed it.

"The solemn, impressive silence of that vast congregation was absolutely painful when a young woman slowly ascended the stairs leading to the pulpit. Instantly assuming the look and manner of a slave-auctioneer, the minister called for bids. 'Look,' he exclaimed, 'at this marketable commodity—human flesh and blood like yourselves. You see the white blood of her father in her regular features and high, thoughtful brow. Who bids? Look at her trim figure and her wavy hair—how much do you bid for them? She is sound in wind and limb. I'll warrant her. Who bids? Her feet and hands are small and finely formed. What do you bid for her? She is a Christian woman—I mean "a praying nigger"—and that makes her more valuable, because it ensures her docility and obedience to your wishes. "Servants, obey your masters," you know. Well, she believes in that doctrine. How much for her? Will you allow this praying woman to be sent back to Richmond to meet the fate for which her father sold her? If not, who bids? Who bids?'

"The congregation was wrought to the highest pitch of excitement. Someone laid a bank-note at the preacher's feet. Then the collecting plates were passed round, and money and jewellery poured into them. Women took off their bracelets and rings, and men unfastened their watches. From time to time Beecher's voice rang out, 'In the name of Christ, Christian men and women, how much do you bid?'

"The congregation was stirred beyond description, and a well-known merchant rose in his place and said that, whatever deficiency in the price demanded remained when the collection was counted up, it would be made good by himself and his friends. 'Then you are free,' said Beecher, turning to the girl beside him, and the pent-up emotion of the audience found vent in sobs."

With such experiences as these to draw upon, no wonder that Harriet Beecher-Stowe could make her narrative thrill and burn.

There can, of course, be no question that "Uncle Tom's Cabin" is the book by which Mrs Stowe's name lives, and will live. But it would, I think, be a mistake to say that all the rest of her thirty books are negligible. "Old Town Folks" has many admirers. Harriet Martineau, no bad judge, thought "Dred" better than "Uncle Tom," and it sold a hundred thousand in a month. But " The Minister's Wooing " is, in my judgment, a better book than " Dred." It is touched, as all Mrs Stowe wrote was touched, by the fire of indignation against Slavery; but, in the main, it is " an endeavour to paint a style of life and manners which existed in New England in the earlier days of her national existence. Some of the principal characters are historic, and the author has executed the work with a reverential tenderness for those great and religious minds who laid in New England the foundations of many generations." The chief interest of the story lies in the struggle between human love and Calvinistic theology—the passionate affection of a jovial young vagabond for a beautiful and saintly girl, who is bound by her creed to regard him as a reprobate, but marries him after all. The book was published in 1859, but had no success. For many years I believe that I was the only man in England who knew it. In 1884 Mr Gladstone was induced to read it; perceived at once its intensely human interest, and sent Mrs Stowe a letter of warm approval. I was told at the time that this letter carried the book into a fresh edition.

Mrs Stowe lived till 1896, when she died in her eighty-sixth year. She was lively and energetic to the last, still worshipping the great cause to which she had given her life, and keenly interested in the fight for Freedom all over the world. But her work was accomplished when the " Constitutional Amendment" formally abolished Slavery in the United States. Her name deserves to be numbered with those of John Brown of Harper's Ferry, and Abraham Lincoln, and Whittier, and Lowell, and Sumner, and Lloyd Garrison, and all that goodly company of whom John Bright so memorably said: "Are they not

"'On Fame's eternal bead-roll worthy to be filed'?"

VII

THE CHANCELLOR

"THE Chancellor is so styled, *a Cancellando*, from cancelling the King's Letters-Patent when granted contrary to law, which is the highest point of his jurisdiction."

Thus Dryasdust, relying on the authority of Sir Edward Coke; but he evidently feels some doubts (which I share) about Sir Edward's etymology, for he thus proceeds:

"The office and name of Chancellor, *however derived*, was certainly known to the Courts of the Roman Emperors, where it originally seems to have signified a chief scribe or secretary, who was afterwards invested with several judicial powers, and a general superintendence over the rest of the officers of the Prince. . . . When the modern kingdoms of Europe were established upon the ruins of the Empire, almost every State preserved its Chancellor, with different jurisdictions and dignities, according to their different Constitutions."

That is true, and to the present day we read about the Chancellor of a foreign State in a sense equivalent to our English Prime Minister, and the *Chancellerie* of an Embassy as meaning an office where diplomatic business is transacted. But here at home we have Chancellors of all sorts and sizes, more than enough to fill this chapter. To begin with, we have the Lord High Chancellor of England, the first lay-subject of the Crown; created by no warrant or letters-patent, but by the simple delivery of the Great Seal. It takes a parchment a yard long, and I know not how many signatures, to constitute a First Lord of the Treasury or the Admiralty; but the Lord High Chancellor is created in an instant by a manual act. Then, as anyone knows, we have a Chancellor of the Exchequer, and, as Lancashire knows, a Chancellor of the Duchy. Every University has a Chancellor; generally, though not always, a blameless nobleman, who looks the part impressively but does not interfere with business. And yet again we have Ecclesiastical Chancellors. The title of Chancellor, says Dryasdust, "passed from the Roman Empire to the Roman Church, ever emulous of imperial state; and hence every Bishop has to this day his Chancellor, who is the principal judge of his Consistorial Court." And furthermore we have Chancellors of Cathedrals, whose functions are not clearly discerned by the outside public; and the Bishop of Oxford, in virtue of the fact that Windsor is in his diocese, is Chancellor of the Order of the Garter, and helps the Sovereign to buckle the embroidered strap round knightly knees.

Amid this multitude of Chancellors, who is *The*

Chancellor? Till within the last three years the question would scarcely have been asked, for it would have answered itself. *The* Chancellor is the Lord High Chancellor, and all the rest are Chancellors of this or that. "The Chancellor said, I *doubt.*" This was Lord Eldon. "The conduct of the Chancellor was most remarkable, skipping in and out of the House, and making the most extraordinary speeches." This was Lord Brougham. "I am glad to have been spared the pain of witnessing the Chancellor's disgraceful exhibition." This was Lord Westbury. "The susceptible Chancellor" of Gilbert's song—was he not Lord H——? Quite lately I have heard the point raised with vivacity and eloquence, by a lady whose father was Lord Chancellor in the reign of George IV. "In my day," she said, "the Chancellor was the Lord Chancellor. When my father was on the Woolsack, people who spoke of 'The Chancellor' did not mean Herries, or Goulburn, or anyone else who happened to be at the Exchequer. They meant the Lord Chancellor of England; and let me tell you that, next to the Premier, he was the most important person in the Cabinet." This must not be dismissed as merely filial enthusiasm, for Mr Gladstone, who amid his endless permutations had once sate in the Cabinet with this lady's father, always said that Lord Nozoo was the most useful man in the general work of Government who had ever filled the office of Lord Chancellor.

But we need not go back to the days of Lord Nozoo for the support of my contention. Even Gladstone at the height of his financial fame; even Disraeli when he was leading the House of Commons and refashioning the Constitution, was never called "The Chancellor." Each in his turn was Chancellor of the Exchequer; and, though Gladstone's financial genius raised that office to a celebrity which it had never known before, neither he nor any of his successors was ever known as The Chancellor. When Sir Henry Campbell-Bannerman formed his Government in 1905, he gathered round him, among other stalwarts, Sir Robert Reid and Mr Asquith. The former he made Lord Chancellor and the latter Chancellor of the Exchequer, and anyone who spoke of "The Chancellor" meant the sturdy Radical who had lately been "Bob Reid" and now became Lord Loreburn. When Sir Henry resigned and the Government was reconstituted under Mr Asquith, Mr Lloyd George became Chancellor of the Exchequer, as all of us know to our cost and some of us to our delight. From that date the style began to change, and, by an insidious process which is hard to trace, "The Chancellor" in journalistic parlance came to mean the Chancellor of the Exchequer. At first it was a little bewildering to old-fashioned people like myself. Our conception of The Chancellor was something ineffably stiff and stately, which could not move a yard without a mace and a seal and a train-bearer, and would sooner perish than appear upon a political platform. So, when we began to read in the headlines of our papers, "The Chancellor in the Hebrides"; "The Chancellor in the Channel Islands"; "The Chancellor at Bethesda"; "The Chancellor at Salem"; "Scathing Oration by the Chancellor"; "The Chancellor indulges in Billingsgate," we rubbed our eyes, and thought that the Great Seal had fallen into strange keeping, and that the old order of Chancellorship had indeed yielded place to new. But then, as Lord Nozoo's daughter indignantly remarked, "When I have read all this fuss about the Chancellor, and have shuddered to think what my father would have said about it, I discover that it is only Mr Lloyd George. Of course, I'm not the least surprised at anything *he* says, but why in the world should he be called *The* Chancellor?"

Why indeed! I think because he is by very far the most conspicuous Chancellor now before the public gaze, and one of the most remarkable people who have ever borne the title in any of its manifold significances. For my own part I have known Chancellors of all denominations—Lord High Chancellors, and Chancellors of the Exchequer, Chancellors of the Duchy, of the Universities, and of every diocese in England; but I have known none so interesting as the present custodian of the national finances (I invent that title by a feat of journalistic art, in order to avoid an irritating repetition).

Mr Lloyd George is, as we all know, a Celt, and

it is the glory of the Celtic races that they can transcend the invidious bars of birth and social station, and rear gentlemen in the shepherd's hut, at the plough-tail, and in the coal-mine. Everyone who remembers "Tom" Ellis—for no more formal designation befits his bright memory—must admit that the Welsh farmer's son was, in all the highest senses of the word, a true and perfect gentleman. Mr Lloyd George has, by the happy gift of nature, that innate refinement which no schooling can bestow, which wealth tends to coarsen, and which learning sometimes makes priggish. His refinement is akin to a kind of spirituality—I know no other word to express it—which sees visions and cherishes ideals, and breathes a soul into the too, too solid flesh of English politics. It is a British convention to assume that everyone has physical courage, and indeed it is true that few people have the moral courage to be physically cowardly. In Mr Lloyd George the two forms of courage are combined. He has displayed them both, or rather they have displayed themselves, at each conjuncture of his political life, and never more conspicuously than when he denounced the infamies of the South African War amid the murderous frenzy of the drunken Jingo mob.

"Who'll wear the beaten colours, and cheer the beaten men?
Who'll wear the beaten colours, till our time comes again?
Where sullen crowds are densest and fickle as the sea;
Who'll wear the beaten colours, and wear them home with me?"

To that challenge our official Liberalism made indeed a lamentable response; but Mr Lloyd George pinned the "beaten colours" over his heart, and carries them there still. His eloquence befits his nature, and is part of it; unstudied, unrehearsed, or, if rehearsed at all, liable to sudden gusts of inspiration which totally transfigure it. He fascinates, persuades, attracts; turns, as lightly as a spirit, from grave to gay, and with a bow drawn at a venture can speed an arrow which goes straight home—and rankles. As lightly as a spirit I said; and, as I write the words, I bethink me of a Shakespearean creation which no other Chancellor of any description has ever resembled. Mr Lloyd George is the "delicate Ariel," the "tricksy spirit," of the political Tempest. He appears, and vanishes, and reappears in unexpected places and at uncalculated times. He is ready, as the moment requires, "to fly, to swim, to dive into the fire, to ride on the curl'd clouds." His mission is to right the wrong, but he is not ashamed to play tricks upon his victims. Though his spells "flame amazement," still he "does his spiriting gently"; and he says, with literal truth, to the usurping Lords, "I have made you mad."

> "You fools! I and my fellows
> Are Ministers of Fate: the elements,
> Of whom your swords are temper'd, may as well
> Wound the loud winds, or with bemock'd-at stabs
> Kill the still-closing waters, as diminish
> One dowle that's in my plume. My fellow-Ministers
> Are like invulnerable. If you could hurt,
> *Your swords are now too massy for your strengths*
> *And will not be uplifted.*"

VIII

THE HEALER

THE 22nd of September 1910 was for Scotsmen a centenary; and not for Scotsmen only, but for all *homines bonæ voluntatis*, as the Vulgate translates the Angelic hymn—for all "men of good will," who find pleasure in calling to remembrance a character of pure virtue and an actively beneficent career.

I believe it is true that I have often written jocosely about Doctors and Doctoring; and, indeed, there are aspects of the medical profession which, in all ages, have afforded material for laughter. Never mind; the doctor "gets his own back," as the phrase is, when he condemns us to bed and slops for a week, or draws "Syme's knife" from its lair in that ornamental casket of lethal weapons. Thus armed, the doctor can stand a little chaff; and, to do him justice, he does not, as a rule, seem to resent it. But to-day I make no demands on his endurance, for I am writing with serious purpose about one who was a doctor, and something more. To call a doctor "a Professor of the Healing Art" is as obsolete as to call a barrister "a Gentleman of the Long Robe," or an M.P. "an Ornament of the British Senate." But the reproach of pomposity and long-windedness cannot, I think, be levelled against the simple phrase—"a Healer." The word is at least as old as the Authorized Version, and it has been made the title of a striking poem in which Whittier addresses a young physician:

> "Beside the unveiled mysteries
>   Of life and death go stand,
> With guarded lips and reverent eyes,
>   And pure of heart and hand.
>
> So shalt thou be with power endued
>   From Him who went about
> The Syrian hillsides, doing good
>   And casting demons out.
>
> That Good Physician liveth yet
>   Thy friend and guide to be;
> The Healer by Gennesaret
>   Shall walk the rounds with thee."

Every doctor who approaches his vocation in the spirit of this high ideal must be, in his sphere and measure, a Healer, and the title is doubly appropriate to the man whom this chapter seeks to commemorate.

Doubly appropriate, I say, for Dr John Brown, of Edinburgh, author of "Rab and his Friends" and "Marjorie Fleming," was not only a skilful and successful physician, but also a writer whose quality was eminently sanative. He had been richly dowered with the gift of the Healer, and it flowed out from him not more conspicuously in his professional practice than in the charm of social intercourse and the cheerful magic of his pen. There must be many among my readers who know and love the books so inseparably associated with his name, and they, perhaps, may care to see a brief outline of his life.

John Brown was born in the town of Biggar, of a long line of Presbyterian ministers who had lived and laboured outside the precincts of the Established Kirk. Both the Presbyterian and the Voluntary elements in his pedigree had their marked effect upon his life. He was educated at the High School of Edinburgh, and at the age of seventeen he chose Medicine as his profession. He was a pupil of the famous Syme (who gave us the knife mentioned in an earlier paragraph), and, when the days of pupilage were finished, his assistant in surgical practice. It was at this period of his life that he encountered the incidents which, twenty-eight years later, he wove into his world-famous story of "Rab and his Friends." Of that story he said, in reply to reiterated enquiries, "It is in all essentials strictly matter of fact." Vague people always imagine that "Rab" is what they call "a story about dogs." Of course it is really a human document; but, in his handling of it the author reveals himself as a true dog-lover. He not only loved dogs, but knew them and understood them. "He has written of dogs with as great fidelity and intuition as Landseer has painted them." He believed that they have not only higher faculties than are commonly attributed to them, but something akin to the Moral Sense. Bacon said, and

Burns repeated it, that " Man is the God of the dog," and thereto Brown added that " it would be well for man if his worship were as immediate, and instinctive, and absolute as the dog's."

But neither the love of dogs nor the love of letters was allowed, at the early period of which I am writing, to come between Brown and his professional work. He had chosen the office of a doctor, and he gave himself to it with all his energies of body and mind—yet with a difference. Surgery, to which he had originally applied himself, could not long detain this delicate and sensitive genius. " He was not fascinated by the excitement of operative practice, and, as those were not the days of chloroform or any anæsthetic, his intensely sympathetic and sensitive nature seemed to recoil from the painful scenes of surgery." So in 1831 he left Edinburgh for a time, and became assistant to a doctor at Chatham, where the first outbreak of cholera gave him an opportunity —which he finely used—of distinguishing himself in a hand-to-hand fight with a new and mysterious enemy. One incident of that fight made a lasting impression on Charles Dickens, who said in later years, " There was a young Scottish doctor at Chatham during the cholera epidemic. He remained with a poor woman whom all had deserted, ministering to her till the end, and then, overcome with fatigue, fell asleep, and next morning was found asleep by her dead body."

By this time Brown had forsaken surgery and

devoted himself wholly to medicine. From Chatham he returned to Edinburgh, took his M.D., and began the career of a practising physician, which, except when occasionally disabled by illness, he pursued for forty years. Yet "frequent contact with suffering humanity unhinged him much, and was indeed one of the greatest burdens of his life." His medical career was marked by no striking incidents. He kept himself studiously aloof from advertisement and notoriety. Though a staunch Liberal in politics, he was in professional matters conservative, and mistrusted new lights. "He could not abide the theories, and hypotheses, and reckless experiments of the period. . . . It was really the *Science of Healing* that he pleaded for, perfected by the practice of its Art." Many of his patients were ladies, who had been attracted to him by his tender and sympathetic writing. Like all good men, he loved the society of good women, but he loved it with discrimination. "A Talking Woman is an awful judgment, and mystery, and oppression." Himself the simplest and straightest of men, he could not tolerate the female patients who played tricks upon the doctor; "running from one 'charming' specialist to another; doing a little privately and dishonestly to themselves or the children with the globules; going to see some notorious great man without telling, or taking with them, the old family friend, merely, as they say, to 'satisfy their mind.'"

What Brown loved and encouraged was a perfect openness and intimacy of confidence between patient and physician, and, where that was established, he was the tenderest, most sympathetic, and most self-sacrificing of friends. His indifference to professional earnings made and kept him a poor man. Quite outside the limits of his profession, "his advice and counsel were sought by scores of young Edinburgh artists and literary men, and he had a felicitous gift of tendering advice with the least possible appearance of preaching." And to this was related another gift. "All natural and unaffected human beings were at once at home with him, and even the most artificial prigs gradually thawed in his presence."

But it is time to turn from Brown the Doctor to Brown the Man of Letters. It was truly said by *The Eclectic Review* that "a man can scarcely hope for immortality by possessing the name of John Brown, but he may walk down to posterity with tolerable individualiy by the epithet of *Subsecivæ* Brown." "Horæ Subsecivæ," or, as he preferred to call them, "Bye-Hours," first appeared in 1858, but long before that date Brown had been at work, or rather at play, with his pen. He started as an art critic; he was one of the first reviewers to acclaim Ruskin's "Modern Painters," and so began a series of studies on all manner of subjects—biographical, artistic, literary, social—which ran, chiefly in *The Scotsman*, for upwards of thirty years. Some of these papers, including "Rab and his Friends," were collected in his first book of "Horæ Subsecivæ"; which was followed by a second in 1861, and a third in the year of his death—1882. Of the papers included in "Horæ," by far the most popular was "Rab and his Friends," first published as a pamphlet which made its author's name famous, not only in Great Britain, but in the colonies and the United States. It is indeed an exquisite idyll of Scottish peasant life, unsurpassed in tenderness and pathos; but, of course, there is no room for quotation here. Next to "Rab," the paper which excited most interest was "Marjorie Fleming," the story of a child precocious in goodness and cleverness, to whom the great Sir Walter turned for refreshment and exhilaration when he found the task of writing "Waverley" hang heavy on his hands.

But even this very cursory sketch of John Brown would be glaringly incomplete without some reference to the quiet but fervent religion which coloured all his life and work. He held that "the greater and the better—the inner—part of man is, and should be, private—much of it more than private." Yet now and then he expressed his faith in words which could not be mistaken. In a letter written in 1864 he made a double protest against Renan's "Vie" and Newman's "Apologia." "I am so glad I was grounded in historic Christianity in my youth, and am almost mechanically screened against these fellows, and their guns and shells, their torpedoes and mines." In a less challenging mood, he wrote, after hearing Jowett preach: "I liked his sermon much, but, with my old-fashioned beliefs, I miss the doctrine of sin and salvation."

On the death of Thackeray, to whom both as man and as author he was devotedly attached, he wrote: "God grant we all get good by this, and indeed by everything! For that, after all, is *the* thing. Are we better or worse now than we were a while ago? Are we ripening, or withering, or rottening?"

And where could one find a more perfectly Evangelical sermon than is contained in the closing paragraph of his "Plain Words on Health, addressed to Working People"?

"Good-night to you all, big and little, young and old; and go home to your bedside. There is Some One there waiting for you, and His Son is here ready to take you to Him. . . . I need not say more. You know what I mean. You know Who is waiting, and you know Who it is that stands beside you, having the likeness of the Son of Man. Good-night! The night cometh, in which neither you nor I can work—may we work while it is day; whatsoever thy hand findeth to do, do it with thy might, for there is no work or device in the grave whither we are all of us hastening; and when the night is spent, may we all enter on a healthful, a happy, an everlasting To-morrow."

We could not fashion a more suitable Farewell to this "beloved Physician," whose whole gospel of life was summed up in this one sentence:

"God must have depths of light yet to reveal, to account for the shadows here."

IX

JAMES PAYN

"SHE," if I remember aright, was short for the fuller title, "She who must be obeyed." I have reason to think that "She" is now numbered among my readers, and She demands, with iteration, a paper on James Payn. The topic has no particular relevance to anything now happening or impending in the actual world; but I am quite willing to forget for a moment all the lore of Second Chambers and Veto Bills and Pantomime Peers—and to recall the winning personality of the man whose name stands at the head of this chapter.

James Payn was born in 1830, and spent his early life at Maidenhead. His father was Clerk to the Thames Commissioners, a keen sportsman, an active man of business, and a leading figure in local society. James Payn was early initiated into the sports of the field, and rode his pony fearlessly with the old Berkshire Hounds. But hunting bored him, and he cordially detested all athletic exercises. It is recorded that his cricket ended when he stopped a ball with the crown of his straw hat. At eleven he was sent to Eton, a sensitive, precocious boy; and he used to say that his earliest experience of misery was the rejection of an article which he sent to the school-magazine. The only traces which "Henry's holy shade" left on him were its gentlemanlike "Tone" (at which he was never tired of laughing) and a dislike of Greek which amounted to a personal enmity. From Eton he went to Woolwich, with the desperate design of entering the scientific branch of the army; but the only result of the experiment was to inspire him with a hatred of all things military. His parents now resolved that he should be a clergyman, and, with that end in view, he went to a private tutor's in Devonshire, where he made his first appearance in print. He began with a poem, which was published in *Leigh Hunt's Journal*, and he soon was writing articles for *Bentley's Miscellany* and *Household Words*.

In October 1849 he went up to Trinity College, Cambridge; read very sparingly, took no exercise, but cultivated, and was cultivated by, all the pleasantest society in College, and published his first book,—"Stories from Boccaccio." The time had now arrived when he must decide on his career. He realized—as everyone who knew him must have realized—that he had no vocation to Holy Orders; whereas he had an even passionate love for literature, and gifts which formed the natural equipment for a literary career. He took his degree in 1852, being already engaged, and was married in 1854. It was, if ever there was, a love match. With his wife he settled at Ambleside, and for some years he "lived an idyllic life at Rydal Cottage, under the shadow of Nab Scar." His writings are full of memories of this time. An essay called " An Exceedingly Cheap Tour " describes a progress which he made from one district of the Lakes to another, telling the landlord of each inn in turn that he was collecting material for a " Tourist's Hand Book and Guide to the English Lakes." The desire to be commended in this guide-book for good accommodation and moderate charges was so strong in each innkeeping breast that the bills grew smaller and smaller as the tour proceeded, and at last " there was quite a difficulty in getting them to charge anything at all."

In the summer of 1857 some old friends from Cambridge, among whom was the ever-beloved " C. S. C.," met Payn at Ambleside. By the magical spell of good-fellowship they induced him to make the unprecedented effort of climbing Scafell ; and as he lagged miserably towards the summit, Calverley made the admirably apt quotation :

> " The labour *we* delight in physics Payn ! "

In 1858 Payn settled himself in Edinburgh as editor of *Chambers's Journal*. He worked so vigorously that the proprietors remarked that, what with his salary as editor, and what with the payments which he received for his contributions, he left very little for the House of Chambers. He liked his work, but he disliked Edinburgh. A Scottish Sabbath was more than he could tolerate, and the east winds were bad for a delicate wife and children. In vain Robert Chambers assured him that the same "isothermal band" passed through Edinburgh and London. "I know nothing about isothermal bands," said Payn, "but I know that I never saw a four-wheeled cab blown upside down in London." So to London he bent his steps, retaining the editorship of *Chambers's Journal*; and settled in Maida Vale. His impressions of the metropolis as it was in 1861 are given in a delightful little book called "Melibœus in London." It was a prime favourite with the writer, who always attributed its failure to its outlandish title. The description of the fire in Southwark, in which the heroic Braidwood lost his life, is one of the most vivid pen-pictures that I know.

Payn's life was now exactly what he enjoyed, for it was one incessant round of literary activity. He took no holidays, for he hated them. If he was forced into the country for a week or two, he used the exile as the material for a story or an essay. The whole burden of editorship was on his shoulders; and, at the same time, he was writing his first novels. "Lost Sir Massingberd," the story of the wicked baronet who fell into the hollow trunk of an oak and was starved to death, ran in *Chambers's Journal* through the year 1864, and raised the circulation by twenty thousand copies. From first to last, Payn wrote more than a hundred volumes of one sort or another. "By Proxy" has been justly admired for the wonderful accuracy of its local colour, and for a masterly knowledge of Chinese character, which the writer drew exclusively from encyclopædias and books of travel. But, for all that, Payn, in my judgment, was at his best in the short story. He practised that difficult art long before it became popular, and a book, called originally "People, Places, and Things," but now "Humorous Stories," is a masterpiece of fun, invention, and observation. In 1874 he became "Reader" to Messrs Smith & Elder, and in that capacity had the happiness of discovering "Vice Versa," and the less felicitous experience of rejecting "John Inglesant" as unreadable.

It was at this period of his life that I first encountered Payn, and I fell at once under his charm. He was not a faultless character; for he was irritable, petulant, and prejudiced. He took the strongest dislikes, sometimes on very slight grounds; was unrestrained in expressing them, and was apt to treat opinions which he did not share very cavalierly. But none of these faults could obscure his charm. He was the most tender-hearted of human beings, and the sight, even the thought, of cruelty set his blood on fire. But, though he was intensely humane, he was absolutely free from mawkishness; and a wife-beater, or a child-torturer, or a cattle-maimer would have had short shrift at his hands. He was intensely sympathetic, especially towards the hopes and struggles of the young and the unbefriended. Many an author, once struggling but now triumphant, could attest this trait. But his chief charm was his humour. It was absolutely natural; bubbled like a fountain, and danced like light. Nothing escaped it, and solemnity only stimulated it to further activities. He had the power, which Sydney Smith extolled, of "abating and dissolving pompous gentlemen with the most successful ridicule"; and, when he was offended, the ridicule had a remarkably sharp point. It was, of course, impossible that all the humour of a man who joked incessantly could be equally good. Sometimes it was rather boyish, playing on proper names or personal peculiarities; and sometimes it descended to puns. But, for sheer rapidity, I have never known Payn's equal. When a casual word annoyed him, his repartee flashed out like lightning. I could give plenty of instances, but to make them intelligible I should have to give a considerable amount of introduction, and that would entirely spoil the sense of flashing rapidity. There was no appreciable interval of time between the provoking word and the repartee which it provoked.

Another great element of charm in Payn was his warm love of life,

> "And youth, and bloom, and this delightful world."

While he hated the black and savage and sordid side of life with a passionate hatred, he enjoyed all its better—which he believed to be its larger—part with an infectious relish. Never have I known a more blithe and friendly spirit; never a nature to which Literature and Society—books and men—yielded a more constant and exhilarating joy. He had unstinted admiration for the performances of others, and was wholly free from jealousy. His temperament was not equable. He had ups and downs, bright moods and dark, seasons of exaltation and seasons of depression. The one succeeded the other with startling rapidity, but the bright moods triumphed, and it was impossible to keep him permanently depressed. His health had always been delicate, but illness neither crushed his spirit nor paralysed his pen. Once he broke a blood-vessel in the street, and was conveyed home in an ambulance. During the transit, though he was in some danger of bleeding to death, he began to compose a narrative of his adventure, and next week it appeared in *The Illustrated London News.*

During the last two years of his life he was painfully crippled by arthritic rheumatism, and could no longer visit the Reform Club, where for many years he had every day eaten his luncheon and played his rubber. Determining that he should not completely lose his favourite, or I should rather say his only, amusement, some members of the Club banded themselves together to supply him with a rubber in his own house twice a week; and this practice was maintained to his death. It was a striking testimony to the affection which he inspired. In those years I was a pretty frequent visitor, and, on my way to the house, I used to bethink me of stories which might amuse him, and I used even to note them down between one visit and another, as a provision for next time. One day Payn said, "A collection of your stories would make a book, and I think Smith & Elder would publish it." I thought my anecdotage scarcely worthy of so much honour; but I promised to make a weekly experiment in *The Manchester Guardian*. My "Collections and Recollections" ran through the year 1897, and appeared in book form at Easter 1898. But Payn had died on the 25th of the previous March; and the book, which I had hoped to put in his hand, I could only inscribe to his delightful memory.

X

GLADSTONE ON HYMNS

As long as Mr Gladstone had a house in London he used from time to time to honour me by dining in Stucco Gardens. Naturally, one did not invite so distinguished a guest casually, but always that he might meet someone whom he wished to see, or who specially wished to see him. On the 3rd of November 1892 he was the subject of an innocent conspiracy. There were a few young, or youngish, men, whom I knew to be enthusiastic Liberals, and who seldom had the chance of seeing their Leader in private life. So I begged Mr Gladstone to honour me with his company, and I invited Lord Acton, than whom no one knew Gladstone's moods more perfectly, and Mr Sydney Buxton, who was one of my colleagues in the Government, to act as my Aaron and Hur, and to bear up my arms through this fateful evening. The other guests were my Oxford friend, H. C. Shuttleworth, then Professor of Pastoral Theology at King's College; Mr H. W. Massingham; Mr E. T. Cook; a young journalist and poet called Fred Henderson; and an Irish curate called Kennedy, from the East India Docks. Smoking was forborne, because Mr Gladstone disliked it;

but Canon Scott Holland, and Arthur Stanton, of St Alban's, Holborn, arrived with the coffee, and the circle was complete. It is easy to guess what would be the drift of the conversation. We were all reformers, some Socialist, some merely Radical; none of us very old, all of us very keen, and attached, with a mixture of wonder and deference, to our Leader, who had just become Prime Minister, for the fourth time, in his eighty-third year. It was obvious, not indeed to "pump" him, yet to listen with eager interest for the slightest hint about a new Home Rule Bill, a democratic Budget, an attempt to meet the growing demand for Social Reform. But on all these topics the Oracle was dumb. My friend Mr Massingham will, I am sure, forgive me if I remind him of the blank perplexity and dismay which expressed themselves in his face, and spread to the countenances of his neighbours, when Mr Gladstone suddenly broke into the subject of Hymnody and its accompaniments—the best hymns, the best tunes, the caprices of village choirs, and the most suitable position for the organ. I have never seem discomfiture more complete, and I nearly perished by suppressed laughter. One episode is specially fresh in my memory. Mr Gladstone waxed enthusiastic over the verses in "The Lay of the Last Minstrel" which begin:

"That Day of Wrath, that dreadful Day."

One of the company, delighted to hear something

that he thought he recognized, mildly observed, "Ah! yes; a translation of 'Dies Irae.'" Gladstone pounced on him like a hawk. "Translation, indeed? Where in the original do you find that splendid image

> "'When, shrivelling like a parchèd scroll,
> The flaming heavens together roll'?

There is no translation there—it's Scott's original genius."

An echo of this discourse reaches me through Mr Laothbury's new book of Gladstone's Letters:

"'Hymns Ancient and Modern' ought some day to receive a drastic purgation. . . . 'Jacob's Dream' is indeed a true and very fine poem, especially the earlier part of it. But 'Jesu, Lover of my Soul,' though a general favourite, I cannot and will not admire. Why, on the other hand, has Mr Goldwin Smith left out those noble, those wonderful verses of Scott in the Lay—'That Day of Wrath, that dreadful Day'—almost the noblest sacred verses since the 'Dies Irae,' of which they are sometimes wrongly called a translation?"

Gladstone's love of hymns was intense but eclectic. He chose for himself, was entirely untrammelled by the authority of criticism, and was swayed by no ecclesiastical preferences. Thus in 1879, after pointing out the growing influence of Anglican

"Ritualism" on the public forms of Presbyterian and Nonconformist Churches, he made the following comment:—

"This is the return of a benefit received. For the present methods of hymnody in the English Church have, I apprehend, in substance been copied from them. And this hymnody will, I think, be admitted to contribute largely, not only to the outward effect, but—which is a very different matter—to the true inward life of her services. The very remarkable 'Communion of Hymns,' so to call it, which now prevails throughout the land, is in truth one among the consolatory signs of the great amount of religious unity still subsisting, though amidst many and even important differences, in this nation."

When Dr Harold Browne was Bishop of Ely he tried to frame a Diocesan Hymn-Book. He asked each Incumbent in the diocese to send him a list of the hymns which were most popular with his congregation. There was only one which appeared in every list, and that was "Rock of Ages." Gladstone shared to the full the general devotion to that glorious "Gospel in Verse," and he showed his devotion by rendering it into rhymed Latin—a compliment which he also paid to "Art thou weary?" "Hark! my Soul, it is the Lord" he deemed only too sacred for promiscuous use; but he rendered it into Italian under the belief—probably mistaken—that Christians in Italy have no popular hymns in their native tongue, but are forced to rely on the Latin hymns from the Breviary.

Writing in 1890 to R. H. Hutton, of *The Spectator*, he said, "'The Dream of Gerontius' is an astonishing flight of genius, incommensurable with anything else. Those closing verses!" Those "closing verses" (profoundly loved also by General Gordon) scarcely constitute a hymn; but, a little earlier in the poem, we find one of the chief glories of English hymnody: "Praise to the Holiest in the Height." This hymn Gladstone loved as it deserves to be loved; but even here he indulged his taste for independent criticism by changing "Holiest" into the inharmonious and tautological "Highest." "Praise to the Highest in the Height"!—I scarcely know a more unfortunate emendation.

Gladstone's disparagement of "Jesu, Lover of my Soul," given in an earlier citation, has attracted general and just surprise. His statement of the reasons for that disparagement—a document in every way characteristic of his mind—is here appended. He gave it to me on the 21st of May 1894:

"I cannot assign a high rank to this extremely popular hymn. It has no unity; no cohesion; no climax; no procession; and no special force. A number of ideas are jumbled together, rather than interwoven. The paths of the metaphors cross one another, not always on the same level. A hymn ought to be what Horace demands in a play—

simplex dumtaxat et unum. This is not a whole, for the parts seem to have no relation to one another.

"The first petition is 'Let me to Thy bosom fly.' It seems to me that the familiarity of a hymn ought not to go beyond that of Scripture. St John undoubtedly lay on the bosom of his Lord. But he alone; and we are not all St Johns. And, further, he does not thus describe himself; he is simply the disciple whom Jesus loved (xxi. 7-24).

"The next prayer is that the bosom may be a refuge from the storm at sea. Surely the more appropriate refuge from a tempest is not a bosom, but a haven or a shore. With another shock, the figure of 'flying to the bosom' is displaced, and the prayer is 'Safe into the haven guide'—a different idea and a different process.

"But we have not yet done. The prayer that follows is another incongruity—'O, receive my soul at last.' But the preceding course of thought is not on escape from the final ordeal of the Judgment; it is on vindicated rescue and repose. Next comes

"'Other refuge have I none,
Hangs my helpless soul on Thee.'

But here again I feel jolted from the one term to the other; the idea of hanging on the Saviour is in itself just, but it is in no unity with that of refuge; dependence being one thing and shelter another; and such a suite ought not to be in a hymn purporting to be continuous. The next prayer is 'Leave, ah leave me not.' This is not emphasis but tautology; the idea that Our Saviour can leave us is not a prevalent one in a Christian's mind, or one on which he should or could lay emphasis. Were the faint one leaving Him the case would be reversed, and any amount of stress might he laid. . . . It would be legitimate emphasis, and not mere tautology. And almost immediately we come across another novelty of metaphor—'Cover my defenceless head.' I do not say that transitions of metaphor are in themselves illegitimate, but surely they should be sparingly used, and not so collocated as to give the idea of incongruity. A step ought to cover the distance between them, but this hymn continually demands a leap. And this metaphor is again immediately broken in upon; a shadow in poetry is hardly to be treated as a cover against attacking forces. Next we have water in a new character. Very good, if there be a bridge to effect the transition. Here there is none, but we must jump to it; the element which at the opening of the hymn was the great enemy and great danger is now presented as the source of hope and life. 'Healing streams' are to abound. Then healing streams are not mere fountains, but the Fountain of Life, and we are to drink of them although they are already within us. They are then invited to spring, though they have already sprung; and to 'rise to all eternity,' with an ambiguity, for it does not appear whether rising means increase or only continuity.

"The central thought of the hymn is without doubt evangelical and good, but it is clothed, as it seems to me, in a pieced and uncomely garment. Every hymn should surely have a movement calm, solemn, and continuous. These zigzags are out of keeping with the nature of the composition. They jar the mind of a reader and set him questioning where he is and where he is going. It is the mass of transitions unsoftened, not the enormity of any single one, that supplies the gravamen of the charge. I know no other hymn, certainly no other hymn of such reputation, against which these objections lie."

XI

MATTHEW ARNOLD

CRITICS have sometimes commented on the frequency with which, in my writings, I refer to Matthew Arnold. They tell me that I am saturated with his diction, that my style is modelled on his prose, and that I quote his phrases with undue iteration. Not long ago the criticism was launched in a humorous form by the promotors of a recreation, to me unknown, called Pop-in-Taw, who wrote thus : " Mr G. W. E. Russell in *The Manchester Guardian* Collects his early Recollections of the game, which go back to his school-days at Harrow. He recalls the late Mr Gladstone's indignation at the simitar play of Beaconsfield, and how as a young man he himself played at Pop-in-Taw with the Duchess of Bedford, Dr Pusey, and Mr Matthew Arnold."

Of " simitar play " (so spelt) and its iniquities I know nothing, but the collocation of names pleases me ; and a game, whether bridge or golf or lawn-tennis or four-handed chess, in which the four persons named were participators, would have presented some interesting features. The Duchess would have contributed grace, Dr Pusey vigour, Matthew Arnold suavity, and the present writer an intelligent appreciation of the performances of the other three. When it was over, all would have agreed that Matthew Arnold was the most delightful playfellow they ever had—he lost so cheerfully, and won so modestly ; never found fault with his partner, and declared that the feeblest beginner only wanted a little more practice to play a capital game. In this judgment Arnold would have himself concurred ; even as, when one quoted from his writings, he would artlessly enquire, "Did I say that? How good that was!" What Arnold would have been at Pop-in-Taw, had the game been invented in his time, that he was in all the transactions of actual life. Lord Morley wrote to me on the occasion of his death, "Never shall we know again so blithe and friendly a spirit" ; and I have always been profoundly grateful for the chance which, when I was still a schoolboy, brought me within the sphere of that fascinating influence.

On the 30th of October 1867 Arnold, whose home was then in London, wrote to his friend Lady de Rothschild : "We are fairly driven out of Chester Square, partly by the number of our children, partly by the necessity of a better school for the boys ; and we have fixed on Harrow. The clay soil is the only objection, but the grass fields and hedgerow elms are a great attraction for me." It was eminently characteristic of this most humane of scholars thus to link the natural amenities with the educational advantages of the place. "I only wish you could eat our strawberries. We have two great dishes every day, and I see no prospect of an end to them." "I have had a long walk with Rover in the fields beyond Northolt, which are quiet and solemn in this gray weather beyond belief." "I have had a capital game at racquets with C——, a friend of the boys, and have been round the garden to look at the wild daffodils, which are coming on beautifully." "Your verses gave me very great pleasure. Nothing will ever eradicate from me the feeling of the greater suitableness and adequateness, for a topic of this kind, of Latin elegiacs than of any other description of verse."

I quote these passages at haphazard from Arnold's letters written at Harrow, in order to show the sort of man who swam into our ken when I was a boy of fifteen. Ignorant as schoolboys proverbially are, we yet knew the name of Arnold, and some of us, a little more alert than the others, knew that Dr Arnold's son Matthew was renowned as a poet and a critic—in short, "a swell." But what we did not expect was to find this distinguished stranger a young, active, and singularly graceful man; interested in all games and sports; a splendid swimmer and fisherman; wholly free from pomposity and stiffness; overflowing with humour, and pleasantly unguarded in speech. "I suppose you know Dr Vaughan, sir," said I, tremulously naming the tutelary deity of Harrow—"he must have been at Rugby about your time." "Oh, yes. I know dear old Vaughan—a good creature, but brutally ignorant." I suppose that there was something iconoclastic in my nature, for this brief epitome of Vaughan's character, and the culture of a Senior Classic, filled me with delight.

Arnold's eldest son was a very delicate and a singularly attractive boy, who soon became a great friend of mine, invited me to his home, and introduced me to his family. Thus began a friendship which has lasted till to-day. Fifteen is a receptive age, and it is not very curious that this early introduction to the chief of critics should have made a permanent dint on a schoolboy's mind. Boys who write are nearly always flamboyant. They adore rhetoric, admire Macaulay, and try to write accordingly. But here was the author of "Essays in Criticism," always kindly interested in the most immature and unpromising efforts, and always ready with the pruning-knife. The perils of "Middle-class Macaulayese," the "note of Provinciality in literature," the difference between "Asiatic and Attic prose," the "desperate attempt to make a platitude endurable by making it pompous"—these were topics to which he introduced us, and the introduction was not in vain. "Tell H. to do more in literature; he has a talent for it; but to avoid Carlylese as he would the devil." Admonitions of this kind fell constantly on our ears, and could scarcely fail to correct the redundancy of youth.

There is another debt, and perhaps a greater, which I owe to this early intimacy. Arnold first taught me to think; before, I only knew how to argue. His "sinuous, easy, unpolemical method" led one almost imperceptibly into new ways of thought. He was always teaching one to "make a return upon oneself," to see "things as they really are," to disabuse one's mind of claptrap, and to challenge hoary conventions. We repeated, as all boys repeat, the shibboleths of Toryism or Radicalism or Ritualism or Rationalism, or any other "ism" to which one had attached oneself; and it was invaluable discipline to be forced back from phrases to things, and to hear, at the end of a florid generalization—"But can we quite say that?" In those days we were Radicals of a utilitarian type. We believed tremendously in Acts of Parliament, and were persuaded that, if only we could disestablish Churches and extend the suffrage and overset the Monarchy, we should precipitate the Millennium. It did us great good, though it irritated us, to be reminded that the most degraded misery, the darkest ignorance, the lowest standards of morals and life, may coexist with a beautifully organized system of government, and that the political machinery with which we wished to be endlessly tinkering was only valuable so far as it tended to make life brighter, happier, and more humane. By being Arnold's disciples we did not unlearn our Radicalism, but we learned to wear it with a difference, and to realize that political reform is related to Social Reform only as the means to the end.

Of Matthew Arnold's theology, once the subject of such acrid controversy, this is scarcely the place to write; and indeed it was marked by a freakishness which often hindered its good effect. Yet he rendered conspicuous service by poking fun at "the old Liberal hacks," the "modern Sadducees, who believe neither in angel nor spirit, but only in Mr Herbert Spencer." To those grim oracles Arnold replied that religion is the most gracious and beautiful thing in the world; that Isaiah and St Paul are writers to be read with human interest as well as spiritual appetite; and that the characteristically Christian virtues, Charity and Chastity—kindness and pureness—are the chief goods of national life. He told me once that his book of "Discourses in America" was, of all his prose-writings, the one by which he most wished to be remembered after his death. It was a memorable choice, for in those Discourses the humorist, the master of style, the fastidious critic, sinks into the background, and the figure that emerges is the uncompromising teacher of an ethical system drawn straight from the New Testament.

"The individual Englishman, whenever and wherever called upon to do his duty, does it almost invariably with the old energy, courage, virtue. And this is what we gain by having had, as a people, in the ground of our being, a firm faith in conduct; by having believed, more steadfastly and fervently than most, this great law that moral causes govern the standing and the falling of men and nations. The law gradually widens, indeed, so as to include Light as well as Honesty and Energy—to make Light, also, a moral cause. Unless we are transformed we cannot finally stand, and without more light we cannot be transformed."

To many—perhaps most—of my readers Matthew Arnold is dearer and more familiar as a poet than as a prose-writer ; but his poetic work and value cannot be properly estimated at the fag-end of a chapter, though perhaps they may some day claim a whole chapter for themselves. Here I have merely been attempting to account for an influence, of which the traces seem to be apparent in my ways of thought and speech. If this be so, I am a proud as well as a grateful disciple.

I first saw Matthew Arnold at Harrow on the 28th of April 1868. On the 15th of April 1888 he wrote to me from Liverpool—his last letter. That day he died. *Lux perpetua luceat ei.*

XII

THE YOUNG DISRAELI

Mr Monypenny is to be congratulated. If the remainder of his book is as good as this instalment, it will rank among our great biographies.[1] The task must have been in any case a difficult one, and it has been said that several writers, eminent in statesmanship or letters, looked at it, hesitated, and withdrew. Mr Monypenny bore himself more courageously, for he accepted a task which, difficult for anyone, was particularly difficult for him. He is said to be a young man, as youth is reckoned in authorship; to have lived a great part of his life out of England; and to be entirely ignorant of politics. Yet he undertook to write the story of a life lived almost uninterruptedly in England, immersed in political matter, and only remembered, in its personal aspects, by people who are growing old. As far as this one volume justifies a judgment, all these difficulties seem to have been overcome; and the biographer's principal aim—to make his hero stand out, vivid and conspicuous from the canvas—has been triumphantly achieved.

It may be presumed that Mr Monypenny is a

[1] "The Life of Benjamin Disraeli, Earl of Beaconsfield." By William Flavelle Monypenny. 1910.

Disraelite, or he would scarcely have been entrusted with the work of depicting Disraeli; but his enthusiasm for his subject is tempered by an admirable frankness. To use a homely phrase, he does not trust his hero farther than he can see him. He has had access to what he calls "a great mass of papers," and some of these papers threw a searching light on the unknown or forgotten episodes of Disraeli's early life. Nothing that awaits Mr Monypenny in the remainder of his task will be equal in difficulty to this portion of it. From 1837, when Disraeli entered Parliament, to 1881, when the harsh winds of Easter killed him, he lived incessantly in the public eye. His name, for good or for evil, pervades the newspapers. Hansard records whole reams of his oratory. Every book of Memoirs or Recollections describes him; and the invaluable page of *Punch* represents that ludicrous aspect of him, which down to 1874 was generally accepted as the true portrait of the man.

For the hero's parliamentary career Mr Monypenny will not have far to seek. His only difficulty will lie in the enormous mass of material with which he will have to deal; but it was not so with the period covered by this volume. Here Mr Monypenny has had to rely on tradition so vague as to be almost impalpable; on letters obviously flamboyant and unreal; on a "Mutilated Diary"—always mutilated just at the most interesting part—and on some scraps of Recollections which Disraeli jotted down in his latter years, when any event or personality recalled the strange vicissitudes of his youth.

It would appear that a perusal and comparison of these various testimonies have led Mr Monypenny to the conclusion that his hero was not pedantically and tiresomely truthful. He permitted a poetic imagination to play gracefully round the events of his early days, and gilded with an Oriental glamour the history of his family. He did not know—perhaps he did not choose to avow—the date or place of his birth. He professed that his ancestors came from Spain, whereas, in fact, they came from Italy. He nursed the delusion that his grandfather, who left thirty-five thousand pounds, was a commercial rival of the Rothschilds. We need not enlarge on these details, for Mr Monypenny gracefully covers them by saying that "Disraeli, all his days, was haunted, more than most men, by a longing to escape from the sordid details of commonplace life into spacious historical atmospheres."

The grandfather who came from Italy in 1748 left a son Isaac, an easy-going character who renounced Judaism, muddled his money, wrote some good books of literary tittle-tattle, and went blind. Isaac Disraeli married Maria Basevi, and their eldest son was born (at 6 King's Road, Bedford Row) on the 21st December 1804. He was duly admitted to the Covenant of Abraham on the eighth day, and received his grandfather's name of Benjamin. He had a sister Sarah, and three brothers—Naphthali,

Raphael, and Jacobus. Isaac Disraeli, though he broke with Judaism, never became a Christian ; but, influenced by the notion that, in the then-existing state of society, it would be better for his children to be Christians than Jews, he allowed them to be baptized. This was done at St Andrew's, Holborn, in 1817, and on the occasion the children's names were slightly modified. Sarah needed no change ; but Raphael became Ralph, and Jacobus James. Fortunately, Naphthali had died in infancy, for his name would have been less easy to transmute or abbreviate.

The infant Disraeli passed through a series of private schools—the last of them kept by a Unitarian minister at Higham Hill, in Epping Forest. "The boys who were members of the Church of England had to walk some distance on Sundays, to attend morning service ; and it resulted from this that they fared rather badly at the midday dinner, which was usually half over by the time they got back. Disraeli was himself among the victims, and his new religion had as yet aroused in him none of the zeal of a martyr ; so he threw out the suggestion to his Anglican companions that it might be as well if they all became Unitarians for the term of their life at school." As to the intellectual results of their schooling, Mr Monypenny believes that Disraeli acquired some Latin and a very little Greek, and adds, with his admirable candour, that "in the list of authors which he claims to have read while at

Higham Hill there is probably a good deal of anticipation of subsequent study."

Then, again, when we come to Disraeli's pecuniary affairs, Mr Monypenny's candour never fails him. He makes no attempt to conceal the various devices and dodges by which his hero, when already a J.P., and aspiring to become an M.P., kept the bailiffs at a distance. He gives us in full the story of the ill-starred "Representative," which Disraeli projected, and John Murray, to his cost, financed; and he seems rather to glory in the fact that "Disraeli, at the age of twenty, had incurred a debt of several thousand pounds—a debt which was not finally liquidated till nearly thirty years later, when he had already led the House of Commons and been Chancellor of the Exchequer." If the writer were not a devotee of his subject, one might suspect sarcasm in the last six words.

And yet once more. When Mr Monypenny prints an extract from his hero's Journal for 1836—"Parted for ever from Henrietta"—he is recording the close of a most discreditable intrigue; and this is his annotation: "Love, after its first rapture was over, had come into contact with the harder side of Disraeli's character, with his masterful will and dæmonic ambition; and, in the clash between will and passion, will had triumphed."

The period covered by this volume saw the publication of some of Disraeli's most remarkable writing. We may dismiss some long-forgotten pamphlets on Trade and Finance, the "Letters of Runnymede" and "The Revolutionary Epick." But we must remember "Vivian Grey," "The Young Duke," "Popanilla," "Contarini Fleming," "Alroy," "The Rise of Iskander," "Ixion in Heaven," "The Infernal Marriage," "Henrietta Temple," and "Venitia." All these are noticed in their proper order, and the biographer has evidently realized (what the present writer discerned long since) that the history of Lord Beaconsfield's early days can be gathered much more accurately from his novels than from his fragments of formal autobiography.

In November 1821 Benjamin Disraeli was articled to a firm of solicitors in Old Jewry; but his heart was in literature; and, when he had been found "reading Chaucer in business hours," it was agreed between all parties concerned that he had better seek a career elsewhere. This lull in his affairs gave him an opportunity for travel, and in the summer of 1824 he set off with his father, and his friend William Meredith (afterwards engaged to Sarah Disraeli), for Brussels and the Rhine. From Ghent he writes: "Cathedral. High Mass. Clouds of incense, and one of Mozart's sublimest Masses by an orchestra before which San Carlo might grow pale. The effect inconceivably grand. The Host was raised, and I flung myself on the ground." In that remarkable prostration one seems to catch a foretaste of "Lothair."

It being now settled that "Young Ben," as his

family called him, was not to be a solicitor, the question arose: What is he to be? He entered as a law-student at Lincoln's Inn, but he was never called, and there is no reason to believe that he ever meant to practise. As regards literary output, it was the most fruitful part of his life; and several of the books which we enumerated above as memorable were produced during this period. But he was low-spirited and downhearted. He was conscious of genius, but not confident of success. Debts and duns worried the life out of him, and he had a serious breakdown of health and nerves. His friends were anxious that he should have complete change of scene and occupation. So he made a rather conventional tour in Italy, and in 1830 he set out on a more adventurous pilgrimage to the Holy Land.

The story of the pilgrimage is adequately told by Mr Monypenny, and also, with a vast amount of decorative romance, by Disraeli himself, in "Tancred." It was a really important period of his career, for then, amid surroundings which reminded him at every turn of the deeds and sufferings of the Jewish race, in climatic conditions to which he was peculiarly susceptible, and in intercourse with seers and rulers who had nothing in common with the homely politics of Europe, he dreamed of a system of government which should be not popular and representative, but Theocratic and monarchical; and he elaborated that curious creed which he called

"Completed Judaism," and which served him as a religion till the day of his death.

Early in the memorable year 1832, Disraeli returned to England, "in famous condition—better, indeed, than I ever was in my life, and full of hope and courage." Meanwhile, his parents had quitted London, and had established themselves at Bradenham House—an old manor-house, standing on the beech-clad slopes of the Chiltern Hills, a few miles from High Wycombe. Thus Benjamin Disraeli became a denizen of what he loved to call "The County of Statesmen"—the county of Hampden and Burke, Grenville and Chandos—which was his home for the rest of his life, and which contains his grave. At Bradenham he now spent a good deal of his time, "working like a tiger" at his novels, and rushing up to London from time to time for a little social recreation. The surroundings of his father's house had not been such as to give him an early initiation into good society, and he had to force his way, by cleverness and audacity, into the circles where he wished to shine. It is curious to trace in his letters to his sister the successive steps of his progress; his delight in each, and his promptness in pushing on to more. At first the Great People, Whig or Tory, would have nothing to say to him, and he lived in "a curious blend of literature, fashion, politics, and Bohemianism." Before the book closes, we find him hobnobbing with Lady Tavistock and Lady Londonderry, Lord Durham and "Dandy Worcester" ; and about half way through his social progress we meet him in a company eminently congenial. He dined one day with Bulwer-Lytton, afterwards Lord Lytton, and the other guests were Henry Bulwer, afterwards Lord Dalling ; Charles Villiers, the Parliamentary champion of Free Trade ; and Alexander Cockburn, afterwards Lord Chief Justice.

Disraeli's grotesque fopperies in dress are among the best remembered incidents of his early career, and on this occasion they figured conspicuously. In after years Lord Dalling used to say, "We were none of us fools, and we all talked our best ; but if we had been taken aside one by one and asked which was the cleverest of the party we should have all agreed that it was the Jew in the green velvet trousers."

But neither literature nor society—still less love or romance—had got the permanent mastery of Disraeli's heart. As he told the astonished Melbourne, he "wanted to be Prime Minister," and as the first step towards that elevation he wanted to be in Parliament. He had begun to attach himself to persons of very different characters and opinions, whom he thought likely to serve his interests. He cultivated Bulwer-Lytton, then a Whig, and was hand in glove with the brilliant and unscrupulous Tory, Lord Lyndhurst. He flattered politicians so diverse as O'Connell, Hume, and Sir Francis Burdett. He paid assiduous court to Sir Robert Peel, though he was always making fun of him ; and there is a tradition that he said to Lord Grey—" My lord, you and I know that in politics there is no such thing as principle," whereupon the conversation was abruptly closed. In truth, he was what Hosea Bigelow called " a Candidate." He was quite clear that he wished to be in Parliament, but he was not very clear about anything else.

His opportunity came very soon after his return from the East in 1832. He arrived to find the country beside itself with the fury of Reform, and, as many people thought, on the verge of revolution. But before long the Lords played their last card and had lost. The Reform Bill received the Royal Assent on the 7th of June, and, as a General Election must come before long, Disraeli determined to stand for High Wycombe. That funny little borough, which subsisted till 1885, then returned two members, and was absolutely dominated by the principal land-owner, Lord Carrington. In the ordinary course, the election would not have been before the winter ; but one of the sitting members suddenly resigned his seat in order to fight elsewhere, and so there was a vacancy at Wycombe. The dominant Whigs produced as their candidate Colonel Grey, son of the Prime Minister, and Benjamin Disraeli came forward to oppose him.

" I start," he wrote, " on the high Radical interest. Toryism is worn out, and I cannot condescend to be a Whig ! " " Whigs, Tories, Radicals, Quakers, Evangelicals, Abolition of Slavery, Reform, Conservatism, Corn-laws—here is hard work for one who is to please all parties." But apparently he did not please any considerable number, for, when the poll closed, the figures were: Grey 20, Disraeli 12. Nothing daunted, the adventurous "Dis," as he now began to be called, again came forward for Wycombe at the General Election in December, and this time as a confessed "Conservative." The figures were: Smith 179, Grey 140, Disraeli 119; and after a third attempt, in January 1835, they stood: Smith 299, Grey 147, Disraeli 126. So "Ben" shook off from his feet the dust of unappreciative Wycombe, but it is worth while to note that the Grey who had thrice defeated him was destined to convey, as Queen Victoria's Private Secretary, her command that Mr Disraeli should form his first Administration.

One more defeat awaited him—at Taunton, in April 1835. Sydney Smith, who lived in the neighbourhood, wrote: "The Jew spoke for an hour. The boys called out 'Old Clothes' as he came into the town, and offered to sell him sealing wax and slippers." But in the meanwhile he had formed a friendship which helped him materially in the fulfilment of his designs. Mr Wyndham Lewis was the Conservative member for Maidstone. He was married to a lady whom Disraeli, when he first encountered her, described as "a pretty little woman, a flirt, and a rattle." Very soon the acquaintance ripened into a warm friendship, and, at the General Election of 1837, Mr Lewis brought Disraeli into

Parliament as his colleague in the representation of Maidstone. Mr Monypenny heads the chapter which records this event with the triumphant legend, "Parliament at last!"

On the 29th July 1837 Mrs Wyndham Lewis wrote: "Mark what I prophesy. Mr Disraeli will in a very few years be one of the greatest men of his day. They call him my Parliamentary protégé!" Disraeli himself wrote on the eve of the meeting of Parliament: "I am now as one leaving a secure haven for an unknown sea. What will the next twelve months produce?" Among other things, they produced the opportune death of Mr Wyndham Lewis; and in 1839 his opulent widow married Benjamin Disraeli, who was nine years younger than herself. There never was a happier or more successful marriage; and it went far to justify the husband's early dictum: "As for 'love,' all my friends who married for love and beauty either beat their wives or live apart from them. I may commit many follies in life, but I never intend to marry for 'love,' which I am sure is a guarantee of infelicity."

(Reprinted from *The Daily News*.)

XIII

THE SCHOLAR

ONCE on a time I wrote a series of "Social Silhouettes." They were attempts to depict various types of men as affected by the circumstances of their life and occupation. One type which I omitted was the Scholar; and this was because the Scholar, as distinct from the Teacher or Professor, is now so rare a character that very few readers would recognize his portrait. For by "The Scholar" I mean the man who devotes his life to the disinterested pursuit of knowledge; with no ulterior aims to serve, and with no intention of applying what he has learnt to any practical purpose. In days gone by, this type of character abounded, not only in universities, which were its natural home, but in all sorts of unlooked-for quarters—in country houses, in Scottish Castles, in Cathedral Closes, in rural Parsonages, in the Temple and Lincoln's Inn, and in the Athenæum Club—even, sometimes, by gross dereliction of official duty, in Whitehall and Somerset House. The Scholar, as then understood, studied because he wished to know; and, though he might, towards the end of his life, put forth a Monograph, a Tractate, or a

Treatise, the object to which he devoted his days was not publication but Learning:

> "This man decided not to Live but Know."

The Scholar, thus understood, has not always been appreciated as highly as he deserved. Though Browning did his best for him, he has generally been the butt of rhymesters and romancists:

> "Did you ever observe in the very ripe scholar
> A silent contempt for all outward display?
> His clothes fit him ill, from his boots to his collar,
> His hair is unbrushed, or else brushed the wrong way.
> With sleeves very long, overlapping his fingers,
> He's spinally crooked, and wanting in grace;
> And mental abstraction provokingly lingers
> In every turn of his figure and face."

George Eliot was downright spiteful about poor old Mr Casaubon, "chewing the cud of erudite mistake about Cush and Misraim." Mrs Ward's Edward Langham was an even weaker vessel than his pupil, Robert Elsmere. Sir Walter made merry over Dominie Sampson's social shortcomings and the erudition of Erasmus Holiday. The author of "The Anatomy of Melancholy"—himself a Scholar, if ever there was one—drew this unflattering portrait of his order: "Hard students are commonly troubled with gowts, catarrhes, rheums, *cachexia*, *bradypepsia*, bad eyes, stone, and collick, crudities, oppilations, *vertigo*, winds, consumptions, and all such diseases as come by overmuch sitting; they are most part lean, dry, ill-coloured; spend their fortunes, lose their wits, and many times their lives; and all through immoderate pains and extraordinary studies."

This string of afflictions is long enough without the addition of moral reproaches. Yet this is the hortation which a famous divine, preaching before the University of Cambridge, addressed to the Scholars of the Cam:

"A man may be a diligent student, and yet 'live to himself.' Indeed there is in that contracted and self-contained life, even in more than one of greater expansion and variety, a peculiar risk of doing so. That daily hoarding of intellectual stores, that daily revelling in literary or scientific pursuits, is one of the strongest illustrations of a refined and elevated selfishness. Let a man who reads in youth read with a view to active work in his generation; let a man who reads on still in age also write, and the charge of mere selfishness must be mitigated or withdrawn—mitigated, if the man proposes to communicate; withdrawn, if he is enabled to consecrate."

It is evident that the preacher had a poor opinion of the Scholar, as defined above. In his eyes the young scholar was only respectable if he was studying with a view to "active work in his generation"; the older scholar, if he was preparing a book. To "communicate" meant, in the preacher's mouth, to teach, to write, in some form to impart; to "consecrate" meant to write definitely for high objects, and the improvement of the reader. Such notions as these, all disparaging to the career and character of the disinterested scholar, have acquired so strong a hold upon the modern world that the few people who read at all seem quite ashamed of themselves unless they can aver that they are reading for some practical object. They are teaching schoolboys or undergraduates; or they are qualifying for a Professorship; or they are going to lecture in America; or they are contributing to a History of Crete in twenty volumes; or they are busy at a new theory of Criticism which will sweep all churches and creeds into the dust-bin. But always and in all things they are practical. They learn, not for learning's sake, but with a single eye to performance—and emolument. A student of this type said to a younger man whom he found busy with a book on geology, "Will geology be of any use to you with your pupils next term?" "No." "Then isn't it rather a pity?" Of a famous Aristotelian it was said—"Does he read Aristotle for pleasure?" "No; he edits him for profit." I myself know a Senior Classic of whom his intimate friends aver that since he got his fellowship they have never known him open a Greek or Latin book. "He is a man of affairs, and reads his *Times*."

From students and study of this type one turns

with a keen sense of refreshment to a case such as that of Walter Headlam, whose Memoir has just been published by his brother.[1] He was a Scholar in the sense in which I defined the term. He read because he wanted to know more—to know all—of a subject which fascinated him. He lived his adult life in the beautiful precincts of King's College, Cambridge, "studying in the grand manner which he held was alone worth while. To him the acquisition of almost all available knowledge seemed necessary in order to prepare for the criticism and elucidation of his chosen authors." Yet "his tendency as an author was to defer the publication of a formal volume." In short, he laboured intensely, but with no immediate object beyond that of intellectual identification with the subjects which he loved. In a curious mood of self-censure he wrote thus to a friend whose letters he had neglected: "It isn't that I forget my friends; but the Scholar's danger of his work becoming too imperious, claiming all his time before any form of writing at any rate. This is what Wordsworth meant when, describing Cambridge in his time, he spoke of seeing 'Learning its own bondslave.'"

Yet, in spite of this complete absorption in pursuits where not one man in a hundred—even among educated people—could follow him, Walter Headlam was neither pedant nor prig. He had no affinity to

[1] "Walter Headlam: His Letters and Poems, with a Memoir." By Cecil Headlam. 1910.

the race of Dryasdust. If, granted a speciality in learning, one can specialize in it still further, Headlam's "special speciality" was the genius of Greek Lyrical Metres. Besides being a Scholar, he was a poet, and still more markedly a musician; and his application of musical tests to the written words of Greek Lyricists was a lantern for his steps, which made dark places seem clear and rough places plain, and enabled him, as it were, to dance and sing while he threaded his way where unilluminated Scholars had laboured and lumbered. The most brilliant classic whom Cambridge has lately produced told me only the other day that he had never known what Greek Lyrics meant till Headlam sang fragments of Simonides and Sappho, accompanying himself on the piano, and wedding the words to traditional tunes of English folk-lore.

Some years ago the present Master of Trinity thus excellently illustrated some of the qualifications for the Teacher's office :—

"Teachers ought to be examples to learners, in body as well as in mind and in character. They ought to be bright, and vigorous, and energetic. There ought to be an open-air look about them, the look of blue skies, and north-easters, and sea, and mountain, and heather, and flowers, and cricket-ground, and lawn-tennis—not the look of the study, and late hours, and the half-digested 'Epoch,' and the 'Outlines,' and the 'Analysis,' and the 'Abstract of the Analysis,' and—more ghastly still—the 'Skeleton.'"

Teaching, in the formal and technical sense, formed a very small part of Headlam's life; but, when he encountered younger people, whether boys or girls, who were eager to follow him into that Earthly Paradise of Greek culture where he was so uniquely at home, he delighted in the task of guiding them; and one cannot doubt that a great part of his attractiveness was due to his truly Greek love of life and form and clear skies and open air. "If I had not been a Grecian," he used to say, "I should have been a Cricket 'Pro.' Cricket, music, Greek poetry, and hunting are the things that I care for." A friend who shared his rides and walks at Cambridge says: "You went through the Fellows' Gardens, where he would stop to look at the double white cherry-tree, 'the whitest white in Nature.'" He delighted to ride down a certain bridle-path that had tall hedges on either side, thick with a tangle of wild roses. "Heaven was a flowery meadow: the Greeks said so, and they ought to know." He was a fearless rider to hounds, but rode, it must be admitted, erratically. "On more than one occasion, when his companions took a turn to left or right, Headlam, lost in the delight of swift motion, would hold on his way like an arrow from the bow, be seen in the distance still going hard, and seen no more that day."

Walter Headlam died suddenly in his forty-third year. If this chapter had been intended for a review of his Life, it might have been necessary to discuss, in an ethical or even a religious light, the best use of time and intellectual gifts ; but my purpose has been quite impersonal. I have only cited a rare and recent instance of a type which the competitive rush of modern life will soon have utterly abolished.

XIV

A GREAT DISAPPEARANCE

THIRTY years ago, the famous "Billy Johnson," most notable of Eton tutors and most exquisite of scholars, wrote thus to his brother:

"I noticed the other day that the lines of Wordsworth on Venice—

'Men are we, and must grieve when e'en the shade
Of that which once was great has passed away'—

are a good modulation of the line which scholars find great, and hopelessly unapproachable:

Sunt lacrimae rerum et mentem mortalia tangunt."

The pathetic thought which underlies both the English and the Latin verse has constantly been forcing itself upon my mind during this last week of controversy and commotion.[1] A Progressive majority composed of three independent sections; an Irish party, for once not homogeneous; and an Opposition frantic for revenge, yet not knowing when or where to strike—these are the elements of a situation in which one of our public men was pre-eminently fitted

[1] 21st February 1910.

to shine. Mr Joseph Chamberlain, like "The Happy Warrior," was

> "endued as with a sense
> And faculty for storm and turbulence,"

and in the present position of parties he would have found full scope for the exercise of his peculiar and characteristic gifts. And yet, just as the plot was thickening, and the sounds of battle filled the air, he was journeying by easy stages to a milder climate, there, if it might be, to recapture some measure of the health which served him so splendidly for seventy years, and then failed him at the very crisis of his career.

> "Men are we, and must grieve when e'en the shade
> Of that which once was great has passed away."

My acquaintance with Mr Chamberlain began when I entered Parliament at Easter 1880. He had not been four years in the House of Commons, and yet he had already established his position as leader of the Radical wing. He was forty-three years old, and, as I suppose, in the very perfection of his powers. It is not easy to describe his physical and mental alertness, his incisiveness of speech, his promptitude in action. In private life he was excellent company, hospitable, genial, and wholly free from the silly formalism which had marked the earlier race of political chiefs, each of whom seemed, on entering the Cabinet, to have swallowed the office-poker whole, and never to have digested it. I always look back upon my social intimacy with Mr Chamberlain between 1880 and 1885 as one of the pleasantest incidents of my Parliamentary life; but it was only towards the end of those years that he began to possess my political allegiance. As a subordinate member of a Government dominated by the transcendent personality of Mr Gladstone, Mr Chamberlaid had no opportunity of showing what was in him or what he meant. In later years it was reported that Gladstone said, "I never knew what there was in Chamberlain as long as we were on the same side." The Liberal Government of 1880-1885 was not conspicuously successful, either at home or abroad, and its dull indifference to the claims of Social Reform filled its Radical supporters with a sense of despair. We had entered Parliament with the hope of doing something for the social service of the people, and the Government, bound hand and foot in the dismal traditions of the Individualist School, gave no sign of even realizing what we wanted. Then suddenly Mr Chamberlain, too long muzzled by official restraints, found his opportunity. *Punch*, in an admirable cartoon called "The Daring Duckling," depicted the Junior Member for Birmingham just escaped from the shell, and sailing out, full of hope and confidence, into the wild waters of Democracy, while the "Grand Old Hen," who had hatched this adventurous infant, ran up and down the bank in throes of nervous apprehension. But at that time the democratic party was rather tired of the "Grand

Old Hen," with her (or his) indifference to all social needs, and welcomed, even enthusiastically, the "Daring Duckling." Mr Chamberlain alone seemed to see the extent and variety of curable misery, and to realize the truth that Politics is the science of human happiness. The Franchise Bill had just passed into law. At the next General Election the whole English people would for the first time have the power of expressing its wishes. To enlighten, embolden, and exhilarate the democracy was the task to which Mr Chamberlain addressed himself. He plied it with tongue and with pen, and, if better speeches have ever been delivered than those in which in 1884 and 1885 he appealed to democratic and humanitarian feeling, I have never come across them. From first to last I was an enthusiastic supporter of the "Unauthorized Programme." I still regard it as a most admirable compendium of social and political reform, and I firmly believe that if it had been made the Authorized Programme the subsequent history of our party would not have recorded so many and such disastrous failures.

And now comes a passage of personal history. On the 2nd of October 1885, I went on a visit to Hawarden. Gladstone and his Government had been turned out in the previous June. It had been arranged that Parliament was to be dissolved in November, and it seemed only too likely that the General Election would find the Liberal Party acutely divided. Even if we accepted Lord Rosebery's metaphor, and all crowded together under Gladstone's umbrella, still, the moment we stepped outside its circumference, we found ourselves on opposite sides of the street. Roughly, there were the old-fashioned Liberals who accepted the Authorized Programme, all the more gladly because there was nothing in it ; and there were the Radicals, who saw their beliefs embodied, for the first time, in Mr Chamberlain's Unauthorized Programme, and were resolved to follow wherever he led. In this state of tension, it was inevitable that conversation, at Hawarden as elsewhere, should turn on the prospects of the election. To what extent would they be affected by the conflict of Programmes ? What did Chamberlain mean ? How far would he push his independence ? Mr Gladstone took me for a solitary walk in Hawarden Park, and asked me to tell him plainly what I thought. I said that, as far as I knew, Mr Chamberlain had no design of trying to oust Gladstone from the Liberal leadership ; but I felt sure that he meant so to consolidate his position in the party as to make himself the indispensable leader whenever a vacancy should occur. I felt sure that, whatever else happened, he did not mean Lord Hartington (the idol of the Moderate section) to be Prime Minister. Further, I ventured to say that, with the young men of the party (among whom I could then be reckoned), the Unauthorized Programme was extremely popular, and that, if only Mr Gladstone could make some concession to it, the result would tend to unity. Then, warming to my work, I said, "The General Election is almost upon us. To go into it with two Leaders and two policies would be disastrous. Chamberlain is your colleague. Surely, instead of ascertaining his purpose through my guesses at it, your best course would be to ask him here, and have it out with him in a straightforward conversation." If I had thrown a bomb into the Temple of Peace, or had proposed an invitation to the Sultan, Gladstone could not have seemed more surprised. He said that he had always tried to keep Hawarden free from politics, and that he had never been in the habit of asking his colleagues to visit him there, unless, as well as colleagues, they were private friends. To this I replied that urgent cases required special treatment, and that this was eminently a case where no preconceived ideas or crusted habits ought to be allowed to interfere with a move which might avert a grave disaster from the Liberal Party. I gained a potent ally in Mrs Gladstone, and with my own hand wrote the telegram which invited Mr Chamberlain to Hawarden. My visit there ended just before his began, but he wrote me an account of his experience. Nothing, he said, could exceed the social pleasantness of it all, but on the points at issue between him and his host no approach to an agreement had been arrived at. Gladstone, in brief, was resolutely opposed to the Unauthorized Programme, and Chamberlain was absolutely committed to it. "If I were now to draw back," he wrote, "the stones would immediately cry out."

I had no further relation to the matter. We went into the election with divided counsels. Mr Chamberlain appealed on his own policy, and did not even mention Gladstone's name. The result of the election was a tie between Tories, *plus* Irish, and Liberals; and the tie precipitated the disclosure of Gladstone's views on Ireland. Not for the first or the last time, Gladstone had underestimated the forces arrayed against him. His hostile attitude towards Social Reform had turned an invaluable ally into an implacable foe. The Chamberlain whom the present generation of Liberals has known and feared was created by the perverse misunderstandings of 1885.

XV

LORD CREWE

THE City of Exeter contains two statues of eminent Devonians, who were thus honoured while they were still alive. These were Sir Thomas Acland (1787-1871) and the Earl of Devon (1807-1888). It is easy enough to choose suitable inscriptions for posthumous statues; not so easy for statues of living men. But Exeter was fortunate.

Præsenti tibi maturos largimur honores

was exactly right for Sir Thomas Acland. In Lord Devon's case the Committee preferred English, and borrowed their inscription from Wordsworth—

> "Who, not content that former worth stand fast,
> Looks forward, persevering to the last;
> From well to better, daily self-surpast."[1]

I have always cordially admired the plan of rendering public honour to living men; for posthumous memorials often bear an uncomfortable resemblance to the "sepulchres of the Prophets" whom our fathers killed. So to-day I eulogize an absent friend, and I write the more freely because (converting the

[1] This quotation was suggested by G. W. E. R.

platitude of the platform) I can say behind his back what I could not so well say before his face.

Robert, Marquess of Crewe, was born in 1858, and my friendship with him dates from 1870, when he came, a little, chubby, round-faced boy, to Harrow, commended by his father to the good offices of a long-legged youth in the Sixth Form, who, if I remember aright, was officially, and appropriately, designated "Russell *Max.*" That father, the first Lord Houghton, I have so often described that I had better refer my readers to a sketch of him in "Collections and Recollections," instead of drawing the portrait afresh. It must suffice to say that he was unique—a poet, a philosopher, and a politician; a Yorkshire Squire and a London Dandy; at once the most original and the kindliest of men. Nature had given him a genius and a heart; and that is a combination which outweighs a great many eccentricities. Lord Houghton was in his fiftieth year when his only son was born, and he concentrated all the resources of his intellect, his knowledge, and his social influence on the boy's education. "Robin," he used to say, "will have to make all his own friends. Mine are dying off so fast that I shall have none left to give him." But this was only a transient despondency; for each generation, as it came on, embraced "dear Yorkshire Milnes," and he had friends all over the world, in every school of thought, and in every rank of life. His profound interest in "Robin's" career always reminded me of *The*

Spectator.—"The Survivorship of a worthy man in his Son is a pleasure scarce inferior to the Hopes of the Continuance of his own Life." His chief delight was to make the boy known to the people of a much earlier generation, and so to link him personally with all that had been notable in social and intellectual life. Let me give an instance of the process. On an appointed day the proud father carried his son to Chelsea, in order that he might do homage at the awful shrine of Carlyle. When the audience was over young Milnes, on taking leave of the Sage, said, "This is a great day in my life. I have seen two philosophers—yourself, sir, and Mr Herbert Spencer, whom Papa pointed out to me in a 'bus." "Eh, laddie," said Carlyle, with sudden animation, "and have ye seen Herbert Spencer? Then ye've seen the most unending ass in Christendom." Surely "unending" is, as the French would say, the just word.

Lord Houghton had been educated at home, and always felt that he had thereby missed a great deal which would have been useful to him in after-life. He was clear about sending his son to a Public School, but hesitated between Eton and Harrow. With a view to helping his decision he invited one of the most famous Eton tutors to stay with him in Yorkshire, and balanced him with the late Mr Edward Bowen, for forty-two years an Assistant Master at Harrow. Bowen carried the day, and Robert Milnes became, as I have already said, a son of The

Hill. He took a good place in the school, and kept it, displaying great facility in Latin and English versification. His Prize Poem, on Gustavus Adolphus, was far above the usual level of such compositions, and attracted the attention of those who speculate in mental heredity. His father wrote:

"It was very discreet of you to keep your own counsel so completely as to the poem. Nobody can now say that I wrote it. . . . The faculty of writing verse (quite apart from poetic genius) is the most delightful of literary accomplishments, and it almost always carries with it the more generally useful gift of writing good prose."

From Harrow Robert Milnes went up to Trinity College, Cambridge, where, half-a-century before, his father had been a contemporary of Hallam, and Sterling, and Tennyson. At Cambridge he did more hunting than reading, and indeed his eyes were already fixed on a prospect of happiness far beyond the precincts of academical distinction. In 1880 he became engaged to a lovely girl, in whom the blood of the Grahams and the St Maurs was blended with the talent and beauty of the Sheridans. Miss Florence Nightingale wrote to Lord Houghton:

"I would, if I could, contribute the sweetest music to inspire the footsteps of the beautiful marriage-pair. . . . With such promise—not only promise, such proof—of so much being in him, it seems a pity that he should not have served his apprenticeship to hard work, which generally forms the best foundation for the future edifice, if there is plenty of stuff ; but that he will do something great for his country —and what times are these !—we do not allow ourselves to doubt for one moment."

Robert Milnes had inherited from his father a vein of keen though independent Liberalism ; and, in fashioning his own career, he became more distinctly an adherent of Party than Lord Houghton had ever been. During the Liberal Administration of 1880-1885 he served as one of Lord Granville's Private Secretaries at the Foreign Office, and he had agreed to contest a Yorkshire seat at the General Election of 1885, when in August of that year his father's death called him to the House of Lords. He accepted office in Mr Gladstone's Home Rule Administration of 1886, but his political activities were soon and sadly interrupted. He lost his young wife in 1887 and his only boy in 1890. He travelled in search of health and change, but returned to England in time to take part in the political campaign which preceded the General Election of 1892. When Mr Gladstone formed his last Administration, Lord Houghton (as he had then become) was made Lord Lieutenant of Ireland. At this period he succeeded to the Cheshire estates of his maternal uncle, the late Lord Crewe, and was created Earl of Crewe in 1895. Four years later he married Lady Margaret Primrose, Lord Rosebery's younger daughter ; but this close alliance with Imperialism did not affect the robust fibre of his Liberal faith. As years passed, he acquired a leading position among the handful of Liberal Peers; and, when Sir Henry Campbell-Bannerman formed his Cabinet in 1905, Lord Crewe entered it as Lord President of the Council. He has since been Lord Privy Seal, Secretary of State for the Colonies, and Secretary of State for India; and, since Lord Ripon's retirement, he has led the Liberal Party in the House of Lords with consummate tact and judgment. A Marquessate was conferred on him at the Coronation of King George V.

Lord Crewe is a man of many gifts and graces. He has a keen and delicate sense of humour, and possesses the dangerous but delightful knack of "abating and dissolving pompous gentlemen with the most successful ridicule." He might almost say with Lord Beaconsfield (and indeed much more truly) that he was "born in a library," and he knows, partly by tradition and partly by experiment, the best that has been said and written. He has taste and fancy and the faculty of appreciation, and that "sense for beauty, that distaste for hideousness and rawness," which Matthew Arnold esteemed the true note of culture. It is, I suppose, some undue fastidiousness which has deterred him from advancing further into that attractive field of authorship which he entered so successfully with his volume of "Stray Verses." Let me give, as a sample of his quality, his "In Memoriam" (written at Capetown) on Browning:

> "The tale of how you found the promised rest
> Flashed fast from North to South, from sea to sea,
> My father's friend, all friendliness to me,
> Dear Scholar-Poet, ever-welcome guest;
> And gone you are to seek your loved one's breast,
> Sped your free soul from Italy the free,
> Soul never flinching from the dim To Be,
> Nor doubting of the Good—and thus, 'tis best.
> 'Tis best—and I, six thousand miles away
> From your and Nelson's Abbey arched in gloom,
> Hear through the surge that thunders on the Bay
> An echo of your verse's roll and boom
> That doubly sanctifies Trafalgar day—
> And wafts this Afric leaf to reach your tomb."

The necessities of public life have made Lord Crewe a speaker in spite of himself. His speaking has not the rush and fervour of oratory; but every word is deliberately chosen, and exactly fits the place for which it is designed. His style of utterance exactly corresponds to his dignified, rather impassive, exterior; and to his manner, which has an appropriate tinge of stateliness. But, after all, these are superficial characteristics, and the words which (let me confess it) I suggested for Lord Devon's statue seem to imply a more intimate appreciation. "From well to better." There cannot be a nobler motto; and I am convinced, by the experience of forty years, that, as life advances, Lord Crewe will render still more worthy service to the State, and will draw yet closer and closer the bonds which unite him to the friends and the scenes of Auld Lang Syne. Let his own lines on Harrow close this sketch:

> "Yet here, 'mid laughter and the ring of cheers,
> Immortal Boyhood keeps his joyous throne;
> With daring eyes aflame, and eager ears,
> He burns for conquest of a world unknown.
> O stay thee, lonely pilgrim of the years,
> Here at the heart of Youth revive thine own."

XVI

A CROWDED HOUR[1]

I HAVE just been enjoying a "crowded hour of glorious life" in my native Loamshire. Electioneering, where one is not the candidate, is certainly the greatest fun in the world, and, as Mr Jorrocks said of fox-hunting, it is the image of war with only ten per cent. of the danger. Loamshire is a small county, and, as all the world knows, it is dominated by the Duke of Omnium, who, from the battlements of Gatherum Castle, keeps watch and ward over the political activities of the Vale below. He speaks habitually of "My People," "My County," and "My Division," for Gatherum is situate in South Loamshire, and it is there that the benevolent despotism of the Castle is most effectively exercised. The Northern Division contains two manufacturing towns, and is therefore more independent. To "My People," "My County," and "My Division" the Duke likes to add "My Member," whose expenses he pays and whose votes he can control. Having returned to successive Parliaments a distant cousin (since appointed to a Colonial Governorship) and a half-pay officer who lost his head and replied blasphemously to hecklers,

[1] Written during the General Election of December 1910.

he determined this time to run his Land-Agent, an obsequious gentleman who looked uncommonly sharp after the rents, and professed the politics which became his situation. But this was a little more than even South Loamshire could stand, and his Grace is to be fought—I say his Grace, for the Agent scarcely counts—in his own Division.

The Liberals have been fortunate in securing a very attractive candidate. In the first place, he is young, and has in full measure that brilliant audacity of youth which its detractors call "Cheek." Luther said that if he had duty to do in Leipzig he would "ride into Leipzig though it rained Duke Georges nine days running," whereon Carlyle justly exclaims, "What a reservoir of dukes to ride into!" But the vision of such a reservoir has no terrors for my young friend Tommy Transome, who means to ride into the citadel of South Loamshire and thence into the House of Commons, in spite of all that Dukes and their Land-Agents can do to bar his progress. "Our Tommy," for so he is universally called, is not only young, but good-looking, clean, smart, and well mannered. He is a keen sportsman and a Football "Blue." The friendship between the family of Transome and my own is hereditary, and Tommy's demand that I should go down to Loamshire and help him could not be disregarded. So I have had my "crowded hour," and have renewed my youth by contact with my native soil.

I went down by an early train, and, having arranged

for a motor to meet me at the station, I took what Tony Lumpkin called a "circumbendibus" before proceeding to Tommy's headquarters. A highroad cuts right across the length of Gatherum Park, and gave the opportunity of observing the enemy at his base of operations. Close to the Estate-Office I discerned an animated group, and, as I drew nearer, I descried the Agent-Candidate mounted on a farm-waggon, and telling a ring of hearers that at times of national danger England had always been saved by its Dukes, so that any attack on their hereditary privileges was at once unpatriotic, ungrateful, and even suicidal. At this a motley audience, composed of office-clerks, game-keepers, lodge-keepers, and upper servants from the Castle, cheered prodigiously; but, when the meeting broke up and the Agent returned to luncheon with his patron, I thought I could discern in the countenances of one or two of the farm-labourers a look of suppressed intelligence which suggested that they wore the ducal colours on their waistcoats rather than in their hearts. Even when Agents are candidates, and ducal emissaries watch the polling-booths, the Ballot keeps its secret.

Before tea-time my circumbendibus brought me to the hospitable residence of Tommy's chief supporter, whom we will call Mr Goodhart. When I rang the bell, I was told that Mrs Goodhart was out canvassing, and that Mr Goodhart was in his study preparing a speech for the evening; but would I go into the drawing-room? There I found a bountifully-spread tea-table, and seated at it a bluff-looking gentleman with a stentorian voice, and an anæmic youth in spectacles. They welcomed me with effusion, as a comrade in the fight. The bluff gentleman poured out tea with exaggerated heartiness, and deluged my cup with cream (which I detest), while the spectacled youth furtively annexed the last scone, and tried to cover his base action by plying me with anchovy sandwiches and plum-cake. We all three ate voraciously (for nothing sharpens the appetite like electioneering), and, when our mouths were not full, we made suitable conversation about the canvass, the contest, and the candidate. To us there presently entered our host, and greeted us all three with unaffected hospitality. At a convenient moment I drew him into a recess, and asked who my fellow-tea-drinkers were. "My dear chap," he answered, "I haven't the slightest idea. Never saw either of them before; but it's all right. I've made over this house to our Tommy, and he asks his friends and workers to stay here, just as it suits him. By the way, I must find out whether these men are going to sleep here, for our spare bedrooms are pretty well filled up. Ah! here comes the best worker of the lot, just in time for a cup of tea. Let me introduce you to Miss Larkins."

As I look round, I see an extremely pretty girl, apparently not more than twenty, dressed in a costume in which the violet and white of "Votes for Women" are harmoniously blended with the scarlet and yellow of Loamshire Liberalism. Miss Larkins, I understand, has been sent down from some central office to fortify Tommy in his unequal contest with the local suffragettes. His conversion to Feminism has been recent and rapid, and his good faith in this particular had been questioned. Miss Larkins's province is to support him on the platform, and to affirm, on her veracity, that the conversion, though sudden, is thorough, and that he is in full sympathy with window-smashing and dog-whips.

At this juncture our party is reinforced by Mrs Goodhart, in an exceedingly muddy riding-habit. She has been canvassing some outlying cottages unapproachable by wheels, but easily reached by a lady whose performances with the South Loamshire Hounds are frequently commended in *The Field*. She knows every gate, gap, and bridle-way in the division, and brings back the most exhilarating reports. Hogstye End is sound to the core, and the Duke's nominee won't score a vote at Duckpuddle Green. Large relays of tea are now brought in by panting servants ; Mrs Goodhart runs upstairs to get her habit off, and, as she crosses the hall, I find an opportunity of enquiring about my fellow-guests. "Oh ! the loud gentleman is Captain Hollowell. He is sent down from headquarters. We don't quite know what he is a captain of, for he is neither a soldier nor a sailor, but the people in the villages think he belongs to the Salvation Army. The young man was a friend of Tommy's at Oxford. He hasn't much voice, and generally loses his place in his notes, but he is useful. We put him up before Tommy comes into the meeting, and he tells the people that he can say behind the candidate's back what he would not say before his face—that Tommy was Dr Welldon's favourite pupil at Harrow, and carried all before him at Oxford. I suppose it means football, for Tommy certainly did not take honours; but that is his cue, and, when young Meakin says 'Oxford,' Tommy comes in from the Committee-room on to the platform, and Meakin trots off to the next meeting."

With these words, Mrs Goodhart flies upstairs, and a manly voice which I know well rings through the hall, commanding the motor to be round again by six sharp, and "our Tommy" bounces into the drawing-room. His good looks are somewhat obscured by motoring clothes, but he is in the very pink of health and vigour, and looks every inch a winner. "What sort of day have you had?" "Oh! ripping. The labourers keep very quiet—and not bad judges either!—but they mean a lot. Even the farmers say it's a bit thick to put up that fellow Jobson, when he's been screwing them up like blazes, till he knew he'd got to stand. As to Tariff Reform—why, Hollowell, I took the tip from you—'Tariff Reform gives you an appetite for your dinner, and Free Trade gives you a dinner for your appetite.' I owe you a good turn for that. It simply did the trick on the village green at Long Turnipfield."

At this moment a third relay of tea arrives, and, as Tommy, ever since his days at Harrow, has been distinguished by an exemplary appetite, the tea-cakes are reinforced by poached eggs, broiled ham, and *pâté-de-foie gras.* Mrs Goodhart, reclothed and beaming, now joins the party. Everyone is eating, drinking, laughing, talking, plotting, planning, hoping, fearing, all at once. The telephone-bell rings every five minutes, and we are triumphing over a Liberal victory, or swearing that Lord Nozoo, who declines to lend his motor for polling-day, is a selfish beast and a Tory in disguise. Presently our host, who is the timekeeper, gives the signal to start. Tommy crams a crowning scone into his capacious mouth, thrusts a plateful of sandwiches into his pocket, and announces himself ready for the fray. He is to "put in" seven meetings that night, and there are twenty-four in the constituency.

The party disperses in different directions. Mrs Goodhart is to chaperon Miss Larkins at Mudford. Captain Hollowell and young Meakin are to keep the ball rolling at Swampstead till the candidate arrives; while I, as the hereditary friend, am honoured by a seat in the car which conveys Mr Goodhart and Tommy. We light our cigars on the doorstep, while our friends shout their counsels from the hall-door. "Don't go by Slopperton; the water is three feet deep in the lane. Go round by Sandford." "Oh! that's worse, for the bridge has broken down." "Does the chauffeur know the way?" "Take care of Dead Man's Corner—it's awfully dangerous in the dark." "I fancy you're likely to have some trouble at Rowdyford. It's in the heart of the Duke's country, and I hear his stablemen and gardeners are going down in a body." "Never mind—there'll be fifty of our fellows there—picked ones—and they've got sticks." "Oh! that's all right." "I dare say the chauffeur will come in for a rotten egg or two, but he's a staunch chap, and would let them empty a grocer's window on him for a quid."

And so, amid these varied voices of benison and warning, we disappear into the encircling gloom.

. . . .

Midnight.—"Safe home, safe home in port." We have all got back alive and undamaged; very proud of our respective meetings, and desperately hungry. We gather rejoicingly round the supper-table. Tommy has grilled chicken and champagne. Captain Hollowell demands cold beef and whiskey-toddy. Miss Larkins sups on strong coffee and a cigarette, and Meakin on hot milk with a plasmon biscuit.

. . . .

Friday, January 16.—Poll declared. Tommy is in by 500.

The Duke of Omnium does not like being beaten, and I pity Jobson with all my heart.

XVII

THE USES OF PROSPERITY

THE "Uses of Adversity" have been greatly over-praised. Commend me rather to the uses of prosperity, as exemplified in the case of my friend Tommy Transome. I have prolonged my stay in Loamshire far beyond its expected limits, and I hear that my friends at the Club have noticed my absence with surprise. But, after all, I am by birth and breeding a countryman. In Loamshire "my foot is on my native heath," and I have been renewing my youth by contact with my early friends. We have all aged a good deal. Unless my ears deceived me, I heard Sir Cingle Headstall exclaim, when he caught sight of me at the Lawn Meet, "Good gad, what a wreck! That's what comes of living in London." And I might certainly have said of Headstall what the Duke in "Lothair" said of Lord Agramont—"I never saw a man so red and grey, and I remember him such a good-looking fellow! He must have lived immensely in the country, and never thought of his personal appearance."

But, in spite of these little shocks of recognition, everything settled itself down very comfortably in the course of a few days, and before the week was over I began to feel as if I had never left Loamshire. Whenever I talked of going back to London Tommy Transome overbore me with hospitable pressure. "Look here, sir, you never will come down for a week-end. You say that sleeping out of your own bed destroys your nights, and that you don't like country churches. Well, now you've got used to a strange bed—your servant says he simply can't get you to open your eyes before nine,—and you admitted that the show at the church last Sunday wasn't bad for a village. All your old pals are jolly glad to see you again; and altogether, now you've come, you'd better put in a fortnight before you go back to that stuffy old Club." Thus the voice of the charmer, and it prevailed; but my chief pleasure in this extended visit is the contemplation of Tommy in his prosperity.

A curious feature of the situation is that the Election seems to have left no bitterness behind it. Rumour, indeed, says that the Duke of Omnium is giving the defeated Agent a bad time, and threatens reprisals at the next election; but Tommy says triumphantly, "Let him 'reprise' as much as he likes. Everyone bars him. I believe I got some of my best support from the villages just round Gatherum. I fancy I've got South Loamshire 'by the wool,' and it'll take a better man than that old Stick-in-the-Mud to unseat me." So much for the Duke; and the other protagonists on the Tory side seem wonderfully softened. The Archdeacon, who at the election denounced Tommy for designing to turn Westminster Abbey into an aquarium, now very handsomely says that he spoke on information supplied by the Church Defence Institution, and regrets that he should have attributed to Mr Transome sentiments which he disavows. The Editor of *The Loamshire Herald* says in effect that the supreme considerations of political principle compelled him to blackguard the Liberal candidate; but that it would be unfair to deny the many excellences of the Liberal Member. The rank-and-file of the Tory party seem friendly enough. Here Tommy's record stands him in good stead. His neighbours have known him all his life, with an unblemished character for manliness and right conduct at Harrow, at Oxford, and in his own home. They like him as a sportsman and an athlete, and, even though they abhor his politics, they secretly admire his pluck. "It was about time," they say, "that the old Duke got a knock. He was getting a bit too Patriarchal. But he has found his match in Tommy."

Among the Agricultural Labourers, who are quite willing to talk when they know that they are talking to a friend, I have found the hereditary sentiment deeply rooted. They know that the Transomes have lived, time out of mind, at Transome Hall. As far back as the village-annals stretch, the forefathers of Sears and Rowkins and Burnage (these are real names) have worked for the Transomes and lived on their lands. In times of sickness and dearth the Transomes have stood between them and destruction. If farmers were tyrannical, there was always an appeal to the Squire, who "would never stand by and see wrong done"; who at the Board of Guardians was always for liberality in outdoor relief, and on the Bench was merciful even to a poacher. These were the hereditary associations which linked the Squire and the labourers of Transome; but there is a more recent recollection which governed a good many votes last month.

Since the Labourers acquired the suffrage, one side has vied with the other in flattering and cajoling them; but the men have good memories, and they know who were, and who were not, their friends in their unenfranchised days. They remember that, at the time when a Tory legislator said they were no more fit to have a vote than the beasts they tended, the Old Squire (Tommy's grandfather) stood up for them through thick and thin; and, when asked to express his wishes at the first election at which they voted, placarded his villages with this reply: "As a lifelong Liberal, I hope that every man on my estate will vote according to his conscience." The agricultural mind is retentive. These things stick, and Tommy is favoured because he is a Transome. But heredity, standing alone, would not suffice. Tommy is favoured, not for his forefathers' sake only, but for his own. The keepers, the woodmen, the labourers, the road-menders, the old women at the lace-pillow, the children in the school, all know his pleasant smile and jolly greeting. He never forgot "Thank you" to a ploughboy who held a gate open for him. He would share his sandwich and flask with a beater; and, if he took a partridge in his pocket to a bed-ridden labourer, he did not—as the manner of some is—choose the oldest in the larder. "It makes the heart bound"—I quote from Mr Gladstone—"to feel that, even in this poor world, truth and justice sometimes claim their own"; and I rejoice to see Tommy in the enjoyment of that Prosperity which personal and ancestral virtues have deserved.

Tommy has only lately come into his property. He lost his father when he was still at Harrow; his immediate predecessor in the estate was his grandfather. Transome was perhaps the most old-fashioned house in England. The Old Squire, though a Radical in politics, was a thoroughbred Conservative in social matters. He used to boast that he still gave beer for breakfast in the Servants' Hall, the luxury of tea being reserved for the Housekeeper's Room. His stud-groom had lived with him all his life, had never slept out of the county, and was called "Old Loam" as an affectionate nickname. He was punctilious about times and seasons; began fires on the 1st of September and left them off on the 30th of April; had his mistletoe hung on Christmas Eve and taken down on Twelfth Night; and never allowed his garden to be planted out before "Old

May Day." He drank a glass of Madeira every night after dinner, and declared (what seemed scarcely possible) that he remembered the introduction of sherry. When he rode about his estate, he always had a pocketful of coppers for bird-scaring boys; and allowed himself to be pillaged by every rogue who could pull a long face and spin a doleful yarn. To succeed such a grandfather, and yet escape opprobrious comparisons, was no easy task; yet, as far as I see, Tommy has achieved it. He is doing a great deal to improve his cottages; but he does not, in his zeal for fresh air, expose the old cottagers to murderous draughts, nor replace the comfortable thatch with chilly slates. He throws open the Park to all comers, leaves every gate on the estate unlocked, and is keen on the preservation of footpaths and rights of way (which the Duke's Agent is always trying to destroy).

The living of Transome happened to fall vacant soon after Tommy succeeded; and he was genuinely anxious to make a right use of his powers as Patron. When Tommy was at Oxford he was sometimes to be met at Pusey House, and he confessed to enjoying what he called a "rowdy Evensong" at St Barnabas. So, when he had to find a new Vicar for Transome, he looked round among his Parson-pals, and had no difficulty in finding a brother Blue, who, as he put it, might be relied on to "make things hum." The first form which "humming" took was the restoration of Transome Church. Tommy flung himself, into the work with characteristic thoroughness; and, when the preliminary clearance began, with his own hands hewed down the Squire's pew. "This Church is going to be Free and Open," he shouted, "and we'll begin at the right end—though what my poor old 'granfer' would say beats me. Lor'! how he used to snore in that corner seat." The "humming" process, thus begun, still continues, and to-day Tommy wears a cassock and surplice, reads the Lessons on Sunday, and enriches the choir with his manly baritone.

All these activities and benevolences come easy enough to a kind-hearted young fellow, trained in the right traditions; but Tommy is such an "all-round good sort" (as his friend the Parson says) that he seems to enjoy even the less exhilarating experiences of remitting and subscribing. "Rather a bore," he says, "these farmer chaps wanting 25 per cent. off again: but still one can't deny they've had awfully bad times, and I don't relish the idea of parting company with men who've held the same farms almost as long as we've held Transome. That old Duke doesn't seem to mind the sort of thing—rather likes it, in fact—and sets that poor devil Jobson on to do it. But I must say that, when I'm shooting my partridges, I like to see a friendly face at the Farm House door." It may be remarked, in passing, that Tommy does not subsist exclusively on agricultural rents. Upper and Lower Transome Streets and Transome Place are neat little thoroughfares not far from the Marble Arch, and between them they pay Tommy £10,000 a year. "Yes, that's right enough," he says, "and I should be a skunk if I was close-fisted." So he sits down to the writing-table in his business-room, pulls out a bundle of letters and a cheque-book, and contemplates them with a smiling face. He is replying to applications for subscriptions. "Now look here," he shouts. "Here's a good one. 'SIR,—We are the Brass Band of Frogmarsh, and we played when you was elected; but a little girl sate down on the drum-head and stove it in. May we ask you to give us another?'"

These are the joys of M.P.-ship; and, as Tommy relishes them, I trust that they may be his for many a long year to come.

XVIII

TWELFTH NIGHT

On the 6th of January 1662 that indefatigable play-goer Mr Pepys recorded in his Diary: "After dinner to the Duke's House, and there saw *Twelfth Night* acted well, though it be but a silly play and not related at all to the name." The final Court of literary appeal—the general consent of the Cultivated Caste in modern Europe—has not confirmed Pepys's sentence on the "silly play"; but when he speaks of it as "not related at all to the name" he makes a palpable hit, or at least indicates a lost opportunity. John Downes, writing a century after the play was composed, says that "it was got up on purpose to be acted on Twelfth Night." And this fact, if fact it be, only makes it more tantalizing that the plot, the action, and the characters should bear no relation to the title. Shakespeare is Catholic as the sea is salt. Did not the very word "Catholicism" suggest to Matthew Arnold's mind "the pell-mell of all the men and women of Shakespeare's plays"? Shakespeare painted the daily life of a rich and free humanity, with the Mass, and all that the Mass represents, for its sun and centre. It is a permissible exercise of literary fancy to imagine the delightful combination of love and frolic and festivity which he might have woven round the traditional observance of Twelfth Night, when, in Baron's Hall and minstrel-gallery, the mirth of Christmas reached its topmost and final note, but not till, in the morning's Mass, men had once again paid their homage to the story of the Star. *Vidimus stellam Ejus in oriente, et venimus adorare Eum.*

But it is idle to speculate on what Shakespeare might have done. What he actually did had in it enough of " wonder and astonishment " to satisfy John Milton, and what satisfied Milton may well suffice for our less heroic age. Only the title—*Twelfth Night*—haunts and tantalizes us, and sets us dreaming of the immortal music in which Shakespeare, had he so willed, might have told us the story and the meaning of the Star.

A poet who lived three hundred years later, when he felt himself to be passing away into the grey mists, had one message, and one only, for the younger minstrels who would take up the task when he laid it down. Round him these young mariners were pressing, who would carry on his adventures, and would sail the seas that had once been his. And to them his farewell word, wrung out of all his long experience, and now charged with the solemn emphasis of the visionary judgment which comes with death, is this only : " Follow The Gleam ! " Follow " the light that never was on sea or land." Follow the quest that is never fulfilled. Follow The Gleam beyond the ocean-margin, and beyond the confines of the world. There is a light which flashes and is gone, and yet survives. There is a light which eludes, but never deceives. There is a light which guides as it flies. There is a light which comes only to those who seek in the night, and can feel after what they cannot find, and can still nurse "the unconquerable hope," and can never lose heart. There is a light which is for ever in motion, and can be retained only by moving with it. There is a light which is always just ahead of where you stand. You must follow, if you would arrive, and the following must never cease. "I am Merlin, who followed The Gleam." The seer's whole character, his whole secret, lies in that, from the first days when

> "In early summers,
> Over the mountains,
> On human faces,
> And all around me,
> Moving to melody,
> Floated The Gleam."

Down to the end, when

> "I can no longer,
> But die rejoicing;
> For there on the borders
> Of boundless ocean,
> And all but in Heaven,
> Hovers The Gleam."

Therefore:

> "O young mariner,
> Call your companions,
> Launch your vessel,
> And crowd your canvas;

And, ere it vanishes
Over the margin,
After it, follow it—
Follow The Gleam."

This was Merlin's charge; and the Message of Epiphany—the story of the Star—repeats it under changed conditions. Those Wise Men from the mysterious East just "followed The Gleam" that broke in upon their patient studies. They could know nothing of the perils and perplexities which lay before them on their long desert-journey; nothing of the place and the circumstances in which they would find the Object of their quest; nothing of the martyrdom which, according to immemorial tradition, awaited their return and crowned their course. All they knew was that the Star had summoned them to a high and difficult enterprise, and whither The Gleam led, there they must follow.

Follow The Gleam. Surely it is the golden motto of adventurous youth, peering into the misty future to see the line of its course through life; the heights to be scaled, the abysses to be avoided. "Follow The Gleam" just where it leads. Cast doubt and fear and misgiving on one side. Press forward with your eyes upon the Star, and when the Star stops, but not till then, you will have found the object of your quest.

"Follow The Gleam." Again and again, not in poetry or romance, but in the solid truth of human history, the Star, seen first in early youth, has guided the man to the haven of his completed ministry and his predestined perfection. St Benedict was at the age of an English Public School-boy when he fled to his cave, and by sharp austerities prepared himself to be the founder of the most permanent society in Europe. St Francis was only a youth when the words—" Take up thy cross and follow Me"—burnt themselves into his soul and sealed him to a life of sacrifice. Lord Shaftesbury was a boy at Harrow when, horrified by a scene of indecency and drunkenness at a pauper's funeral, he devoted his life to the service of the poor. Gladstone had only just entered on man's estate when he pledged himself before God to put first among the objects of his ambition the rescue of the fallen. All these followed The Gleam, from the hour when it first flashed upon their " inward eye," till the journey was accomplished and the quest was won.

After such heroic examples of devotion to high ends, it may seem a bathos even to recall the pursuit which, according to Bacon, is of all others the most immersed in matter. Yet even the life of Politics has its ambitions and its inspirations, its guiding stars and its visionary gleams; and they to whom in early youth Our Lady of Freedom has revealed the divine beauty of her face will be found fighting her battles when their hairs are grey. One need not be a Scotsman to feel one's heart beat quicker when Sandy Mackaye on his deathbed sends to his fellow-workers for the Charter the dying counsels of " ane o' four-score years and mair—ane that has grawn grey in the People's Cause—that sate at the feet o' Cartwright, an' knelt by the deathbed o' Rabbie Burns—ane that cheerit Burdett as he went to the Tower, an' spent his wee earnings for Hunt an' Cobbett—ane that beheld the shaking o' the nations in the Ninety-three, and heard the birth-shriek o' a new-born world—ane that while he was yet a callant saw Liberty afar off, an' seeing her was glad, an' followed her through the wilderness for three-score weary, waeful years."

Yes. "Follow The Gleam." It may lead you into unpopularity and contempt, the scorn of the vulgar, and the world's disesteem; even, perhaps, to definite hardship, and the loss of much that makes life sweet and smooth. But "Follow The Gleam." It is worth all the struggles and the sorrows, even though they were agonies, through which it leads you; for when at length the Star stops, and by stopping tells you that your work is done, you will know that you have not "been disobedient unto the heavenly vision," nor closed your ears to the voice which spoke to you from on high.

"Is not this reward enough—
To have helped to smooth the rough,
To have made the toilsome way a little clear;
To have fallen in the van,
Though but one forgotten man,
Of the army that is bringing the New Year?"

Such thoughts as these, though suggested in the

first instance by the ecclesiastical season, are not, I think, inappropriate to the Civil struggle on which all England is just entering.[1] If the worshippers of Liberty will "follow The Gleam," it will guide them through the quicksands and morasses which beset their way more surely than all the constitutional treatises and fiscal pamphlets that ever were written. And to my younger brothers in the great family of Liberalism, more emphatically than to any other class of readers, I say: "Follow The Gleam," and follow it so whole-heartedly that, when you look back upon the crisis of 1910, the memory of the fashion in which you then played your part may animate your maturer age with the enthusiasm of your prime.

P.S.—If anyone should accuse me of having in part of this chapter plagiarized from Canon Scott Holland, I welcome the accusation; and I exhort my readers to make themselves acquainted with Sermon III. in a book called "Vital Values." It is certainly one of the most inspiring utterances that I ever heard or read.

[1] The General Election, January 1910.

XIX

THE THYESTËAN BANQUET

EXACTLY forty years ago—on the 2nd February 1871—Matthew Arnold addressed (from Grub Street) his Dedicatory Letter to his friend Adolescens Leo, of *The Daily Telegraph.* " We are now," he wrote, " on the point of commencing what Arminius, with his fatally carping spirit, called our 'Thyestëan banquet of clap-trap'—we are on the eve of the meeting of Parliament." Arminius Von Thunder-Ten-Tronckh (who had fallen in the Franco-German War of the previous autumn) had certainly been an unsparing critic of our national foibles ; but I cannot conceive that, even in his bitterest moment, he would have applied to any of our institutions the epithet " Thyestëan," in all its dread allusiveness. Rather I must suppose that he used it in the more general sense conveyed by Dr Smith's Classical Dictionary, which speaks of a " horrid meal," and that this seemed to him a fit description of the feast of Parliamentary eloquence which February brings with it.

For my own part, I do not share the opinion of that rather overbearing Prussian. In fact, I rather enjoy the " Thyestëan Banquet," especially at the opening of a new Parliament. I enjoy the ample, dignified, yet easy, rhetoric, drawn from the best period of our English tongue, in which the newly elected Speaker submits himself for the approbation of the Crown, and the Crown approves him, and grants him all that he claims. I admire the stilted vagueness of the Speech from the Throne ; and I am agreeably affected by the modesty of the gentlemen who move and second the Address. *Punch* at one time compiled a list of occasions on which a man does not look his best ; and certainly among them may be reckoned the occasion when, in a House full of men in ordinary garb, a full-blown Colonel bursting through a Hussar Uniform, or a pavid youth in black velvet and silk stockings, rises to move that this House has heard with loyal gratitude the gracious sentiments of the Front Bench—for this is what it comes to.

So far, the *menu* of the Thyestëan Banquet is invariable ; but these, after all, are only the *hors d'œuvre*. (It is curious that a culinary metaphor always involves one in the language of the *Haute Cuisine*.) But what comes after ? What are the *entrées* ? What is the *pièce de résistance* ? Mr Asquith would say, with gnomic wisdom, " Wait and see " ; and the flippant, looking forward to Monday, might chorus, " Now we sha'n't be long." But, in the meantime, my attempts to acquire information have left me as wise as I was before. Jawkins is quite sure that all is plain sailing. The Veto Bill will pass unamended into law. As to the Five

Hundred, or Pantomime, Peers, he is confident that the Lords will never consent so to "water their stock." The national conscience would revolt from civil discords at the time of the Coronation, and we may rest satisfied that, before six months are over, we shall see that Constitutional crisis, which at one time looked threatening, peacefully solved; not, perhaps, without resort to that spirit of compromise which is so characteristic of the national temper, and which has played so great a part in our Parliamentary history.

Thus Jawkins, who, when he can get no one else to listen to him, empties the vials of his wisdom on me. From Tommy Transome I hear quite different language. He rushed up from Loamshire to "do a swear," as he calls it, and take his seat; and then he rushed back again to get two more days' hunting before business begins. He looked in at the Club for luncheon, and was full of fight. His reverence for Jawkins, never overpowering, has yielded place to an active and vehement contempt. "No, really, I can't stick him. He is such an absolute old rotter. If I'd listened to all he said about moderate counsels, fighting with the gloves on, *noblesse oblige*, and the right line for an educated gentleman, I should have found myself at the bottom of the poll instead of Jobson, and serve me jolly well right too. No. If you enjoy that sort of tosh, you can go and have it. Don't let me stop you. I've got to catch a train at Paddington at three. The motor's in dock. We had a

' binge ' for the election workers at Slopsby—that's our biggest town—last week. Sing-song, supper, speeches, smoker—all in one. And I suppose my chauffeur ' binged ' a bit too freely—drinking success to the Liberal cause, for he's a very steady chap usually. Anyhow, we ran up a tree coming home, and the motor won't be out again for three weeks."

Having indeed had enough for one day of Jawkins on the crisis, and bethinking me of a duty-call overdue in Hyde Park Gardens, I join Tommy in a taxi, and as we speed along he unfolds to me his artless views and desires. " By Jove," he says, " I'm spoiling for a fight, and I shall be awfully sick if the Lords give in. I suppose it all depends on the proportion of ' Funks ' among them. Of course they all hate the Veto Bill like poison ; but some of 'em would like to fight it, and some would rather take it lying down. Now there's our old man at Gatherum—he had a Caucus of his pals last week. Called it shooting, but it was really politics. To do the old bird justice, he's a fighter—fought me, I know, for all he's worth, and will again if he has the chance. And he wants the Lords to fight now—says they've nothing to lose and everything to gain by showing a little pluck : tells 'em they can only die once, and may as well die like gentlemen. At least, that's what Jobson goes about saying, and he pretends he was at the Caucus, though I believe he was listening at the door, or read the notes on the Duke's blotting-paper. Well, if they want a fight, I'm quite ready to oblige them, and so's South Loamshire; and, if Asquith wants five hundred peers, we'll contribute Goodhart, and Laura Larkins's father. Not me, thank you—no, not for Tommy! When you've got a seat like Loamshire, taking a peerage is a mug's game. True, it's only a small majority; but, if we put up a good fight against old Omnium and his friends, we shall multiply it by ten. All I bar is a Compromise. That would make my chaps fairly sick, and me too. I haven't been at the game very long, but from what I can make out a Compromise always means giving in to the Tories and saying it's a triumph of moderate and statesmanlike policy. If the Government comes that game, I'm off, and I think that, what with the Irish and what with the Labour-Members, we shall be able to make things lively. Oh! here we are in Hyde Park Gardens. I'll take the taxi on to Paddington. See you again next week."

. . . .

Tea and muffins are over; and, strolling homeward in the chilly twilight, I ponder on the prospects of the Thyestëan Banquet—whether its successive courses will be acceptable to Tommy; and, if not, in what form his displeasure will manifest itself. The healthiest trait in my young friend's mental constitution is his dislike of humbug and solemn plausibilities. Though he is an Oxford man, I doubt if he is deeply versed in the history of the Oxford Movement. If he were, he might recall a downright controversialist who said: "When a man is called moderate, I distrust him; but, when he is called moderate and venerable, I set him down as a double-dyed old humbug." Though my friends tell me that I ought to be ashamed of myself, I must confess that this judgment still commands my assent. The "moderately fresh egg" of familiar story is typical of all moderation under the sun. It is the advanced men, the extreme men, the zealots, the enthusiasts, who do the fighting and face the storm. It is the moderate men who garner the fruits of victory, and abide under cover till the storm has rolled by. Now, as of old, *Regnum cœlorum vim patitur, et violenti rapiunt illud.*

Compromise is a word of evil omen in Liberal ears. The Educational Compromise of 1870 bequeathed us forty years of sectarian warfare. The Compromise with the Tories over the Franchise Bill of 1884 taught the Lords their power. Compromise on the question of Scottish Disestablishment robbed us of a majority in 1885, and in 1892 lowered Gladstone's own poll from thousands to hundreds. Compromise, informal but not the less real, between Tories and Liberals over the South African War surrendered the election of 1900 into the enemy's hands, and gave the Tories five more years of absolute power. It may be that some of these instances are already forgotten; but it would not be safe for our leaders to rely on the proverbial shortness of political memory; for, unless I am greatly misinformed, the new Parliament contains an element which remembers old scores, and means to pay them off. So, if for simple Veto—the plain and satisfying joint of the Parliamentary Bill of Fare—is substituted the mysterious and unwholesome compound which bad cooks call "Compromise," a baulked appetite may express itself in unseemly demonstrations:

> "Like cats in air-pumps, to subsist we strive
> On joys too thin to keep the soul alive."

If Tommy Transome is dissatisfied with the fare set before him, I shall introduce that couplet to his notice, and shall watch with interest his attempts to secure something more substantial.

XX

SPRING HOLIDAYS

PARADOX is not in my line. I have no delight in tilting against received opinions, or in showing that obvious deductions are necessarily fallacious. These exercises I leave to the genius of my friend Mr Chesterton (which, by the way, I ardently admire), and I content myself, as a rule, with humbly thinking and doing as others think and do. But to all rules on earth (except those of arithmetic) there are exceptions; and I practise some mental independence with regard to Holidays. Supposing that the laborious year allows one only three or four weeks which one can call one's own, I feel sure that one ought to claim them at the end of April and the beginning of May. I am more than sufficiently familiar with the boisterous joys of Christmas, and I understand, though I do not share, the rapture of the parched citizen when he smells the sea on the August Bank Holiday. I hold September the most perfect of all months, alike as regards its weather, its temperature, and the length of its days. But somehow the fall of the year, however gently it descends, seems inconsistent with the genius of a Holiday; for its prevailing tone is pensive and a holiday should speak, to all the senses, of

"Hope, and a renovation without end."

That is exactly what Nature gives us just now. Everywhere there is the triumphant sense of a great reaction. We have escaped from the frosts and fogs of winter, and have survived the still more murderous winds of March. In our calmer moments we know only too well that mid-May can be colder than Christmas, and that snow may be covering Epsom Downs on the Derby Day; but the persistent dominance of hope over experience, which is one of man's best gifts, insists on telling us that the worst is over, and that the Mighty Mother has forgotten how to be stern. The sympathy of Nature is indeed a "pathetic fallacy"; but it is impossible to believe that she cherishes sinister designs, when we gaze on an English landscape just as spring is yielding place to summer. As I sit down to write these words there comes to me from far Mashonaland the voice of an exiled poet who has not forgotten the country from whence he went out:—

"Tell the tune his feet beat
On the ground all day—
Black-burnt ground and green grass,
Seamed with rocks of grey—
'England,' 'England,' 'England,'
That one word they say.

Now they tread the beech-mast,
Now the ploughland's clay,
Now the faery ball-floor
Of her fields in May,

Now her red June sorrel, now her new-turned hay;
Now they keep the great road, now by sheep-path stray;
Still it's 'England,' 'England,'
'England' all the way!"

Perchance there may be among my readers one or two who share my feelings about a Holiday in spring, and to such I address myself, believing that my accumulated experience may supply some useful counsels.

In the first place, let me speak of Companionship. I do not commend a solitary holiday. It is true that Wordsworth was "wandering lonely as a cloud" when he saw the daffodils by the lake, and learned from them the loveliest of short poems; but few of us have Wordsworth's gift of being at our best in solitude. Even the companionship of Nature is more enjoyable when we can share it with a friend. Most of us would say about the finest view in England:

"A scene to me more strangely fair
Because we sate together there."

We. Yes, but who is to be the other? I hope that I shall not be reproached with want of gallantry (for I am really the most chivalrous of mankind) if I say that the presence of Femininity is incompatible with a Spring Holiday. Viatrix and the children can go to the sea-side later on; but let Viator for once assert his natural independence and choose his companions from among his male friends. Of how many should the party consist? Two is not enough. If we happen to possess a friend with whom we are so absolutely one that it is safe to commit ourselves for three weeks to his undivided society, he is certain to be busy, or ill, or abroad, or in some way hindered just when we want to start; and a friend not absolutely one is out of the question. Four is too many; for they will inevitably split into two sections of two apiece; and, when A. and B. wish to climb, C. and D. will insist on fishing. No, the right number is three. The instinct of self-preservation will make them stick together, for no one wishes to be "odd man out," with the moon shining on his solitary walk (Wordsworth again), while the other two are hobnobbing in

> "The Village Inn, our evening resting-place."

Our party, therefore, consists of three intimate friends of the same age, tastes, and habits; and, if not strictly of the same opinions, yet temperate in the statement of what they respectively believe, and averse from "Ructions." Argument and a Spring Holiday are palpably incompatible. And how shall we travel? The train is hopelessly commonplace. An aeroplane is more romantic, but has a perverse knack of dropping one where one has no wish to be. A driving tour has undeniable merits, and still more so a riding tour; but both require a knowledge, which perhaps not all the three possess, of horses, and both depend for their enjoyability on fine weather. It is difficult to be cheerful under a macintosh in a dogcart, or on a slippery saddle, when a storm is beating on one's face and the reins are slipping through one's fingers. Motorists and cyclists, and those strange hybrids the motor-cyclists, seem to disregard weather; and yet somehow they do not look as if they were enjoying themselves. The passion of record-breaking, the pain of competitive effort, the ill-concealed ambition to see one's performance recorded in *The Car*, are jarring elements in a scheme of pure enjoyment, and that is what a Spring Holiday should be. And then, again, the wheelman, of whatever type, is confined to the hard highroad, whereas the choicest beauties of England are to be found on heathery moors and slippery downs, and in woodlands and deer-parks, and amid the tall, lush grass which fringes running water.

Sir Walter Scott, to whom all manly exercises came easy, and who understood Nature as well as he loved her, declared, plump and pain, for a walking tour:

"Dr Johnson thought life had few things better than the excitation produced by being whirled rapidly along in a post-chaise; but he who has in youth experienced the confidence and independent feeling of a stout pedestrian in an interesting country, and during fine weather, will hold the taste of the great moralist cheap in comparison."

On the whole, I vote with Sir Walter. The supreme joy of a Spring Holiday is to go wherever you wish; and this joy (so far as our Land Laws permit it) is possible to a stout pair of legs and to no other form of conveyance. So, in imagination, I form my party of three—strong, active, and cheerful, on the best of terms with the world, themselves, and one another; and I stand on my doorstep and wave Farewell as they set off on their Spring Walking-tour. My best wish for them is that they may fare as well as that prince of good fellows, John Evelyn, and his companions, fared three centuries and a half ago. "Sometimes we footed it thro' pleasant fields and meadows; sometimes we shot at fowls and other birds, nothing came amiss; sometimes we play'd at cards, while others sung or were composing verses." "We had a supper that might have satisfied a prince." "We lay that night in damask beds, and were treated like Emperoors."

When we have arranged our party, and fixed our method of travelling, we must choose our route. For my own part, I love to travel in good company, and, if one of my favourite writers has described my journey, I find it more enjoyable. So now in springtime we may tread the Pilgrim Way to the shrine of St Thomas at Canterbury, stopping on the way to crack a joke with R. H. Barham at Tapton Everard. With Pope as our guide, we may plunge into the Garden of England, which is Windsor, and thence may follow Shakespeare to the stone walls of the Cotswolds, or Charles Kingsley to the depths of the New Forest, or Tom Hughes into the Vale of

White Horse; or with Matthew Arnold we may explore the Valley of the Thames, or with Milton gaze on Oxford from the heights of Shotover. Eastward, Essex has its prose-painter in Mr Baring Gould, and westward the genius of Blackmore will guide us over Exmoor. In the Midlands, Cowper will introduce us to the quiet beauties of the Ouse and the Nene; Whyte-Melville will show us the way across Northamptonshire, and Macaulay will make our hearts beat high with the tale of Naseby. When we touch Sherwood Forest we want no better company than Mr Richard Whiteing and his Yellow Van. As we press northward, Sir Walter will welcome us where the Greta meets the Tees in the woods of Rokeby, and, when we enter Lakeland, will hand us over to Wordsworth, only to reclaim us when we touch the Border; and thence he will lead us, through the ever-ascending scale of Scottish landscape, till we encounter Dr Johnson on the terrace at Inveraray.

But all this time we have been walking; the day begins to draw in, and we are both tired and hungry, exactly to that degree which invests the thought of Supper with unspeakable charms. And now once again we change the venue, and find ourselves at the door of a roadside inn, twelve miles inland from Portsmouth town. The landlord tells us that there will be "a hot beefsteak pudding, with potatoes," ready at nine. We believe him, and are justified. A fellow-traveller invites us to share a bowl of punch, which "appears steaming in a manner quite exhilarating to behold, and sending forth a most grateful and inviting fragrance." We have supped with Dickens and all is well.

VERSES SUGGESTED BY THE FOREGOING CHAPTER

"Matilda, dear, you recollect—
Tho' Time is on the wing—
The day you vowed to love me
In the Spring.

A year passed on, and then for you
I bought a golden ring,
And took you to the altar
In the Spring.

You know how true I've been, my dear ;
I've never had my fling ;
But thought perhaps you'd let me,
In the Spring.

I'll stay with you at other times,
As happy as a king,
But let me stretch my legs, love,
In the Spring."

WILLIAMS LEIGH.

XXI

PUBLIC DINNERS

THE Public Dinner is an institution peculiarly British. That it should have established itself among our national observances is in itself a conclusive proof of racial vigour. It argues a most royal digestion thus to combine banqueting with oratory. The sensations of Juvenal's friend who carried a crude peacock with him into his bath were not more painful, though perhaps more perilous, than those of the man who, full of *hors d'œuvres*, soup, fish, *entrées*, lamb, chicken, macédoine, caviare, Stilton, ice, strawberries and cream, let alone vinous accessories, "rises to propose a toast." One cannot digest when one knows one has got to speak, and one cannot speak when nature is trying to digest. The audience is as uneasy as the orator. Some have wished to speak but have not been invited to do so. Some have been placed below their proper rank, or next the co-equals whom they most dislike. Some, having eaten and drunk in excess, are longing for fresh air. Some are anxious to catch their train. All alike join in condemning the oratory. "How infernally long-winded Smith has become!" "Brown's style of speaking is awfully pompous—like himself." "I have heard Jones make the same speech ten years running." "Did you ever hear a fellow mumble like Robinson? He must have lost all his teeth." Amid this chorus of disparagement, well understood even if not heard, the successive speakers stagger to their goal; and then we shake the crumbs from our laps, and stretch our legs, and once again breathe freely.

Yet these strange rites, so unwillingly endured, survive from generation to generation. Kings come and go. Ministries rise and fall. Coronations and Elections engross our thoughts. Men make wars, and Science makes discoveries. But, through all permutations, the Public Dinner stands unshaken, unchallenged, and, in the main, unchanged. I insert these qualifying words because, as the programme of the Coronation shows us, the most public of all Public Dinners—the supreme instance of this national observance — has perished unwept. All through the centuries which made England great the Kings of England were no sooner anointed and crowned than they fell to dining in public; and King George IV., who, in spite of Thackeray's acrid criticism, was a very fine King in his way, dined even more publicly, elaborately, and expensively than any of his predecessors.

"The first course consisted of 24 gold covers and dishes, carried by as many Gentlemen Pensioners; they were preceded by six attendants on the Clerk

Controller, by two Clerks of the Kitchen, by the Clerk Controller in a velvet gown trimmed with silver lace, by two Clerks and the Secretary of the Board of Green Cloth, by the Controller and Treasurer of the Household, and by Serjeants-at-Arms with their maces. The Duke of Montrose performed the office of Serjeant of the Silver Scullery. At the end of the dinner the Sovereign's health was drunk with nine times nine. The National Anthem was sung with incomparable effect, and the King quitted the Hall at a quarter before eight, *when the company was indiscriminately admitted to partake of such refreshments as remained on the tables.*"

That was something like a Public Dinner, before which the Coronation Banquet given by King George V. and Queen Mary sinks to the level of a private party.

As far as I know, Religious Societies do not dine in public. They breakfast ; and discuss Missions or Disestablishment over coffee and muffins, and break up, at midday, in a highly dyspeptic state of mind. But Societies of a more secular type conform to the world, and dine. The most famous dinner of the year is the Banquet of the Royal Academy, where some of the most inartistic people in the world are put up to utter enormous fibs about the spiritual character of British art. The Royal Society dines on St Andrew's Day, and Matthew Arnold "liked dining with it very much." "The Royal Society," he said, "is our one truly great Society, a sort of Institute." Regiments dine enormously, and the month of May is sacred to their martial orgies. The dinners at the Guildhall, the Mansion House, and at the Halls of the City Companies are too well known to need further description. Thackeray's account of "A Dinner in the City"—food, wine, music, oratory, and all—is as true as if it had been written yesterday; and the only material fact which has emerged since his day is that the Companies spend £100,000 a year on meat and drink, irrespective of servants' wages and upkeep of premises. Sion College dines. The Dean and Chapter of St Paul's dine. The Colleges of Physicians and Surgeons dine. Hospitals dine, but solely with a view to collecting money. The Inns of Court dine publicly and often, but more by way of entertaining their friends than of glorifying themselves. The Eighty Club dines sparingly and speaks profusely. Colleges dine annually, but, as their dinners are generally held in their own delightful abodes, they have a touch of romance about them which is not attainable at the Savoy or the Ritz. The "gentlemen educated at either of the two foundations of St Mary Winton"—in other words, New College men and Wykehamists—have a dinner which combines the dignity of Oxford with the free and easiness of school. Winchester is the mother and mistress of Public Schools, but every school that claims the title of Public has its annual or triennial dinner, where ancient friends, perhaps long separated, renew their youth, laugh and chaff, or secretly recall the time when life seemed to promise brighter things than it has given.

> "Forgotten cheers are in our ears ;
> Again we play our matches ;
> And memory swells, with magic spells,
> Our boyish scores and catches.
> Again we rush across the slush,
> A pack of breathless faces,
> And charge, and fall, and see the ball
> Fly whizzing through the bases."

What is the conversation on these occasions? It was sketched for us, some years ago, by an author, himself educated at Eton, who, for obvious reasons, preferred to write anonymously. "Let us suppose that the company were Etonians—what will form the theme of their discourse? The genius of Canning? The poetry of Gray? Will they favour you with descriptions of the old 'Montem,' or talk pleasingly or sensibly of the good to be derived from a residence in those classic shades? No such thing. They will gabble about Cotherstone Major—how he licked a bargee; about Swabbs, who flirted so shamefully with his tutor's fat Scotch cook; about Bogglinton, who was six feet high, and had fags when he was himself in the Lower School." Though these latter themes do not sound particularly inviting, I should prefer them to the suggested alternatives. It would bore me dreadfully to sit at dinner by a man who discoursed of Canning, or Byron, or Clough, or the first Lord Selborne; who described Montem, or "Hills," or "Bigside"; who "talked pleasingly and sensibly" about the good which he had derived from residence at Eton or Harrow or Winchester or Rugby. Unlike Wordsworth, I "much and oft delight to season my fireside with personal talk" and memories of Cotherstone, and Swabbs, and Bogglinton, or their equivalents among my own contemporaries, would interest me much more keenly than high discourse about the respective places of literature and science in public education, or the claims of Eton to be considered the School of Statesmen.

. . . .

To-night is the Triennial Dinner of Roslyn School. (The name is Dean Farrar's, but it will serve as well as another.) Lord Lumpington is in the Chair. Why? His career at Oxford, and the "feat of mental gymnastics" in which it culminated, are known to all readers of "Friendship's Garland." I should make a much better chairman than Lumpington, who cannot string two words together; or Mr Justice Wigsby, who cannot pronounce his h's; or the Bishop of Barchester, who presided last time, and delivered a Confirmation Charge enlivened by bad jokes.

Two hundred of us are crammed into a room which would barely hold a hundred and fifty. The air is already mephitic, and before long will recall the Black Hole of Calcutta. We are all hunting for our places, exchanging noisy greetings with each other, peeping furtively at our neighbours' names, and looking with some dismay at the List of Toasts. "Good heavens! we shall be here all night." "Gentlemen, pray, silence for Grace, by the Rev. Dr Smithers." "Good old Smithers! I haven't seen him since the last day he swished me; but, as the sack followed next week, that isn't odd." "For what we are going to receive——" "Thick or clear, sir?" "Thick, please. I wonder if it's made of tinned pease." "I believe the clear is Bovril and water." "I seem to remember your face, though you've changed a good bit." "Let's see, whose House were you in? Oh! Creakle's. What a brute Creakle was!" "Yes; but he was better than Gushy."

Thus harmlessly, if not improvingly, the stream of talk meanders for an hour and a half, till suddenly we are again called to order. "Gentlemen, pray, silence for the Chairman—the Right Honourable the Earl of Lumpington." Lumpington rises amid tumults of applause: "My Lords and Gentlemen, there is one toast . . . King George reigns over an Empire on which the sun never sets, but he has no more loyal subjects than Old Roslynians." (*Immense cheering.*) "Gentlemen, the King." Next we toast Gracious Ladies and Hopeful Princes, and every member of a Family universally beloved. And now comes the toast of the Houses of Parliament coupled with the names of that grand old Roslynian Lord Mumbles, and of young Sydney Snap, M.P. Old Mumbles replies. We live in perilous times. New and strange doctrines are abroad. Venerable institutions are threatened; but of one thing Lord Mumbles is confident—that, if the House of Lords is to die, it will die, as it has lived, with dignity. Lord Mumbles is not seldom seen drunk at the C—— Club, his bills are notoriously unpaid, and Lady Mumbles has long since parted company with her lord; but we feel that he is inherently a good judge of dignity, and say "Hear, hear," in the solemn bass of deep conviction.

Young Snap is on his legs. He is the latest-born of Under Secretaries, has an uncommonly good opinion of himself, and would like to insult old Mumbles if he dared. But the audience, like every gathering of Public Schoolmen, is Tory as the sea is salt; so Snap keeps his impertinences locked in his own bosom, and contents himself with saying that the House of Commons closely resembles a Public School, where everyone fights fairly, and the best man comes to the top.—(*Ironical applause, and cries of "Bravo, Snap," from disappointed competitors.*)

"The Church, and the Bishop of Barchester"; "The Army, and General Nogo"; "The Navy, and Admiral Breezy"; "The Reserve Forces, and Sir Anthony Lumkin," of Territorial fame; and so on, and so forth, till the oldest of living Roslynians rises amid deafening applause to propose his dear old friend—our admirable Chairman of to-night—one of those whose undeniable merits will be the effectual safeguard of the august assemblage to which he belongs against the assaults of an unscrupulous demagogy. "Gentlemen, I give you the health of Lord Lumpington." In reply, Lumpington, who, to do him justice, wastes no time in superfluous rhetoric, expresses his conviction that, as long as the House of Lords is manned by Public Schoolmen in general, and Roslynians in particular, it is as safe as the Bank of England. We spring to our feet, wave our napkins, join hands all round the table, and burst into the National Anthem of our beloved school:

"FIFTY MILES OFF."

XXII

THE CORONATION

I HAVE an hereditary right to be interested in Coronations. In J. W. Croker's Journals, under the date 19th July 1821, we read :

"I went to the Speaker's House this morning. . . . The King heard I was there, and sent for me. He was waiting for the public officers to proceed. Even after he had put on his robes and hat, most cumbrous and heavy, he had to wait full half-an-hour for the Great Chamberlain, Lord Gwydyr, who, it seems, had torn his robes, and was obliged to wait to have them mended. I dare say the public lays the blame of the delay on the King, who was ready long before anyone else."

The King, of course, was George IV. The day was the day of his Coronation ; and, according to the custom then observed for the last time, he slept overnight at the Speaker's house, "his sofa-bed being brought from Carlton House." Next morning he walked in procession, on a raised platform, from Westminster Hall to the Abbey. The cause of the delay which Croker mentions was an accident to Lord Gwydyr's train. Lord Gwydyr's page was a little

Westminster boy,[1] lively and larky, who tugged so hard at the vast expanse of velvet which it was his duty to carry that it came off (at what I believe ladies call the "gathers"), parting company with the ermine cape, and leaving the Lord Great Chamberlain an object of derision. Seamstresses were hastily summoned, and the damage was repaired; but the procession was delayed for half-an-hour, and the page used, in old age, to say with infinite gusto, "I did my best to keep that old rascal off the throne."

The Coronation, thus inauspiciously commenced, cost £240,000 of public money; and, although this was all very well in the days of a restricted franchise and a gagged populace, it scarcely harmonized with the "Peace, Retrenchment, and Reform," which were the watchwords of the ensuing reign. William IV. came very near to not being crowned at all. When, at the crisis of 1831, he determined to go down at a moment's notice to the House of Lords and prorogue Parliament with a view to immediate dissolution, he took his Crown from the nobleman appointed to carry it, clapped it on his own head, and turning to the Prime Minister, Lord Grey, exclaimed: "Now, my Lord, the Coronation is over." This probably delighted Lord Grey, who was an utilitarian Whig of the most offensive type, and condemned the ceremonies of the Coronation, as "at variance with the genius of the age we live in, and suited to another period of Society."

[1] Lord Charles James Fox Russell (1807-1894).

However, the historic sentiment prevailed, and William IV. was duly crowned on the 3rd of September 1831, though with a debased and truncated ceremonial. Charles Greville, who as Clerk of the Council was present when the arrangements were made, records this quaint story about the Homage:

"It is first done by the Spiritual Peers, with the Archbishop at their head. The first of each class (the Archbishop for the Spiritual) says the words, and then they all kiss the Sovereign's cheek in succession. The King said he would not be kissed by the Bishops, and ordered that part to be struck out. But, as I expected, the Prelates would not stand it; the Archbishop remonstrated, the King knocked under, and so he must undergo the salute of the Spiritual as well as of the Temporal Lords."

By 1838, when Queen Victoria was crowned, the squalid temper of the previous decade had passed away. The Gothic revival had affected public taste, and the Oxford Movement had recalled men's minds to the spiritual significance of visible forms. The young Queen's Coronation became a National Ceremony, of the highest interest and importance. It was estimated that five hundred thousand people flocked to London for the occasion, and that £200,000 was paid for seats alone. "The great merit of this Coronation," wrote Greville, "is that so much has been done for the people; to amuse and interest them seems to have been the principal object." Prince Esterhazy, steeped in the absolutism of Vienna, said: "Nothing like it can be seen in any other country in the world." Among the spectators were the Rev. R. H. Barham, who described the scene in the amusing but rather irreverent verse of "The Ingoldsby Legends"; and a lad of more refined and susceptible genius, who lived to preside over the Abbey Church.

"The last Coronation," wrote Dean Stanley in 1867, "doubtless still lives in the recollection of all who witnessed it. They will long remember the early summer morning, when, at break of day, the streets were thronged, and the vast city awoke—the first sight of the Abbey, crowded with the mass of gorgeous spectators, themselves a pageant,—the electric shock through the whole mass when the first gun announced that the Queen was on her way—and the thrill of expectation with which the iron rails seemed to tremble in the hands of the spectators, as the long procession closed with the entrance of the small figure, marked out from all beside by the Royal train and attendants, floating like a crimson and silvery cloud behind her. At the moment when she first came within the full view of the Abbey, and paused, as if for breath, with clasped hands; as she moved on to her place by the altar; as, in the deep silence of the vast multitude, the tremulous voice of Archbishop Howley could be faintly heard, even to the remotest corners of the Choir, asking for the Recognition ; as she sate immovable on the Throne when the Crown touched her head, amidst shout and trumpet and the roar of cannon, there must have been many who felt the hope that the loyalty which had waxed cold in the preceding reigns would once more revive, in a more serious form than it had, perhaps, ever worn before."

The Girl-Queen whose fair and touching youth had won all hearts in 1838 reigned so long that when, in extreme old age, she laid down her Crown, people in general had forgotten the forms with which her successor must assume it. But there, safely treasured in the Abbey, which it has never left, was the splendid order of the *Liber Regalis*, which from the Coronation of Richard II. till now has regulated this supreme ceremony, and modern researches into liturgiology and ceremonial have thrown instructive light on its successive permutations. The increasing sense for visible beauty in the daily life of men, which had so conspicuously marked the last quarter of Queen Victoria's reign, found its highest satisfaction in a rite which was both Sacramental and Constitutional. Two prelates there had lately been—Benson and Creighton—who, the one from the liturgical and the other from the historical point of view, would have been admirably qualified to represent the Church in this great solemnity ; but both were untimely dead; and of Archbishop Temple, in many respects admirable, it may be safely said that no human being was ever less fitted to play a ceremonial part. However, the service is in itself so majestic that no ineptitude on the part of the ministrants can destroy its effect; and the Coronation of King Edward and Queen Alexandra remains to the present day an imperishable memory.

And now we are once again making ready for our part in this great act of national devotion, and it may not be out of place to remind ourselves of its precise nature and significance. Most nobly and most aptly, it begins with the Recognition. The Coronation does not make the King; he is made by the Act of Settlement; and, from the moment when King Edward VII. breathed his last, King George has been our lawful Sovereign. He is King of England, and not all the Crowns and Unctions in the world could make him more. It is this truth that is so grandly testified by the first act of the great solemnity. The King stands "and shows himself to the people," while the Archbishop of Canterbury, as first subject of the realm, proclaims him for what he is, saying: "Sirs, I here present unto you King George, the undoubted King of this Realm." "Whereupon the People signify their willingness and joy, all with one voice crying out, 'God save King George,'" and then "the trumpets sound."

Is not this as simple as it is noble? The King is King already; his people accept and acknowledge him as such; and the Church blesses him and prays that he may have grace to fulfil the great office to which he is called. So then the whole congregation falls to prayer, as the chanted litany lifts the heart to Heaven. And then the Archbishop, laying aside his civil, and assuming his spiritual, function, goes to the High Altar, and there begins the great service of the Eucharist; and, when the King and Queen have confessed their faith in the immortal Creed of Nicea, the Archbishop approaches the King and demands the Oath; and, as he does so, the Great Charter is behind him, and the memories of Runnymede and of Whitehall. Then the King, having made the prescribed answers to the three great questions which concern Law, Justice, and Religion, lays his hand on the open page of the Holy Gospel, and, kneeling on the altar-step, confirms his promise with an oath.

And then he bows his head, and the *Veni Creator* rolls over him as he kneels, and the Archbishop takes the consecrated oil, and anoints him thrice, and signs him with the Cross, and then act after act of the Investitute is duly rendered, and each act has its own significance. "The Orb with the Cross is brought from the altar and delivered into the King's hand by the Archbishop pronouncing this exhortation—'When you see this Orb thus set under the Cross, remember that the whole world is subject to the power and empire of Christ our Redeemer.' " And so the supreme moment arrives and the Crown of pure gold is set upon the Sovereign's head ; and then he seats himself upon the Throne of his ancestors, and the chief Estates of the Realm render him their willing homage. And then the Archbishop resumes the service of the Eucharist at the point where it was broken off for this majestic interlude. The King and Queen, having laid aside their Crowns, kneel down to receive the Sacred Gifts ; and then the final benediction is pronounced, and the most glorious hymn of Christendom is sung as an act of thanksgiving for the safe accomplishment of a nation's desire. " Surely the life of the whole People will feel the transfiguring force which comes from the achievement of so great an action."

XXIII

A MIDSUMMER DAY'S DREAM[1]

MIDSUMMER DAY this year is to be marked by such a spectacle as may well set Englishmen a-dreaming. The King of England, himself a sailor, is to review his fleet. The hereditary Sovereign of the Seas will see marshalled round his floating throne the most wonderful creations of science and skill and wealth and courage that the world has ever known —the science of the designer, and the skill of the artificer, and the courage as keenly tested in construction as in action, and the national wealth which buys all these. Truly there is a magic in this Pomp of the Sea which stirs the Viking-blood of Englishmen as no tramp of cavalry, no blare of trumpets, no crash of artillery can stir it. The salt water sets our veins a-tingle ; the most lethargic wax delirious, and the most prosaic dream dreams. No one can escape the contagion. It goes rollicking down all our national minstrelsy, from Shakespeare, who, though a son of the Midlands, yet reeks of " the rude imperious surge," to Swinburne, whom, in spite of his cosmopolitanism, the sea inspires

[1] 21st June 1911.

with something dangerously like the strain of insularity.

> "Let Russian with Prussian
> Exchange the kiss of slaves;
> But sea-folk are free folk,
> By grace of winds and waves."

"Rule Britannia" shares the rank of a National Anthem with what the Frenchmen called "Le god-save." Tennyson is never more majestic than when he chants the repulse of the insolent Armada:

> "Ship after ship, the whole night long, their high-built galleons came,
> Ship after ship, the whole night long, with her battle-thunder and flame;
> Ship after ship, the whole night long, drew back with her dead and her shame."

Less stately, indeed, but as passionately patriotic, are Dibdin, and Campbell, and Cunningham, and the nameless bard who claimed the Sovereignty of the Seas in a verse beloved by schoolboys:

> "Oh! 'tis a wonderful Island—
> All of 'em long for the Island,
> Hold a bit there: let 'em take fire and air,
> But we'll have the Sea and the Island."

Lord Beaconsfield handled this vein of maritime Imperialism with characteristic humour:

"I must say," said Waldershare, "it was a grand idea of our kings making themselves Sovereigns of the Sea. The greater portion of this planet is water; so we at once became a first-rate Power. We owe our Navy entirely to the Stuarts. King James the Second was the true founder and hero of the British Navy. He was a worthy son of his admirable father, the Blessed Martyr, the restorer at least, if not the inventor, of ship-money—the most patriotic and popular tax that ever was devised by man. The Nonconformists thought themselves so wise in resisting it, and they have got the Naval Estimates instead!"

That last is a barbed sentence which strikes home to-day.

We may be pardoned if, dazzled by the splendour of our Midsummer Day's pageant, we forget for a moment the uses to which ships are, or may be, applied, and think of them only in their intrinsic strength and beauty.

"Take it all in all, a ship of the line is the most honourable thing that man, as a gregarious animal, has ever produced. By himself, unhelped, he can do better things than ships of the line; he can make poems and pictures, and such other concentrations of what is best in him. But, as a being living in flocks, and hammering out, with alternate stroke and mutual agreement, what is necessary for him in these flocks to get or produce, the ship of the line is his first work. Into that he has put as much of his human patience, common sense, forethought, experimental philosophy, self-control, habits of order and obedience, thoroughly-wrought handiwork, defiance of brute elements, careless courage, careful patriotism, and calm expectation of the judgments of God, as can well be put into a space of three hundred feet long by eighty broad. And I am thankful to have lived in an age when I could see this thing so done."

It is Ruskin who is speaking, and I can rejoice with him in the contemplation of these magnificent masterpieces of human skill. But what is the next step? Having built our ship, and christened her, and manned her with our best flesh and blood, and crowned her with the Threefold Cross which is the emblem of our sovereignty, what are we to do with her? In another place, and writing under a different inspiration, Ruskin tells us that wherever there is war there must be injustice on the one side or the other, or on both. "War," he says, in words which might well have been written during the South African frenzy—"war may be so involved with national prejudices or ignorances that neither of the contending nations can conceive injustice as attaching to their cause; nay, the constitution of their Governments and the clumsy crookedness of their dealing with each other, may be such as to prevent either of them from knowing the actual cause for which they have gone to war."

Wars of self-defence—wars for the maintenance of home and freedom and national existence—may be necessary and even noble. But of all the wars which can be traced down the long, red battle-line of human history, how many can be justly called wars of self-defence? How many have been created by insensate ambition, by the lust of aggrandisement, by cruel and clamorous jealousies, by the blundering diplomacy of miscalled statesmen? If we believed that our British fleet was to be employed for purposes of challenge or attack, we ought to pray that the lightning of heaven might send it to the bottom.

But that England should be "confident from foreign purposes," and impregnably secure against aggression, is a duty which she owes to God, to the world, and to herself. "The white wake of her vessels is the avenue to her palace-front, along which no enemy may approach." A few years ago, fear and doubts and misgivings on this score would have been unthinkable. It seemed as if the nations of the world had learnt the lesson of mutual forbearance, had recognized the obligation of the strong to the weak, and had realized that war is the greatest calamity which can afflict the human race. But all these optimistic dreams—all these Beatific Visions of the Brotherhood of Man already existing and operating on earth—were dispelled in an instant by the tragedy of South Africa. We learned in three years of agony that the brutal passions of mankind are as strong as ever, that the idea of chivalry towards the weak and the defenceless had perished from the minds of men, and that the ministers of the Prince of Peace could be the shrillest inciters to bloodshed. What we did then, other countries may do now. After that miserable experience, it is folly to indulge in millennial dreams; and, as we gaze on the assembled battle-ships of England, we are forced to consider the possibility that, on some unforeseen alarm, arising at a moment's notice in a district severed from us by half the compass of the globe, they may be forced to strike in defence of an Empire which, just because it is world-wide, is also vulnerable.

It was the contemplation of some such possibility as this that suggested to George Canning, speaking at Plymouth in 1823, one of the noblest images in the oratory of either the ancient or the modern world:

"Our present repose," he said, "is no more a proof of inability to act, than the state of inertness and inactivity in which I have seen those mighty masses which float in your harbour is a proof that they are devoid of strength, and incapable of being fitted out for action. You well know, gentlemen, how soon one of those stupendous masses, now reposing on their shadows in perfect stillness—how soon, upon any call of patriotism or of necessity, it would assume the likeness of an animated thing, instinct with life and motion—how soon it would ruffle, as it were, its swelling plumage—how quickly it would put forth all its beauty and its bravery, collect its scattered elements of strength, and awaken its dormant thunder. Such as is one of those magnificent machines when springing from inaction into a display of its might—such is England herself, while, apparently passive and motionless, she silently concentrates the power to be put forth on an adequate occasion. But God forbid that such occasion should arise."

XXIV

"POMP AND PRODIGALITY"

OF course the verbal felicities of the greatest poets were unintended. It was not by study or effort or the laborious file that Homer and Shakespeare and Dante produced those "jewels five words long" which "sparkle for ever" in the grateful memory of mankind. Wordsworth said that "Goethe's poetry was not *inevitable* enough"; and Matthew Arnold, contrasting the two men, adds that Wordsworth's poetry, when he is at his best, "is inevitable—as inevitable as Nature herself," whereas there is not a line in Goethe "but its maker knew well how it came there." Exactly the same criticism applies to Gray. The "Elegy" contains a greater number of frequently quoted lines than any other poem of its size in the world, and every one of those lines is a triumph of skill and care. It is so with the line from which I quote at the head of this chapter. When Gray wrote of "Pomp and Prodigality," we may be quite sure that he was acting, not under the irresistible impulse which drives the poet whither it will, but with the deliberate purpose of choosing effective and memorable words to express his thoughts. And he succeeded to perfection. The words sound well and mean much—indeed, in their combination they express a thing for which human nature yearns. Nature is a good deal stronger than philosophy, or logic, or political economy. And, though the philosopher and the economist may affirm, and the logician may try to prove, that "Pomp and Prodigality" are things mischievous and undesirable, still mankind goes on delighting in them, and is never so happy as when it can enjoy them to the full.

For the last month we have lived on nothing else, and the nation has never been so cheerful. The words which Gray picked out of a copious vocabulary express with curious precision the forms of pleasure which we have been enjoying. "Pomp" is *Pompa* —"a solemn or public procession—a train, suite, retinue, or row of persons—hence parade, display, ostentation, POMP"—the very word we wanted. And then "Prodigality." Here the derivation at first suggests only what is "wasteful or lavish"; but it soon merges, through various shades of meaning, into "rich, abundant, profuse, PRODIGAL." The common speech of Bible-reading English folk has made us familiar with "the Parable of the Prodigal Son," and has thereby given the epithet an evil colour; but we might just as reasonably speak of "the Prodigal Father," whose wealth of love let byegones be byegones, and gave the repentant wanderer such a splendid home-coming.

So Pomp, freed from its debased associations of

"Pomposity," and Prodigality, as signifying not waste but abundance, have furnished the delights of this memorable summer, and the supply is not yet exhausted. London, as became the capital of the Empire, led the way, and there, if anywhere, the poet's vision was realized:

> "The golden Pompa cometh,
> The Pompa streams along,"

representative of a world-wide dominion such as no "purple Cæsar" ever dreamed. To Imperial Rome, Africa was a commonplace, and India a mystery, and Britain a rough island in the northern seas. To-day all the world knows that Confederacy of States which we call the British Empire, and in the national "Pompa" our English roses were blent in strange harmony with the Canadian maple-leaf and the silver fern of New Zealand.

And then the "Pompa" crossed the Irish Channel to a land where it is peculiarly at home. The Irish love splendour, whether in the observances of religion, or in military display, or in civil administration. When Queen Victoria paid her first visit to her Irish capital, *The Times* burst into unwonted dithyrambics: "No ovation of olden Rome, enriched with the spoils of conquered nations, and illustrated by the wealth of captured kings, was so glorious as the triumphant entry of Queen Victoria into Dublin." When O'Connell, at the height of his demagogic fame, was made Lord Mayor of Dublin, he lived habitually in his official robes, and "appeared at meetings a hundred miles from Dublin in his red velvet gown and cocked hat." Thackeray laughed at him for it; but he knew the people with whom he was dealing. The most popular Viceroys of Ireland have not always been the wisest or the most liberal rulers, but those who best knew how to maintain the traditional stateliness of the Viceregal Court. "Give me Abercorn," said one enthusiast—"give me Abercorn, who looks at you over his beard as if you were so much dirt."

From Ireland the "Pompa" sailed to Wales, and there again a Celtic population, with a strong spirit of nationality, and an historic sentiment now for the first time gratified, showed its unmistakable delight in ceremony and symbolism. Surely the idea of "Inaugurating" the Heir Apparent in the northern capital of his picturesque Principality was a master-stroke of political genius.

At the last stage of the Royal progress, the popularity of "Pomp and Prodigality" might have seemed less well assured. The Scotch are a mixed race, and at Edinburgh the poetry and romance of the Gael have to contend with the prosaic and businesslike qualities of the canny Southron. But Edinburgh is a city framed alike by the bounty of nature and the genius of man for processional display; and, by retaining some at least of the outward forms which belonged to her polity when she was a separate State, Scotland has borne a standing witness to the value of ceremonial.

"Ye suld mind the riding of the Parliament in the gude auld time before the Union—a year's rent o' mony a gude estate gaed for horse-graith and harnessing, forbye broidered robes and footmantles, that wad hae stude by their lane wi' gold brocade. But Scotland was Scotland in those days."

And Scotland is Scotland still, and knows how to lay aside the cares of money-making, and the strife of politics, and even the purer delights of metaphysical theology, when the descendants of the Bruces and the Stuarts keep Court at Holyrood.

At a moment when "Pomp and Circumstance" are asserting themselves so universally and so beneficially, it is curious to reflect that only a few years ago they were thought by some hard-headed people to have disappeared for ever from practical life. We were reminded, only quite lately, that when William IV. came to the Throne, some of his advisers were in favour of dispensing with the Coronation, as inconsistent with the spirit of the times. It became an accepted belief among utilitarian Radicals that forms and ceremonies of all kinds were contemptible and even harmful. I remembered Professor York Powell murmuring against the ceremony (something like a Confirmation) with which a Degree is conferred at Oxford, and saying that it would be quite ceremony enough for the B.A. to pay a fee and write his name in a book. When the Primrose League was beginning its remarkable career, Sir George Trevelyan said, with his habitual emphasis, "I decline to believe that England will allow itself to be governed by Knights and Dames and Badges and Habitations." This view of forms and ceremonies never commended itself to Mr Gladstone. Like his great master, Edmund Burke, he knew "the sacred virtue of parchment and sealing-wax." He saw that the same principle underlay the vestments of the Church, and the robes of the Judicial Bench, and the uniforms of Army and Navy, and the insignia of Freemasonry and Oddfellowship. "How many men," he asked me during the Parliament of 1880, "how many men would vote for *unwigging* the Speaker?" I suggested Mr Labouchere. Mr Gladstone assented, but said that in that case the vote would represent freakishness rather than conviction. He could think of only one man who would unwig the Speaker on conscientious grounds—and that was Mr T. C. Thompson, then Radical member for the City of Durham.

It is certainly inconceivable to me that anyone who habitually watches the life of the populace can doubt that the great mass of Englishmen love "Pomp and Prodigality." Lord Shaftesbury, who knew the poor as no man in his class has ever known them, poured scorn on the theorists and economists who disparage ceremony. In the year of revolution —1848—he told the Prince Consort that the best service which the Prince could render to the Throne was to preside at the annual meeting of the Labourer's Friend Society, having previously visited some of the worst dwellings in St Giles's. "I said, 'you should come with three carriages, and have the footmen in red liveries—these things are not without their influence.'"

What people really dislike is a shabby "Pompa." They want money's worth for their money. If they suspect that the show is conducted on money-saving principles, they feel that they are cheated. The only occasion on which I have ever heard a murmuring word about a procession was when, at a royal wedding, the principal persons drove past with a pair of horses, instead of four, to their carriage. The populace is quite inaccessible to Political Economy, recks nothing of Bastiat or Fawcett, and is convinced that splendour is good for trade. Whether that is so or not is a question which I leave to the "sophisters, calculators, and economists" whom Burke so justly disliked. I know that splendour adds to the agreeableness of life, and whatever does that is good.

XXV

EDINBURGH

I SAID just now that the bounty of nature and the genius of man alike have done their best to make Edinburgh the beautiful city that she is. There perhaps I might have stopped; but the events of the week which ends to-day have awakened some happy memories; and, as I know that I number some enthusiastic Scots among my readers, I hope I may be pleasing them as well as indulging myself if I dedicate this chapter to the capital of Scotland.

As a matter of fact, one-fourth of my blood is Scottish, but my forebears were more familiar with the Spey than with the Forth; and I owe my love of Edinburgh not to my Jacobite but to my Whiggish ancestry. At the beginning of the nineteenth century the English Universities were supposed to be hotbeds of Toryism. Gibbon's sneer at "Port and Prejudice" still held good. Sydney Smith likened Oxford and Cambridge to "enormous hulks confined with mooring-chains, everything flowing and progressing round them, while they themselves stood still." Lord John Russell wrote in old age: "My father thought that there was nothing useful to be learnt at the English Universities, and determined to send me to Edinburgh." A similar step was taken by the Duke of Somerset, and Lord Lansdowne, and others who cared seriously for mental and moral freedom.

The University of Edinburgh was then in its days of glory. Dugald Stewart was Professor of Moral Philosophy, John Playfair of Mathematics, John Hill of Humanity, and James Gregory (a name to be eternally execrated by reason of the Powders which he invented) of Medicine. The University was in close relations with the Bar, then adorned by the great names of Francis Jeffrey, Francis Horner, and Henry Brougham; and in a society thus highly charged with intellectual activity *The Edinburgh Review* made its first appearance, clad in that famous livery of Blue and Buff, which the Whigs had copied from Charles Fox's coat and waistcoat. The intellectual and political effects of Edinburgh were so satisfactory in the case of the lad who was destined to win the battle of Reform in 1832 that his younger brothers were submitted to the same discipline. Lord Charles Russell entered the University in 1825, and before long found himself a delighted member of the circle which surrounded the central figure of Sir Walter Scott. A contemporary wrote: "The tall form and white head of Sir Walter may be seen rocking in the distance, with his patched old gown flaunting behind him, his under lip tucked within his teeth, and the upper part of his body thrown eagerly forward, taking long steps and long thoughts, and quite unconscious of the gaze of a knot of little Cockneys, male and female, who bustle after the Ariosto of the North, wondering if this can really be the charming man who writes the Scotch novels."

The place and the time and the intellectual atmosphere combined to make an indelible impression on a young and responsive nature. "The principles of the French Revolution were fully afloat, and it is impossible to conceive a more violent and agitated state of society." The passionate love of freedom, which Pitt and Dundas had striven in vain to crush, and which the barbarous Trials for Sedition had dignified with the honour of martyrdom, was beginning to take heart of grace, and was looking to English statesmen for vindication and deliverance.

> "Bliss was it in that dawn to be alive,
> But to be young was very heaven."

And yet, concurrently with all this, there still lingered, principally within the obscure precincts of the "Suffering and Episcopal Church," a theoretical Jacobitism, which recalled memories of Charles Edward encamped at Duddingston, or holding his transient Court at Holy Rood.

The scene of all this excitement was one of the most inspiring cities in the world, and it is not strange that, fifty years later, the pupil of Pillans and the guest of "auld Sir Harry" brought his sons to it in happy pilgrimage.

"Here is all the sublimity of situation and scenery, mountains near and far off, rocks and glens, and the sea itself, almost within hearing of its waves. Everywhere, all around, you have rocks frowning over rocks in imperial elevation, and descending, amid the smoke and dust of a city, into dark depths such as nature alone can excavate. Here the proudest palaces must be content to catch the shadows of the mountains, and the grandest fortresses to appear like the dwellings of pigmies perched on the bulwarks of creation. It is this singular combination of the grandeur of nature with the grandeur of art that distinguishes Edinburgh from all other cities in the world."

But, after all said and done, the best guide to Edinburgh is the man who wrote "Waverley" and "The Heart of Midlothian" and "Guy Mannering" and "Old Mortality." He will show us its landscape from Salisbury Crags and its architecture from Parliament Square. In one mood he will teach us speak of "High Dunedin," in another of "Auld Reekie." He will introduce us to the grimmest tragedy in the scene of the tortured Covenanter, and to the broadest farce in the orgies of Counsellor Pleydell. But, whatever be the impression of the moment, this he will certainly do—he will make us feel at home in Edinburgh. Guided by him, we shall realize that "The Heart of Midlothian" is a synonym not for the city, but for the Tolbooth,—and we shall avoid the droll blunder of the Southron orator who praised the "comforts of the Grass-Market" (where the Covenanters were executed), when he meant "the Salt-Market," where the opulent Bailies of Glasgow dwelt secure. Under the constraining influence of the magician's wand, we shall almost learn to love what Stevenson called "the wind which blows so softly towards the West," and to forget the fact that it turned a four-wheeled cab upside down, and thereby drove James Payn from the service of *Chambers's Journal.*

. . . .

But we must not be content to dwell on the material charms of a city in which every street and bridge and wynd speaks to us of people whom we admire, and of actions which have their place in history. It was in 1786 that Burns, visiting Edinburgh for the first time, found at length the social recognition which he had so long deserved. "I am in a fair way," he wrote, "of becoming as eminent as Thomas à Kempis or John Bunyan"—strange trio—"and you may expect henceforth to see my birthday inserted among the wonderful events in the almanac." Those were lively days in Edinburgh, and would have exactly suited Robbie, when Jane Maxwell, Duchess of Gordon, rode down the High Street on a pig; when ladies at their tea-tables read aloud the romances of Aphra Behn; and when an itinerant vendor of what boys now call "Tuck" stood outside the College-gates dangling at the end of a string a bit of bacon dipped in treacle, with the alluring cry: "Twa dips and a dollop for ane bawbee." Those were the days of a conviviality which knew no bounds, and of a barbarous jollity which was preparing the way for a vehement reaction. Thirty years later, the greatest preacher of the modern world flung himself on the bewildered society of Edinburgh with all the passionate severity of a modern Baptist, and Edward Irving "turned the whole population out of their beds at three in the morning," to hear him denounce Apocalyptic judgments on a backsliding society. Meanwhile a Scottish painter, strong enough to withstand the atmospheric influences of "the grey metropolis," was asserting for himself the place which he still holds as the greatest colourist of British birth; and a young student of medicine was embarking on that mysterious voyage of discovery which in the end gave him mastery over human pain.

And yet one more event remains to be recorded—the most glorious of all—when on the "grey and cloudy afternoon" of 18th May 1843, all Edinburgh waited in tense expectancy outside the door of St Andrew's Church, and four hundred ministers and licentiates of divinity came forth from the prison-house of legality and Erastianism to form the Free Church of Scotland. "Before them the waters of the Firth gleamed under the blue and bitter north, and beyond it stretched many a moor and strath, with the manses which the old men were the next day to leave, and the young men were never to enter."

Edinburgh, with all her glories, has known no prouder day than that.

XXVI

CRISES

SCIENTIFIC students of the English language tell us that the word "crisis" is not found in the sense in which we now use it until times comparatively recent. "Junius" wrote in 1769 of a political "crisis full of terror and despair." A century later Mill borrowed the word and wrote of a "commercial crisis"; and, ten years after Mill, Tyndall applied the word "crisis" to a dangerous moment in Alpine climbing. So, by degrees, the word, in its derivative and corrupted sense, became embedded in the language; and to-day "crises" are as common as blackberries. "Crisis in Cotton," "Crisis in Shipping," "Crisis in the Church," "Crisis in the Publishing Business," follow one another in brisk succession, and no one takes much notice of them. We know, by long experience, that on the pen of the modern journalist a crisis generally means nothing except a local dispute or a temporary difficulty; and those who love "the joy of eventful living" have again and again been bitterly disappointed to learn in next day's paper that "the situation has been materially relieved," and that "the crisis is averted."

Some years ago a large number of excellent people persuaded themselves, by mysterious methods of eschatological research, that the end of the world would occur on the 14th of July 1875. Here was indeed a crisis, and those who believed in it assembled in a church not a hundred miles from Euston Square, and with intense eagerness awaited the event. One can imagine the state of nervous tension which pervaded the assemblage. A thunderclap or a trumpet —nay, a banging door or a penny whistle—might have produced one of those scenes of indescribable panic which are the familiar phenomena of religious revivals. But nothing happened. Hour after hour the expectants waited and watched and wondered —and still nothing happened. And presently the shades of evening descended, and one by one the disillusioned congregation broke up and crept home to bed. Nothing had happened. I write the story in no derisive spirit, but in deep sympathy with people who had built high hopes on the imminence of a tremendous event, and then had to return to the humdrum ways of everyday life amid the mockery of an unbelieving world.

In regions less exalted than those of Eschatology we have again and again been threatened with "crises" which did not come to pass. The year 1832 was esteemed a crisis, but, thanks to the good sense and statesmanship of William IV. and his Ministers, it issued in nothing more formidable than the first Reform Act. Three years later another crisis arose, and it presented some features which recent events have recalled to memory. Lord

Howick, afterwards Lord Grey and the stiffest of Whigs, "talked of the Lords having played their last trump, of the impossibility of their going on, of the hostility towards them in the country, and the manner in which suggestions of reforming the House of Lords were received in the House of Commons." "He said that the Lords must give way or a collision would be the consequence, and he knew which would go to the wall." This is just the language which even experienced men use when they believe that there is a crisis at hand; but, as usual, nothing happened. The Whigs jogged on in office; Queen Victoria ascended the throne amid universal acclamation, and the House of Lords pursued its course unchecked for seventy-six years. When the Queen had reigned ten years, it was time for another crisis. This time it was the Chartists who were supposed to make it. 1848 was the year of Revolution, and on the 10th of April their "Monster Petition" was to have been borne in triumphant procession to the Bar of a terrified House of Commons. But "the people would not rise. The meeting, which was to have been counted by hundreds of thousands, scarcely numbered its tens, and broke up pitiably piecemeal, drenched and cowed, body and soul, by pouring rain, while the monster Petition crawled ludicrously away in a hack-cab, to be dragged to the floor of the House amid inextinguishable laughter." The Duke of Wellington had made military preparations on the most elaborate scale, and an army of Special

Constables had broken a good many unoffending heads; but the crisis failed to come off, and Chartism died a natural death.

When the country is really engaged in serious business no one talks of crises. The Crimea and the India Mutiny tried the metal of English manhood as gold is tried in the furnace; and nobly it stood the test. The issues at stake were too momentous, and the national suffering was too keen, to admit of hysteria or tall talk. The work of fighting was done on the Euxine and on the Ganges; and, while it was doing, the work of citizenship at home went on as usual. There is no need to discuss the fictitious crisis of 1868–1869, which disestablished the Irish Church; for no one outside Ulster, and a few Vicarages in the remoter parts of England, believed that the Loyalists of the North would really fulfil their threat of "kicking the Crown into the Boyne." But the downfall of the French Empire was, no doubt, a crisis for France, and some undefeated idealists tried to manufacture a sympathetic crisis here. Solemn men talked of serious danger to the Monarchy, and more mercurial spirits hoped to see the last king strangled in the bowels of the last priest. But again nothing that was expected happened. The Prince of Wales contracted typhoid fever; the nation, united as one man, watched by his sick-bed and rejoiced in his recovery; and the result of the crisis was the destruction of English Republicanism, and an unprecedented access of devotion to the throne and the person of the Sovereign. In 1879–1880, when we deposed Lord Beaconsfield and installed Mr Gladstone in his place, I believe that some of us really thought that we were assisting at a crisis. Well, well. We were young, and credulous. The greenness of youth is a beautiful thing; but it soon turned to the jaundiced complexion of disappointment when we found that our crisis only resulted in five years of unusually dull government, and the reduction of a Liberal majority from a hundred to less than nothing.

Next it was Mr Gladstone's turn to produce a crisis, and he went to work with a will, following in the wake of the "Hawarden Kite," which started on its ill-starred voyage on the 17th December 1885. When genius and eloquence, parliamentary skill and passionate conviction, are joined in an effort at crisis-making, some disturbance of the atmosphere is inevitable. In the spring of 1886 there were a good many people, on one side, who believed that, if Home Rule were granted, "Ulster would fight, and Ulster would be right"; and not a few on the other who believed that, if the Bill were thrown out, we should all be stabbed in the streets or dynamited in our beds. Yet how short are political memories! On the 10th of August 1911, I was standing in the House of Lords near an excited politician who firmly believed in the political crisis, and kept on ejaculating, "This is the most dramatic thing I have ever seen." If only he had seen the interior of the House of

Commons in the early morning of 8th June 1886, he would have been much more profoundly moved. This August nothing hung upon the division, except the anticipated Coronets. The Government was bound to win, if not in the Lobby, then by the creation of Peers. With all due deference to the sincerity of the Die-hards, crisis there was none. But in 1886 the fate of the Government and the Liberal party, of Mr Gladstone himself, and, as some thought, of Ireland, hung on the issue of the division, and the result was to the last moment uncertain. This was something like a crisis, and yet the country took it so calmly that its only result was sixteen years of Tory rule. Sir Henry Campbell-Bannerman was not a man disposed by nature or training to believe in crises, and still less to create them. But what he would never have done for himself the crime of South Africa and the blunder of Tariff Reform did for him. They made him Prime Minister, and when he formed his Government, in December 1905, he started a series of "crises" which, like the bumps of coupled railway-trucks, have gone on startling nervous people from that day to this. How often have we been told, as in Lord Rosebery's thunderous perorations, that the Budget, or the Pensions Bill, or the Parliament Bill, or whatever else might be uppermost at the moment, was the end of home, and religion, and time, and space! And yet all these things go on as before; and *nondum est finis*.

An acute critic has said of Charles Kingsley:

"The belief, which he never lost, that something tremendous was going to happen about the middle of next week kept him always on the stretch, and half spoiled him for a man of letters." It would have wholly spoilt him for a man of affairs. "Miracles do not happen," say the Critics. "Crises do not come off," says the Politician.

. . . .

To the politician, more than to most men, "years bring the philosophic mind." He amuses himself for half-an-hour with the "red fool-fury" of a Sunday paper and a monthly review, and then turns to the sedative pages of *The Spectator* or *The Westminster Gazette*, with the renewed conviction that crises never come off; that Crowns, and Parliaments, and Ministries will go on very much in the same way as they have always gone; and that Disestablishment in Wales and Home Rule in Ireland will make uncommonly little difference to the daily life of the British citizen.

Thus the Politician. Tea-time, Hal, and all well—but is it? This cream tastes rather odd. "Yes, sir, the milkman says that all their supplies are cut off. Their farm is near Reading, and the G.W.R. men have struck. And, oh! if you please, sir, I'm afraid there'll be a difficulty about the ice for the champagne to-night. We are quite out of it, and Wenham's carters have struck in sympathy." Hardly has our Politician's spirit risen from these stunning blows when a telegram is placed in his hand. It is dated from a dale in Yorkshire, where he has shot grouse for twenty years. "Owing to the disturbed state of things in the North, I have put off our party." Gracious heaven! Can these things really be? The luxuries of life are cut off at one fell swoop, and even its necessaries are threatened. How about my week-end at the sea-side? Of course, it is out of the question to trust to the train, and I must motor down; but it's a long run in this broiling weather; and, good gad! if the chauffeur strikes——! I believe I should if I were in his place. And all this happens to me, who have always been saying that "crises don't come off!"

. . . .

It was, as we now know, a short agony, but it brought a good many people to their bearings. The delicate machinery of the Constitution might creak and groan, the "Thunderer" might bellow about Revolution and the "Henchman" snivel about Treachery; five hundred patriots, not created peers, might moan over the vanity of human wishes; and no one cared a jot. But the moment that the ordinary conveniences and pleasures of life were touched, the comfortable classes woke with a start. It was a rude awakening. They learned in three days what social reformers have been trying to teach them for thirty years: that, if the State will not guard the interests of Labour, Labour must look after itself, and—Milnerize—the consequences.

XXVII

POPULAR MONDAYS

SIR WILLIAM GILBERT depicted in haunting verse the Normal Youth:

> "Who thinks suburban hops
> More fun than Monday 'Pops';
> Who's fond of his dinner, and doesn't get thinner
> On bottled beer and chops."

It is in order to avoid any confusion with those musical orgies that I have inverted the title, and write, not of "Monday Pops," but of "Popular Mondays." The entertainments which I purpose to describe take place on Mondays, and, in this waning season of the year, have a popularity which is all their own. London is just now very pleasant, and, in spite of fashion, very full. Every prospect pleases, and man is not at all vile. He is French and courteous and lively, or German and serious and bent on a scientific study of the town. Or he is American and vivid and breathless, has just done London in twenty-four hours, and means to be at Ober-Ammergau by dinner-time to-morrow. Or he is the Excursionist—my own flesh and blood—with enjoyment oozing out of every pore of his face, or listening with solemn interest to a topographical lecture by a bronzed clergyman in a black straw hat. There is a splendid show at "His Majesty's." There is plenty of fun going on at music-halls and small theatres; and such as love an innocuous dissipation can find what they want at the Anglo-Japanese Exhibition.

All this is true of every weekday, but Monday has, as I said above, a special attraction of its own. The performer, the scene, the audience, and all the surrounding circumstances are so unlike anything which one sees elsewhere that our "Popular Mondays" are worthy of a rather full description. And first as to the locality. "Baldwin's Gardens" has, methinks, an attractive sound, as of some chivalrous scene illuminated by the historic genius of Sir Walter Scott. Indeed, tradition affirms that "Baldwin" was one of Queen Elizabeth's gardeners; but all traces of him have disappeared as completely as the odour of his flowers—which has been replaced by that of fried fish. The traveller who had nothing but his nose to guide him would probably take some time before he discovered the nook called Baldwin's Gardens, which lies in an angle formed by the junction of Gray's Inn Road and Holborn. High-sniffing people might call the district a slum, but it is haunted by great names. In it dwelt Fulke Greville, Lord Brooke, who was "servant to Queen Elizabeth, counsellor to King James, and friend to Sir Philip Sidney." One of his neighbours was that good knight of whom his epitaph records that:

> "Sir Thomas Leigh, by civil life,
> All offices did bear,
> Which in this city worshipful
> Or honourable were."

Here, two centuries after fashion had fled westward, the unhappy Chatterton, maddened by hunger and despair, poisoned himself in his lonely garret; and the surroundings amid which he lived and died were as miserable as his fate. Wholesale demolitions of overcrowded and insanitary dwellings have of late years altered the place almost beyond recognition; but, when I first knew it, an area of five hundred yards by two hundred contained some eight thousand souls. Decent people seldom ventured into its courts and alleys. The very policemen appeared rarely, and then in pairs. The central attraction had been a Thieves' Kitchen of deserved popularity, and its frequenters lived all round it.

The existence of such an area in close proximity to one of the principal thoroughfares of London was scarcely suspected, and when, through disclosures at the Police Court, it was brought to light, two private citizens took in hand a work of reformation which the public authorities had long evaded. On a site given by Lord Leigh (descendant of Sir Thomas named above), Mr J. G. Hubbard, afterwards Lord Addington, built, in the very heart of Baldwin's Gardens, the beautiful and famous church of St

Alban's, and that church became the centre of a reforming movement which touched every department of life—religious, moral, educational, sanitary, and structural. The church itself is a masterpiece of Butterfield's Gothic skill. It has "the most beautiful arches in London," and it was one of the first churches in which red brick was employed for internal decoration. Partly because of these peculiarities, partly because of a ritual deemed in those distant days elaborate, and partly because of the unconventional lines on which it was worked, St Alban's became from the very first a target for the unwelcome attentions of descriptive reporters and interviewers. These gentlemen were by no means always unfriendly, but by their vivid imaginations, their too-graphic pens, and their curious knack of misreading all ecclesiastical actions and objects, they brought St Alban's and its clergy into a peculiar prominence. By doing this they did much to prepare the way for a long series of harassing prosecutions which had for their object the expulsion of the Vicar and the destruction of his work. The steps by which this amiable design was frustrated can be read in Archbishop Tait's "Life," and for the last twenty-five years and more St Alban's has been at peace.

Meanwhile a remarkable influence has been evolved by the vicissitudes through which the church and its congregation passed. The Rev. Arthur Henry Stanton was born in 1839. He was ordained to the service of St Alban's, even before the church was consecrated, and since Advent 1862, he has lived and worked in the alleys of Baldwin's Gardens. An analysis of Mr Stanton's character would here be out of place. I am concerned only with those characteristics which pertain to the subject of this chapter. To begin with, he was, as a young man, strikingly handsome. Then he is a natural orator, with all the orator's gifts of speech and voice and gesture, and can ring the changes on every phase of human emotion. And yet again he has a sense of humour which he allows to play with unfettered freedom round the subject of his discourse, and he can turn with the ease and lightness of a bird from grave to gay, and back again to grave.

And now I come to close quarters with my "Popular Mondays." On every Monday in August (as also on every Monday in Lent) Mr Stanton holds a special service at eight o'clock in the evening in St Alban's Church. What Puritans amiably call "meretricious attractions" are utterly banished. The service is plain enough to satisfy Dr Clifford. Even the choir is absent. Yet an hour before the appointed time a great company of men and women, old and young, is pouring up Brooke Street, or winding into the church through the more devious ways of Baldwin's Gardens. By half-past seven the church—men's side and women's side alike—is full. A quarter of an hour later it is uncomfortably crowded. Every seat is occupied. Late-comers are driven into the chancel. All the choir-stalls are full. Rows of extra seats are brought in. Men who can find no room to stand or sit, crouch on the altar-steps.

As the clock strikes eight, Mr Stanton climbs into the pulpit, huddling on his surplice as he goes. From the pulpit he reads, in a slightly shortened form, the ordinary Evening Service of the Church. We read the Psalms, verse by verse, and say the Canticles all together, as if we were in some old-fashioned village church, untouched by the Ritualistic movement. When the Prayers are ended, we burst into a hymn—perhaps of Faber's type, perhaps of Sankey's; but, in either case, "burst" is the right word; for the whole congregation sings with a fervour of devotion, pent-up but now liberated, and the great volume of male voices gives to the singing a massiveness not usual in mixed congregations. Then Mr Stanton rises from his knees and begins to preach. His sermons are not easy to describe. They follow none of the conventions of the pulpit. They range widely over the broad field of faith and duty. The appeals to conscience are vivid and pointed; but they are interspersed with touches of humour and sarcasm which provoke a responsive sound dangerously like a laugh. Most notable is the preacher's wide-mindedness—his intense grasp of his own beliefs, his absolute charity towards those who do not share them, and his abounding humanity.

Backwards and forwards he sways his graceful form, unbent and undisfigured by age. He turns to the sea of faces in front of him. He wheels round to the "overflow" in the chancel. His voice, as Mr Gladstone said of Bishop Wilberforce, is "sometimes like a murmuring brook, sometimes like a trumpet-call." Now it sinks till it is nearly inaudible, and now you see the preacher's hold upon his hearers, for they stretch forward with hands to ears, and strained and anxious faces, lest they lose the smallest word of the spell which this great magician is weaving round their hearts. And all this, remember, year after year, in a slum-church, in the holiday season, on a week-day evening. I know no "triumph of the Pulpit" to equal it, at any rate in the Church to which I belong.

Now the preacher has come to his end. The service has lasted a little over the hour. Two thunderous hymns again shake the roof. The blessing is given, and we stream out towards Holborn and Gray's Inn Road. A "Popular Monday" indeed; and what is the meaning of it? "Dynasties come and go, Empires rise and fall, literatures vanish from the memory of man, forms of polity wax old and perish, and the ancient homes of great peoples survive only as the sepulchres of the dead; but the broodings of the soul on the dim hereafter never fade or die. To any fresh or earnest word on those most solemn and mysterious of themes men listen with the eagerness which a fond imagination ascribes to the Ages of Faith." That is a true testimony; and on these five Mondays in August it has been verified anew.

XXVIII

HEATHER

I WAS reared among the Barbarians, and such days as the 12th of August, the 1st of September, and the 1st of October are still marked dates in the almanac of memory. Fox-hunting asserts its superiority to shooting, as in other things, so also in its majestic latitude as to times and seasons. Indeed, the whole year belongs to the fox-hunter, save only May, June, and July; and, if his lot be cast in a woodland country, he can even claim an interest in May. But the dates of the Shooter's Kalendar are as precise as quarter-day, and "the Glorious Twelfth," as flamboyant writers call it, is the Feast of Heather and the Heather-bird. Even in a chapter devoted to the heather it would argue an impiety to disregard the bird. The Scottish blood in my veins calls out against the Southron pock-puddings, who profane their roast grouse with bread-sauce, as if it were no nobler fare than a barndoor-fowl. Let such wrong-doers learn a lesson from the Highlands. Lay each bird on a slice of buttered toast; bid avaunt to all vegetables except French beans or a tomato salad; and then you may fancy yourself feasting with Fergus MacIvor in the feudal hall of Glennaquoich.

The late Lord Sherbrooke, not commonly regarded as a sentimentalist, when addressing a Scottish audience on his lifelong love of Scotland, spoke thus of her charms :

"My affection has been a disinterested one, for I have neither the power nor the will to make war on your deer, your fowl, or your fish. I come simply to enjoy your romantic scenery, to cherish the memories it calls up to my mind, to breathe your invigorating atmosphere, and to visit those many kind friends whom I am fortunate enough to possess on the northern side of the Tweed."

I have paid my tribute to the Heather-bird when slain by others, but, like Lord Sherbrooke, I have neither part nor lot in the slaughter. I can lay my hand on my heart, and affirm that I have never killed anything larger than a wasp, and that only in self-defence. My love of the heather is totally unconnected with sport. It is disinterested love of a beautiful thing, and a thing which is never found except amid beautiful surroundings. In this matter, I range myself side by side with Mr Frederic Harrison, who unites an exquisite sense for beauty with a faculty, not less exquisite, of expressing it.

"I love," he says, "the moors much too well to carry a gun when I walk over them. . . . I have heard the grouse swirl up from almost every moor in

Scotland, from the Cheviots to Skye, and from Arran to Dunrobin. I have seen, perhaps, as much of the hills as most sportsmen; but I never thought it would add to my enjoyment of them to kill anything. If I were compelled to kill something, I would rather shoot a broken-down cab-horse than a pheasant or a stag. I should at least feel that I had put a poor thing out of its misery, and that I had not wantonly destroyed a beautiful creature."

Mr Harrison writes of heather in its more exalted habitations, by "dangerous Corrievreckan," and "where roads are unknown to Loch Nevish." I have loved it in less majestic, but not less beautiful, surroundings, before time had sucked the colour out of life, and left it dry and brown as a moor in October. It was "C. S. C." who discovered, in his painfully close parody of Jean Ingelow, that "Heather" and "Weather" are inseparable rhymes, and that the inevitable third is "Together."

> "Through the rare red heather we danced together,
> (O love my Willie!) and smelt for flowers:
> I must mention again it was gorgeous weather—
> Rhymes are so scarce in this world of ours."

Poor Miss Ingelow was not exactly an inspired singer, but here the very fact that rhymes were "scarce" helped her to a happy collocation of ideas. The glory of the heather is in memory inseparably connected with "gorgeous weather," and we enjoyed them both, not in solitude, but "together," with hearts which beat as one with our own, and with faces which have long since vanished from our ken. Do my readers know the Shropshire hills? If not, let them take the next train to Church Stretton or Craven Arms, and thread the beautiful valley which lies between Shrewsbury and Ludlow. "On the one hand, the Longmynd rolls its great sheets of grouse-moor and scarps of rock up, fold beyond fold; while, on the other, the sharp peak of Caradoc takes the evening, and smiles upon his distant brother, the towering Plinlimmon; while Plinlimmon, in the west, with silver infant Severn streaming down his bosom, watches the sinking sun after Caradoc and Longmynd have lost it, and, wrapping himself in purple robes, sleeps in majestic peace."

Purple robes, indeed! White Heather is admired, I suppose, because it is rare. Perhaps it may bring luck, and it certainly was once the title of a delightful play; but, for the pure enjoyment of the eye, commend me to "the hue of empire and of martyrdom" in which August dyes the slopes of Longmynd. In their recesses, if anywhere in England, you can enjoy the beauty of heather. To complete your joy, you can catch the music of falling water from the silvery "Light-spout," and all around you is the glory of the everlasting hills. These are "the country places which God made and not man," and to have known them at a receptive age is indeed a joy for ever. "Again we roam in that fairy valley that lies behind each of us, into which come nothing but children and children's sports, into which nothing foul can enter, for the simple reason that only what was pleasant has remained in the memory of that magic time."

And, if we could discover these beautiful islands in the broad ocean of commonplace, we need not travel so far north as the Longmynd or the Woodhead Moors, let alone Schehallion or Lochnagar. Heather has a wonderful way of asserting itself amid unlikely surroundings, and, wherever it shows its purple flush, it brings with it an unique sense of freedom and activity and buoyant life.

Within twenty miles of London there is a hideous villa called Addington, built by a stockbroker in the eighteenth century, and inhabited for a hundred years by a series of Archbishops, who had little enough to do with beauty or freedom. Yet the park which surrounds it is like a slice of Scotland transported to the South, with bracken, and gorse, and "the bonny rowan tree," and heather as purple as ever bloomed on the braes of Loch Lomond. Then, when we strike South-westward, through the true Garden of England, which has Windsor for its centre and Beaulieu for its bound, it is heather, heather, all the way. Enclosures are few, and bird and beast are wild, and the peasants are half poachers, by right of their forest blood, and everything invites to rapid motion and manly exercise, and all about one there is that invigorating sense of freedom unrestrained by rule, which one can never feel in a walled park, or a padlocked fox-covert, or a fenced deer-forest, or where the selfishness of man, in any form or grade, has circumscribed the beauty and beneficence of the natural world.

But Windsor and the New Forest, the Highlands and the Border, and the rugged Grampians, and "the stormy hills of Wales," and the "blue and purple foregrounds which look down upon the Severn Sea"—all these have had their sacred bards. The Midlands, of which the present writer is an unworthy son, have been left unsung—at least since Drayton published his "Polyolbion." Yet as I sit here, in sweltering Stuccovia, I can shut my eyes and see with my mental gaze a breezy upland, as purple in August as the sky which overarches it; and around it is a stretch of golden gorse, and beyond the gorse on three sides a dark expanse of fir-wood; and on the fourth side a view, as far as the eye can reach, across the level pastures of North Bucks; and, on the sky-line, the dim shades of the Pytchley woodlands—Salcey Forest and Whittlebury and Yardley Chase. "It is a place to open a man's soul and make him prophesy, as he looks down on that great vale spread out as the Garden of the Lord before him." So wrote Tom Hughes, and he had nothing to inspire him but the short turf and chalky sheep-walks and steep hillsides of the Vale of White Horse. What would he have said if he had been standing knee-deep in heather? Then he would indeed have opened his soul and prophesied in all the fulness of the joy of living.

. . . .

My eyes are unclosed again, and I see all round me such town-bred objects as inkstands, and arm-chairs, and electric fans. But "that inward eye, Which is the bliss of solitude," retains the faery vision, and the inward ear still hears the voices which it heard when all the world was young.

> "Oh, it's ill to loose the bands which God decreed to bind—
> Still will we be the children of the heather and the wind;
> Though far away from home, it's still for you and me
> That the broom is blowing bonny in the North Countree."

XXIX

THE SEA

Suave mari magno—but the tag is something hackneyed. Clough tried to popularize it in his "Tales on Board"; and the great Sir Robert Peel, with platitudinous magniloquence, rendered the first word. "It is a source of melancholy satisfaction." Despite the absurdity of the phrase, I hold with the orator rather than the poet. I feel no desire to hear "Tales on Board"; and, indeed, even if Scott or Cervantes told them, I should be in no condition to relish, or even to understand, them. But *Suave* exactly expresses my feeling: it is the psychological word at the psychological moment. All round me, as I write, my friends and neighbours are packing up and making ready for "the Sea," and I feel a "melancholy satisfaction" in contemplating their condition and their prospects.

George III., when he heard of Bishop Watson's "Apology for the Bible," remarked that, in his opinion, the Bible needed no apology; and there are those who think, or profess to think, the same about the Sea. Certainly there have been plenty of people to sing its praises, and even to gush over it; but this sea-worship, like mountain-worship, is a modern growth. "The Ancients," as Lord Morley would call them, took a more rational view alike of Alps and of oceans. The schoolboys in "Eric" disputed whether a famous phrase of Æschylus were better translated as Keble translated it, "The many-twinkling smile of ocean," or, as Dr Farrar preferred, "the innumerable laughter of the sea." But the unfriendliness, the separativeness, the gloom and tragedy of the Sea, were more familiar thoughts, and a Latin poet hit it off in an epithet which Matthew Arnold, most classical of moderns, rendered "estranging." Byron, who, in spite of his genius, was a mass of affectations, extolled the sea in memorable verse. But Lewis Carroll, whose genius was dominated by sincerity, took a different view :

> "It is pleasant and dreamy, no doubt, to float
> With 'souls as boundless and thoughts as free' ;
> But suppose you are very unwell in a boat,
> How do you like the Sea ?"

Ay—there's the rub.

The example which Byron set was followed by a host of imitators. Robert Montgomery cribbed from him, and was trounced by Macaulay for his pains. Kingsley tried hard to make us believe that we were Vikings, and enjoyed being driven "sea-ward round the world." Mr Swinburne hurls defiance at "Russians and Prussians," and boasts that "Sea-folk are free folk, by grace of winds and waves." There is, I think, a note of hypocrisy in all this sea-worship, and the note was heightened by

Barry Cornwall, whose poem on the Sea was the delight of all well-regulated drawing-rooms, and the choice gem of all " Selections," in the earlier part of Queen Victoria's reign. To him, enduring the torments of the lost between Dover and Calais, and rolling in a livid agony, enters his tender wife, and murmurs in his ear his own immortal refrain:

"The Sea! The Sea! The open Sea!
The blue, the fresh, the ever free!
The Sea! The Sea! I love the Sea,
For I was born on the open Sea."

Perhaps the citation was malignant, but hypocrisy should never go unrebuked.

The dislike of hypocrisy was a leading characteristic of Sydney Smith, and it sometimes betrayed him into undeserved severity. William Carey, the shoemaker-missionary, was a man whose devotion and learning might have placed him beyond the reach of ridicule, but the Baptist Missionary Society rather invited sarcasm when they printed in their Official Report: " Brother Carey, while very seasick, and leaning over the ship to relieve his stomach from that very oppressive complaint, said that his mind was even then filled with consolation in contemplating the wonderful goodness of God." Certainly the " Acta Sanctorum " contains no more striking instance of the triumph of Spirit over Flesh; and Sydney Smith made the most of it in his famous essay on " Indian Missions." But we may leave to Thackeray and Dickens (both of whom knew it experimentally and described it graphically) the miserable plight of those who go down to the sea in ships, and think to recruit their energies by a run to Madeira and back or ten days' cruise among the Faroe Islands. It is indeed the awfulness of their lot which makes me feel the suavity of my own; but I have some compassion left even for those whose notion of a holiday is a month at the seaside. To Matthew Arnold Margate seemed "a brick-and-mortar image of English Protestantism, in all its uncomeliness and all its salubrity." Against the salubrity of the seaside I say nothing; except that sea air always makes me bilious, that lodging-houses are often stuffy, and that the sewage of the town, scarcely masked by the pungent odours of decaying seaweed, not seldom mingles with the invigorating breeze. It is the "uncomeliness" of the Sea which specially distresses me. Bishop Mackarness of Oxford was a man of virtue and of solid learning, but there was in his nature a certain lack of what Lord Beaconsfield called "picturesque sensibility." One day he was talking to the children of the Sunday School at Cuddesdon about some passage of Holy Writ which involves the Sea—perhaps that most comfortable of all texts which the Vulgate renders: *Et mare jam non est.* "Now, my dear children, you have never seen the sea. We live in Oxfordshire, and Oxfordshire is a long way from the Sea. But you all know Farmer Jones's pond at the bottom of his big field. Well, if you can fancy that pond made much larger, and stretching away so that you couldn't see the other side, that would be like the Sea." Very like; and so say I, and so said Lewis Carroll:

> "Pour some salt water over the floor—
> Ugly I'm sure you'll allow it to be;
> Suppose it extended a mile or more,
> *That's* very like the Sea.
>
> I had a vision of nursery-maids—
> Tens of thousands passed by me,
> All leading children with wooden spades,
> And this was by the Sea."

Can anything in the world be uglier than the sea-front at Brighton, with its unending and manurious street, its vulgar vagaries of bizarre architecture, its total lack of trees and shade, its parched lawns, its jagged shingle, and its shipless sea?

My favourite poet has told us that:

> "Two voices are there; one is of the Sea,
> One of the mountains; each a mighty voice."

I do not dispute it. I never dispute with my beloved and honoured Wordsworth; but I say, quite honestly, that both those mighty voices bore me. In particular, I detest the monotonous murmur of the Sea, with its occasional bursts of angry clamour—like a discontented temper breaking into passion. But I am well aware that on better-constituted natures those sea-sounds produce quite a different effect. "Now, for the first time, a new voice—the great voice of the Sea—broke with its grand but awful monotony upon his listening ear. As he gazed upon the waves, glowing and flashing with the golden network of autumnal sunbeams, it seemed to dawn upon him like the discovery of a new sense. He longed to have his brother with him there. . . . He picked up handfuls of the hard and sparkling sand; he sent the broad, flat pebbles flying over the surface, and skimming through the crests, of the waves; he half filled his pockets with green and yellow shells and crimson fragments of *Delessaria Sanguinea* for his little sisters." What need to say that this high-toned youth was one of Dr Farrar's creations, and that this vivid realization of the beauties of the Sea occurred on his first day at a Public School? Alas! I cannot emulate him. From the summit of Harrow Hill one can see an extensive and a pleasing prospect, but (like the view from Cuddesdon) it includes no glimpse of the Sea. "Little sisters" I have none to gratify with *Delessaria Sanguinea,* and, even if I had, I am certain that they would prefer strawberry ice (*Glacies Sanguinea* of the classical pastry-cook). I cannot "long to have my brother with me," for I know that he hates the sea as cordially as I or Lewis Carroll, and would indeed be a dismal companion on

> "the sandy tracts,
> By the hollow ocean ridges roaring into cataracts."

Mr Anstey Guthrie tells us of a seaside place where

the iron benches on the Parade bear this inscription:

> " Presented to the Town
> By Joseph Buggins, Esq., J.P.
> 'The Sea is his, and he made it.' "

I can quite believe that he did, but no such boast is mine. I did not make the Sea—indeed, if I had ever had the chance I should have made something entirely different. And I was not made for it, nor it for me. I am a son of the English Midlands, and meadows and woods and streams make my notion of an Earthly Paradise.

XXX

SEPTEMBER

YEAR by year, as the month comes round, I sing the praises of September. The theme appeals to me in my twofold nature of Londoner and Countryman; for alike in Stuccovia, my present habitation, and in Loamshire, from whose generous soil I spring, it is the choicest month of all the year. The days are exactly the right length, and the temperature is neither too hot nor too cold. One needs neither fur coats nor electric fans. One can take such exercise as one wants without exhaustion, and can lounge without inviting pneumonia.

Here in Stuccovia there is a general sense of unaccustomed space and freedom, for every true Stuccovian has quartered himself on his friends in the country, and will presently take his wife and children to the seaside. The parks are at their prettiest, for the Board of Works excels in autumnal planting. As a consequence of our abnormal August,[1] the Virginia creeper which veils the natural hideousness of Stuccovian architecture, is turning red before its time, and some yellowish leaves are already beginning to fall from the plane-trees in

[1] 1911.

Stucco Square. Here, in a season of calm weather, my soul has sight of that immortal sea which brought me hither—I apologize for turning Wordsworth into prose—and, aided by the sights around me and the thoughts they bring; I "can in a moment travel thither." But not to the literal sea. Of that I have expressed my dislike more than once in these pages, and have thereby brought down upon myself the satire of breezy gentlemen, with blue jackets and gilt buttons and white caps, who daily make the adventurous voyage from Brighton Pier to Worthing, or even brave the terrors of the Solent. No; when Wordsworth spoke of

> "that immortal sea
> Which brought us hither,"

he was thinking of our earliest memories, reaching back into a past even beyond memory itself, and of the surroundings in which our childhood was passed. But there is no need to analyse here the incomparable Ode (Lord Houghton held it to be the finest poem in the language). It has supplied me with the phraseology which I want when I meditate upon September in the country. I "can in a moment travel thither," and see the landscape now as I saw it then, amid the towering beech-woods of Woburn or Ashbridge, "when merry haymaking and merrier harvest were over, and the September sun was blazing down due west." For the pure joy of living I can recall nothing more perfect than an evening ride in a bright September, through a country still rich with its summer foliage, yet, by the cool breath of its sunset-breeze, reminding one that autumn is not far off. And then again, amid the jaded window-boxes of Stucco Square, I can recall the glories of a September garden. What a "pomp and prodigality" of colour! What a riot and revel of the eye's delight! Purple Dahlias, and scarlet Gladiolus, and Heliotrope as yet unbrowned by frost, and the foliage-plants running up the whole gamut of crimson and orange, till they strike their top note in the Ampelopsis on the southward wall.

And yet again, though perhaps it is something of a bathos, what is more delicious than a blackberry bush in September? In Loamshire we deemed it unwholesome to eat blackberries after Michaelmas Day; thenceforward they were only used for Harvest Decorations, but even that limitation allowed us three weeks of rich enjoyment. Mushroom-hunting is indeed good sport, but tamer; it leads you across flat lands and oozy meadows, and, as long as backs are supple, it affords no element of pain or risk. But the gallant blackberry loves a wilder venue; he glories in the woodland and the forest; the graceful convolutions of his form, the glorious complexion of his mellowing leaves, and, above all, the lusciousness of his fruitage, all tempt to impetuous pursuit; and well he knows how to avenge himself on the rash invader.

> "I ate the blackberries: you scratched your legs.
> I took the nest: you blew the addled eggs."

'Tis a perfect parable of life ; but I have no time for moralizing.

The only defect of September, to a humanitarian mind, is that it is a month so much given to sport. To stump across the stubbles under the September sun has been time out of mind an Englishman's favourite recreation. Charles James Fox loved it. Sir Barnes Newcome condescended to it. The sportsmen of Dingley Dell made it an occasion of high revel. Sir George Trevelyan aspired after it, and, amid the heat and humbug of the House of Commons, longed to be

> "Tramping after grouse or partridge through the soft September air,
> Both my pockets stuffed with cartridge, and my heart devoid of care.

The most delightful of all writers on the rural life of England records that " Partridges in vast plenty are bred in good seasons on the verge of Wolmer Forest, into which they love to make excursions ; and in particular, in the dry summer of 1740 and some years after, they swarmed to such a degree that parties of unreasonable sportsmen killed twenty and sometimes thirty brace in a day." Unreasonable sportsmen, says the admirable Gilbert ! But then he had never shot at Six Mile Bottom.

Of those who have essayed to follow " White of Selborne," none, I think, has so nearly reached his charm as Arthur Gibbs, whose early death twelve years ago closed a life of singular beauty and robbed nature-lovers of a most sympathetic companion. He had his dwelling among the Cotswolds, and described them with curious felicity. "There is no time of year one would sooner spend at home on Cotswold than the month of September. Nature is then at her best; the cold, bleak hills are clothed with the warmth of golden stubble; the autumnal haze now softens the landscape with those lights and shades which add so much of loveliness and mystery to a hill-country; the rich aftermath is full of natural life; birds of all descriptions are less wild and more easily observed than is the case later on, when the pastures and downs have been thinned by frost and there is no shelter left. Now you may see the kestrels hovering in mid-air, and the great sluggish heron wending his ethereal way to the upper waters of the trout-stream. . . . A country never looks so well from the roads as it appears when you are in the fields."

That last remark is very true; only, if you wish to enjoy the fields, you should not be walking over them in pursuit of Partridges; for, while you admire the scenery, you will miss your bird. Shooting-men, a little ashamed of their unworthy sport, used to say that they liked it for the opportunity which it gave of seeing the dogs work. Certainly a setter is one of the most beautiful creatures that exist, and a pointer, though hideous, one of the most intelligent; but it is quite possible to enjoy their company without killing partridges. Modern alterations in shooting have tended to destroy this particular hypocrisy.

Mr Gibbs, I am happy to say, cared little for the gun; but he was a keen fox-hunter, and yet, being a lover of natural scenery, he did not despise cub-hunting. Surely an English woodland never looks more enticing, its air never feels more exhilarating, than at eight or nine on a September morning. "The hounds turn up punctual to the appointed time. How beautiful and majestic they look, as they suddenly come into sight amid beech, and ash, and walnut, whilst the bright pageant advances leisurely and in order over the ancient, ivy-covered bridge which spans the silent river, where the morning mist still hangs, and the grass shines white in the silvery dew. With the ground in its present state, this mist and this dew give you your only chance of a scent. . . . You greet the genial Master, and then, in answer to his inquiry as to where you would like him to draw, you point to the hanging wood on the brow of the hill, and tell him that, as you heard the cubs barking there this very morning, it is a certain find. No sooner are the words out of your mouth than a holloa breaks the silence of the early morn. . . . And soon the whole valley re-echoes with hound music as the pack come crashing towards us through the thick underwood." I protest that this writing stirs the blood in my veins, but I will quote no more, lest I should forget the country in which I was reared, and imagine that I am sailing across the stone walls and high tablelands of the "Cotsal" where Shakespeare hunted.

I have expressed my dislike of shooting; but I must confess to a passionate love of the thing shot. I say, with Izaak Walton's friend "Auceps," that "the very birds of the air are both so many and so useful and pleasant to mankind that I must not let them pass without some observations. They both feed and refresh him—feed him with their choice bodies, and refresh him with their heavenly voices." That particular "bird of the air" to which, in September, one's thoughts instinctively turn, has, as far as I am aware, nothing much in the way of a voice; but a "choice body" indeed he has, and, more than any of his brethren, he "pleases the curious palate." Were I to attempt, in emulation of Dr Johnson, to "write a cookery-book on philosophical principles," I should certainly devote a long chapter, with an infinitude of divisions, subdivisions, and cross-divisions, to the contemplation of the Partridge. But it would argue an irreverence to essay this high theme at the fag-end of a chapter on something else. So to-day the oracles are dumb; but, that I may not seem to run into the opposite error, and to dishonour the delectable bird by ignoring him, I will quote from the ingenious "A. Hunter, M.D., F.R.S.," whose "Culina Famulatrix Medicinæ," published in 1810, is still worthy of close study and respectful attention: "After trussing the Partridges, stuff their craws with forced meat, and lard them down the sides; then roll a lump of butter in pepper, salt, and powdered mace, and put it into their bodies. Fry them to a light brown ; then put them into a stewpan, with a quart of gravy, two spoonfuls of Madeira or white wine, a spoonful of mushroom catchup, two teaspoonfuls of lemon pickle, an anchovy, a quarter of a lemon sliced, and a sprig of sweet marjoram. Cover up close, and stew for about half-an-hour ; after thickening the gravy, pour it over the partridges, and serve them up with boiled artichoke-bottoms, cut in quarters. *This is a savoury dish.*"

It sounds so. Is anyone brave enough to risk it ? If so, I will not be outdone.

One of my favourite poets is the mild and pedestrian Thomson, who deserves to be remembered for his line on coursing :

> "Poor is the triumph o'er the timid hare."

Of Field Sports in general he remarks with dignity :

> "These are not subjects for the peaceful Muse,"

and invites her to accompany him on his rural walk, where he courts

> "Th' inspiring breeze, and meditates the Book
> Of Nature, ever open ; aiming thence,
> Warm from the heart, to learn the moral song."

Like the present writer, Thomson found it easier to "learn the moral song," and sing it, in September than in any other month.

"Here as I steal along the sunny wall,
Where autumn basks, with fruit empurpled deep,
My pleasing theme continual prompts my thought,
Presents the downy peach, the shining plum,
The ruddy, fragrant nectarine, and, dark
Beneath this ample leaf, the luscious fig."

I trust that my favourite bard will not be deemed to have lowered his ethical standard when he goes on to praise the ripening grape, and even its fermented juice. He waxes enthusiastic over the glories of the Vintage and the "mashy flood,"

"Which, by degrees fermented and refined,
Round his rais'd nations pours the cup of joy;
The claret smooth, red as the lip we press
In sparkling fancy, while we drain the bowl;
The mellow-tasted Burgundy, and, quick
As is the wit it gives, the gay Champaign."

A few pages back the Poet has been very severe on the hard-drinking habits of the brutal fox-hunter; but surely "Nimrod" himself, or Hugo Meynell, or Warde of Squerries could scarcely have sounded a more bacchanalian note—wit given by "gay champaign," whole nations "raised," or, as we say with reference to individuals, "elevated," and "the cup of joy," widely dissimilar, indeed, from that which Cowper drank and sang! One can only exclaim with the critic in the Gallery, when he heard the distinguished line:

"O Sophonisba! Sophonisba, O!"

"O Jemmy Thomson! Jemmy Thomson, O!"

XXXI

CHRISTMAS CARDS

"IF ever I live to enjoy a respite from Politics, I intend to occupy my leisure in composing an epic poem." So said Mr Gladstone, in the spring of 1892, to the present writer, who naturally replied, "What is to be your theme?" To this question Mr Gladstone answered, with indescribable emphasis, "The Praise of the Post-Card. Did not Cowper write a poem about the Sofa? I am sure that the Post-Card is a much worthier theme, as regards its serviceability to man. Cowper began, with fine abruptness, 'I sing the Sofa.' I shall imitate him, and begin, 'I sing the Post-Card.'"

The contemplated epic remains, I believe, among those unfulfilled designs of literature which, like Mr Casaubon's "Key to All Mythologies," would, if only they had been published, have conferred undying fame upon their authors. Myself unskilled, as Milton would have said, "to build the lofty rhyme," I am constrained to celebrate the objects of my devotion in lowly prose. Among those objects a chief place belongs to the Christmas Card, and as I cannot, like Cowper and Mr Gladstone, glorify it in an epic poem, I will render it the highest honour in my power by making it the subject of this meditation.

Like that honoured Master whom I am never tired of quoting, but whose name I forbear to mention lest my readers should grow weary of it, I eschew the words "science" and "scientific" for fear I should be understood to admire the blue lights and bad smells of a chemical lecture. Yet something of philosophic stringency—something, if you will call it so, of "scientific method"—should go to the handling of a theme like this; and therefore we must not be content to discuss Christmas Cards as they are, but, in the first place, must peer into "the dark backward and abysm of time," and try to discover how they came to be. In these matters of obscure research there is no such capable guide as Mr Frederic Boase, who wrote that priceless book, "Modern English Biography, containing many thousand concise memoirs of persons who have died since the year 1850." Well, Mr Boase, who, like William of Deloraine, is "good at need," and never failed one at a pinch, informs us that the first Christmas Card which can be traced in the far-reaching history of the human family was designed by Edward Bradley (1827-1889), who, under the pseudonym of "Cuthbert Bede," attained immortality as the author of "Verdant Green." The epoch-making work of art—the first Christmas Card of recorded time—was given to the world by Joseph Cundall (1818-1893), who carried on business as a publisher in Bond Street, and the date of this great event, worthy to be ranked with the discovery of the Steam-Engine and the Telegraph, was December 1845. It has often been remarked that even the most beneficent inventions are extraordinarily slow in winning their way to general acceptance. Ignorance, stupidity, prejudice, laziness, habit, and custom deter mankind from availing itself of newly-discovered boons; and the history of the Christmas Card illustrates this truth. As far as I can calculate, it must have been quite thirty years before the Christmas Card attained its rank as a social institution. But, though it won its way slowly, it has held its place securely; and for the last five and thirty years it has made its substantial and increasing contribution to the happiness of the world. That happiness is Protean in its forms, and each form deserves recognition.

In the first place, there is the joy of the Designer—the artist who sketches a graceful figure or an effective landscape; the illuminator who supplies the often beautiful lettering in gold and colours; the humorist who discovers an as yet unused joke, and the motto-maker who enriches his fellow-artists' handiwork with

> "Things unattempted yet in prose or rhyme."

I have been told by those who have the opportunity of knowing the conditions under which Christmas Cards are produced, that crippled boys, and delicate girls, and ladies broken down by illness and poverty, can often make substantial additions to narrow incomes by the exercise of this graceful art; and that, at an expensive time like Christmas, is a joy not to be despised.

Then there is the joy of the Buyer, and I protest that this never palls. The sense of being able to purchase on a large scale, to plunge recklessly, to order dozens of each object that pleases your fancy, in the consciousness that the more you spend the happier you will be making your fellow-creatures—these are experiences which some of us taste only once a year, and only in relation to Christmas Cards. Then there is the delicate exercise of judicious selection and the tactful adaptation of card to recipient. Far from all well-conducted homes be the "Insulting Christmas Cards" with which Lupin Pooter greeted his friends, and which, by a cruel perversity, ricochetted on to the blameless head of Mr Pooter, senior; but there is a type of card, at once humorous and inoffensive, which may be safely addressed to intimate friends (though even with them it behoves the sender to work warily, for different people have different notions of a joke). Sporting Christmas Cards seem a little on the wane, possibly because the designers, "in populous cities pent," had such very odd notions of a fence or a foxhound, that their productions lacked verisimilitude and provoked laughter instead of gratitude. But Ecclesiastical Cards flourish in an ever-increasing profusion, and

I know more than one ingenious curate who reaps a substantial harvest for his Boys' Club or Drum-and-Fife Band by designing cards which reproduce sacred pictures and the most ornate passages of ritualistic worship. Of purely Religious Christmas Cards—cards designed to teach the sacred lessons of the season—this is not the place to speak. But this year I have had a new experience, in the shape of a Controversial Christmas Card, on which some highly disputable propositions of polemical theology were set forth with much pomp of type and illustration, and barbed, if I may so say, by references to some peculiarly pungent texts.

And then, above all, there is the joy of the Recipient. One need not be a child to feel this, though perhaps one must have kept something of

> "The young lamb's heart among the full-grown flocks."

One of the cheapest, and yet most valuable, joys of life, is the receipt of a Christmas Card from someone on whose remembrance one has no claim, but who is kind enough to recall some casual meeting, some slight intercourse, some common interest in places or people or pursuits, and who will take the trouble to let one know that one is not forgotten, although he who remembers and he who is remembered may be separated by half the compass of the globe. From one's kinsfolk and neighbours and intimate friends one has, perhaps, some right to expect the assurance that one still has a place in their thought; but when a similar assurance comes, though even in the form of a Robin Redbreast and a verse of doggerel, from a far land or a scarcely-known correspondent, it warms the cockles of the heart. "Fellowship is Heaven; lack of it is Hell," and of Fellowship the Christmas Card is the almost sacramental symbol.

And here let me urge two absolute and imperative duties. The sender should make his identity and address quite clear, and the recipient should acknowledge without an hour's delay. Disregard of these two canons of card-sending leads to endless confusion, mortification, misunderstanding, and disaster. No one, however stoical he may profess to be, can really like to find the humblest token of his goodwill disregarded; and yet sometimes the recipient cannot, with all the will in the world, testify his gratitude and reciprocate the benediction—simply because the sender forgot to affix his name. There lies on the desk before me as I write a small square envelope, bearing the postmark of "Devonport, December 24, 1898." It contained the counterfeit presentment of a jovial-looking Highlander in a kilt, and the Highlander conveyed, in good broad Scotch, the sender's kind wishes for Christmas thirteen years ago. From that day to this I have never been able to throw the faintest light on the origin of that card; and, as I have never received another directed in the same hand, I have a sad suspicion that, by no fault of my own, I lost a friend. I feel inclined to add to this discourse: "*Devonport papers, please copy.*"

There remains one last joy of Christmas Cards, and that is the joy of handing them on. I do not mean the paltry baseness of trying to palm them off, as though they were newly purchased, on the acceptance of our friends; but I mean the practice of collecting them and sending them to an Orphanage, or a Cripples' Home, or a Children's Hospital, where they are welcomed as the benefactions of a belated Santa Claus. One of Liddon's most celebrated sermons was called "The Lessons of the Holy Manger"; and of all those lessons there is surely none more obvious than the blessedness of doing something for helpless and suffering infancy.

XXXII

POLITICAL NOVELS

Mr R. H. Gretton must be a remarkably bold man. He has published a Political Novel called "Ingram" (which, by the way, sounds to Londoners more like an ecclesiastical novel, with a bishop for its hero). In his "Foreword," for he is much too modern to speak of a Preface, he tells us that his book is "an exercise in the Disraelian manner," and that behind this description he hopes to find protection. Now all this is bold, and very bold. In the first place, to write a Political Novel is to attempt the almost impossible; for the essence of a novel is a Love-story. Scenery, style, dialogue, description, epigram, and all the rest, are merely accidents. If we are to be interested we must see that A. wishes to marry B., and our one care is to know how he sped in his wooing. Now I am far from affirming that Love and Politics are incompatible; but they are terribly liable to clash; and, when that happens, love commonly goes to the wall. Politics are, as Bacon said, of all pursuits the most immersed in matter; but Love belongs to the supra-sensuous world. Mr Monypenny, depicting the remarkable composure with which Disraeli dismissed his adored "Henrietta," says that "Love had come into conflict with the harder side of Disraeli's character, and, in the clash between will and passion, will had triumphed."

What then happened in real life generally happens in political fiction. The Politics and the Love-story strive for the upper hand; Politics gets it: and the Political Novel, ceasing to be a love-story, ceases to be truly a novel. So far, then, Mr Gretton is bold in his attempt; and he is bold again when he tells us that his book is "an exercise in the Disraelian manner." That word "Exercise" gives me pause. We read in "David Copperfield" that "an unhappy culprit, found guily of imperfect exercise, approached at Mr Creakle's command," and that Mr Creakle "cut a joke before he beat him." I feel rather like Mr Creakle; but, at any rate, if I am forced to beat, I will not joke. Yet once more Mr Gretton is bold when he hopes that his description of his book will protect him. Rather, it increases his danger, and tends to enhance severity; for he who professes to write in the Disraelian manner challenges comparison with the supreme master of political fiction. When "Lothair" appeared Lord Houghton wrote: "There is immense and most malevolent curiosity about Disraeli's novel. His wisest friends think that it must be a mistake, and his enemies hope it will be his ruin. He told Longman that he believed he was the first ex-Premier who had ventured on a work of fiction. If he had said this to me I should have suggested M. Guizot's 'Méditations Religieuses.'" Disregarding this rather Creakle-like joke at Guizot's religious experiences, I may point out that Disraeli had an unique equipment for the work of political novel-writing. He had been in close contact with politics from his boyhood; he had been an active politician from his youth. He had been in Parliament for more than thirty years. He had entered the Cabinet in 1852, and he had just been Prime Minister during a peculiarly disturbed and critical time. Add to this his intimate acquaintance with society in all its grades, his mordant humour, and his arresting style, and one sees a combination of qualifications for the task such as no other author has ever been able to approach. In "Lothair" at any rate, though one could not say as much of "Coningsby" or "Sybil," Love holds its own even against the master-spell of Politics, for Theodora is a heroine whom, as Froude pointed out, Disraeli himself thoroughly likes, and we sympathize with all our hearts when Lothair falls prone under her spell. Now Mr Gretton has written an extremely clever and interesting book; but I confess that, without his "Foreword," I might have failed to recognize the "Disraelian manner." Rather should I liken "Ingram" to the earlier part of "The New Machiavelli." The opening scene is laid outside the National Liberal Club on the night of the 15th of January 1906. "Out on to the screens came the astonishing news of the black defeat of the Tory leader by a completely unknown man, in a constituency he had held for years." The sayings and doings, the performances and the failures, of the Liberal Party between that date and this supply the material of Mr Gretton's book.

Although, at the outset, I spoke disparagingly of Political Novels, I must confess that I am fond of reading them; but I must defend my consistency by saying that I read them for their Politics and not for their Love. Some of the best are scarcely known. Who nowadays remembers the masterpieces of Edward Jenkins, M.P. for Dundee—"Barney O'Geogehan" and "Lord Bantam"? No one ever read "Breakers Ahead"—a very clever study of politics at the end of Lord Palmerston's reign, by a friend of mine who chose to call himself "Ralph Vyvyan." "The Next Generation," by J. F. Maguire, M.P. for Cork, was a prophecy of Women's Suffrage, as "Barney O'Geogehan" was a prophecy of Home Rule. But they all alike are forgotten. Henry Kingsley has, indeed, his admirers; but unfortunately they never read anything except "Ravenshoe" and "Geoffrey Hamlyn." They ignore "Austin Elliot," with the incidents, drawn from life, of the session of 1846 which repealed the Corn Laws. In "My Novel" Bulwer-Lytton used his own political experience, in the constituencies and in the House, to singular advantage. "The Newcomes" and "Middlemarch" give us excellent bits of electioneering, but stop short at the door of the House. Does the ascendancy of a beautiful woman over an inflammable statesman make a political novel? If so, "Diana of the Crossways" may claim the name. Not so "Bleak House"; and yet Sir Leicester Dedlock is a truly political figure when, to Volumnia incautiously asking, "What for?" about the "Hundreds of thousands of pounds" which the Constitutional Party has spent at the election, he replies: "For necessary expenses; and I trust to your good sense, Volumnia, not to pursue the subject, here or elsewhere." Anthony Trollope had a curious fondness for politics, though he knew little about them; and in "Phineas Finn" he caught the broader aspects of Parliamentary comedy. Mr Justin M'Carthy, in "Waterdale Neighbours," drew a Tory Democrat long before Lord Randolph Churchill was heard of.

Of Disraeli I have already spoken. "Lothair" stands conspicuously at the head of all political novels, and, besides being a social satire of the most brilliant kind, it is a real chapter of European history. I am therefore paying the highest compliment at my command when I say that "Democracy," published in America in 1880, is the finest novel dealing with politics which has appeared since "Lothair." "It combined, with a skill which Disraeli himself could not have bettered, the deliberate purpose of exposing the sordid side of American politics, with a dashing story in which the central figure of Mrs Leigh remained ever fresh and charming and sympathetic." The book was indeed a capital love-story, as well as a pungent satire on political corruption. What made it additionally stimulating was the fact that it was anonymous. The guesses at its authorship were innumerable. Even the author's sex was uncertain, and a crucial passage by which critics sought to decide this point was the description of a Parisian ball-gown, which Worth, its creator, called "The Dawn in June." The story of its creation is worth repeating. The Master had struggled all night for an idea, but had not caught it. He woke careworn and perturbed, and flung open his window. "There, before his bloodshot eyes, lay the pure, still, new-born radiant morning. With a cry of inspiration the great man leaned out of the casement, and rapidly caught the details of his new conception. Before ten o'clock an imperious order had brought to his private room every silk, satin, and gauze within the range of pale pink, pale crocus, pale green, silver, and azure. Then came chromatic scales of colour; combinations that vulgarized the rainbow; symphonies and fugues; the twittering of birds; the great peace of dewy nature; maidenhood in her awakening innocence; '*The Dawn in June.*' The Master rested content." That was the crucial passage, and the judgments on it were curiously divided. All men said it proved that the author was a woman, for no man could describe a gown so beautifully. All women said the author must be a man, for no woman would write such dreadful nonsense. Quite lately it has been revealed that the book was written by Professor Henry Adams, the historian of the United States; but I, being a man, cling to the belief that the episode of "The Dawn in June" sprang from a woman's brain.

XXXIII

THE AGRICULTURAL LABOURER

LORD MORLEY tells us that Mr Gladstone, when enumerating clergymen who had written poetry, mentioned Frederick Faber, "who had written at least one good poem—'The Old Labourer.'" The present writer has some reason to believe that he, indirectly, brought this poem under Gladstone's notice, and certainly he has always loved it for its melodious pathos. Faber, in his Anglican days, had lived and worked among the agricultural poor, and he knew by observation the hidden tragedy which so often underlies their apparently vapid lives.

> "Peace! he is dying now;
> No light is on his brow;
> He makes no sign, but without sign departs.
> The poor die often so,—
> And yet they long to go,
> To take to God their over-weighted hearts.
>
> Born only to endure,
> The patient, passive poor
> Seem useful chiefly by their multitude;
> For they are men who keep
> Their lives secret and deep;
> Alas! the poor are seldom understood."

To a man brought up in rural England, the truth

conveyed by those stanzas, and indeed by the whole poem from which they are taken, must always make a strong appeal; and my mind has been recalled to it by the extremely interesting paper on the Agricultural Labourers' Union which Mr Charles Roden Buxton contributed to the *Nation* of 16th September 1911. That paper, though dealing specially with Norfolk, revived the memories of Bedfordshire and Buckinghamshire as I knew them in the sixties and seventies. In the North of England, as Mr Buxton points out, there was always a "Democratic spirit," even among the agricultural labourers, which prevented them from becoming serfs or cyphers. But this was not so in the South. So far as registers and other records could show, the same families had dwelt in the same villages from time immemorial. Sometimes their names were Saxon; sometimes, by a curious half-French twist, they suggested the notion that they had been bestowed by the insolent Normans on the drudges who tilled their fields and tended their flocks. The men, and their forefathers, had been agricultural labourers—had "worked on the land," in their own phrase—as far back as tradition reached. They knew no other craft, nor wished to know it. Their hopes, their fears, and their general view of the world were bounded by the village where their forefathers had always lived, and almost by the farm on which they had laboured. They were a race wholly dependent for existence on the goodwill of those above them. They, with their wives and children, depended for food on the farmer who employed them, and for lodging on the landlord who owned their cottages. They could not, like artizans, follow their work whither it led them. They were, if any human beings could be, bound to the soil. At the worst, their lot was that which Kingsley described, with painful realism, in "The Poacher's Widow"—at the best, it was a life of hard labour and little food, lived under the strictest supervision of hereditary masters, and having the Workhouse for its goal.

It was natural—nay, inevitable—that a race of men, deduced from such an ancestry and living under such conditions, should develope a quality of secretiveness. Indeed, it was their only defence against all-powerful forces which, if offended, might at any moment destroy them. No wonder that, in Faber's phrase, they "kept their lives secret and deep," and their thoughts were even more secret than their lives. But they knew their friends. They had no class-hatreds. If the Squire was a "hard man" about his cottages, screwing the last penny out of their poor pockets; if the Parson on the Bench sent a man to gaol for picking leaves or "sleeping out"; if the Farmer raved and bullied, thrashed the boys, or was insolent to the women; then they remembered it, and hated the oppressor, not for his class but for his conduct. The awful song about the burning farm, at the Village Revel in "Yeast," is scarcely, if at all, an exaggeration. But, when the Squire was open-handed and the ladies of the Hall were kindly visitants ; when the Parson was in and out of the cottages, with a genial word for all ; when the Farmer spoke civilly and shared the work at times of pressure ; the labourers were perfectly willing to be friendly.

Outwardly, their demeanour was much the same in either case—stolid with a stolidity born of necessary caution. But such as visited their cottages or trudged alongside of them on their way home from work knew well enough the difference of feeling which different sorts of treatment engendered. Those, too, in whom the Labourer could place confidence—to whom he could open his mind without risk of pains or penalties—knew that, in spite of narrow opportunities and the most beggarly elements of education, he was to the full as shrewd and as clear-seeing, though not, perhaps, as far-seeing, as his betters. And, as the old generation passed away to their nameless graves in the village churchyard, and a younger race sprang up, it was not difficult to discern the workings of a new spirit. Labourers who were still boys when the Education Act of 1870 was passed were, by the eighties, a race of comparatively educated men. They were beginning to realize their manhood in a sense in which they had not realized it before, and to feel after something in the way of citizenship of which their fathers had never dreamed. Encouraged by what they read of Trade Unions in the towns, they began to think that the way to more endurable conditions of living lay through combination; and hence, in 1872, sprang the Agricultural Labourers' Union, inspired and controlled by Joseph Arch, himself a Labourer and a Methodist Preacher.

Everyone who knows the life of rural districts—the ascendancy claimed by even benevolent squires—the devotion to the established order which animates even exemplary clergymen—the intolerance of new ideas which is stamped on the British Farmer more deeply than on any other man on earth—can picture to himself the reception accorded forty years ago to the Agricultural Labourers' Union. An eminent Bishop of the Established Church prescribed a ducking in a horse-pond as a suitable discipline for Mr Arch, and every man who had the pluck to join the Union knew that he did so at the imminent risk of ruin. Still, undeterred, the poor fellows tramped the country, halting at dinner-time or sunset on some common or village-green, where at any rate the "Powers that be" could not stifle, though they might punish, free speech. I recall one such scene, in the rich twilight of an August evening; the earnest, passionate, rugged eloquence of the speakers; the sympathy, palpable though awed into muteness, of the listeners; and the rather mournful cadence of the slowly sung chorus:

> "Where Freedom may call you, there fearlessly go,
> And stand like the brave, with your faces to the foe."

About the same time, I recall a happy gathering

in a Village Church, where an enlightened clergyman held a special service for the men of the Union (who had asked for it), and preached them an admirable sermon.

"How much happier would it be for the labourer (and how much better for the rates too!) if adequate wages had enabled him to put by enough to keep him in his failing years—if he could, by the aid of his own savings, still sit at ease in the chimney corner, where he rested in winter evenings after work—if he could still linger, with feeble step in the familiar garden-plot amid the flowers, and end his days in the home where, from time to time, a few dear and bright associations had gleamed upon his toil."

But, in spite of occasional encouragements, the odds against the Union were too heavy; after a few years of vain struggle it collapsed, and now, as Mr Buxton tells us, it has, at any rate in a limited area, revived. No doubt the new Union will find plenty of work and plenty of fighting before it attains its ends; but when compared with what befell in 1872–1874 its work and its fighting will be child's play. The vote has made the difference. Richard Jefferies wrote, out of full knowledge, about "Hodge and his Masters"; but now Hodge's Masters supplicate for his favour, and the Agricultural Labourer is a power in the land. Here, in passing, let me pay my tribute to the present Bishop of Truro, who, long before the Labourer obtained the vote, and in days when nothing was to be gained by caressing him, founded a voluntary "Parish Council" at his parish in Buckinghamshire, and habitually took counsel with the labourers in all matters affecting the Parish Church, the Schools, the Charities, and other interests of village life. If any man in those days deserved the title of "The Labourers' Friend" it was Charles Stubbs, Vicar of Granborough; and this fact was present to Mr Gladstone's mind when he made him Dean of Ely.

Another warm and consistent friend of the agricultural poor was the saintly Bishop of Lincoln, Edward King. The first twenty years of his ministerial life had been spent in Oxfordshire villages, and he knew, not only the wants and sorrows, but the merits and capacities, of the ploughmen and carters. Although he was a stiff Tory in political opinion, he earnestly supported the extension of the Suffrage to the Agricultural Labourers; urging, characteristically, that they must be trained to be citizens of the Kingdom of Heaven by being citizens of the Kingdom of England. In 1877 he wrote as follows to his friend Henry Scott Holland (now Regius Professor of Divinity at Oxford), whose special interest has always lain in the reconciliation of Religion and Philosophy: "The relation of Ethics and Politics is becoming a practical question, and I very much hope that some of you good people will bring out an edition of 'The Republic' adapted for a Christian Plough-boy, with notes in his own language, and illustrated not by arguments but by stories. These poor boys are now beginning to feel that there is a big world round about them, and lots of new Powers and Hopes ; and so they are dashing about. But we must put them upon the real Principles, and then, after a bit, they will go on, and up, in order, dear things. It is grand to know that there is all this undeveloped power, and to feel sure that it has order, and beauty, and value, if we can only get the dear People to watch patiently, and work with its laws."

The same thought was always present to the Bishop's mind, and, eighteen years later, he wrote to the same friend : "I don't think the *minds* of the Poor have been treated with sufficient loving, reverent ability. We want a book (like Darwin on Earth-Worms) on the intellectual, moral, and spiritual capacities of the poor. Do write it."

This reverence for the minds of the Poor, as well as their souls and their bodies, is a comparatively rare form of humanitarian zeal. The Ploughboy's edition of "The Republic" has not yet been produced. I have some Platonists among my readers. Will one of them set his hand to the work ?

XXXIV

ASSOCIATION

My title has a seasonable sound, and suggests "Rugby" as its antithesis. But "Association" for the purposes of football is only a small and special application of an all-pervading principle, and recent occurrences have led me to consider the effects of Association, or Combination, or Co-operation, or whatever we prefer to call it, on human life and affairs.

Quite lately, I have addressed a considerable gathering of men and women more or less interested in religion and in social reform. I took my hearers through the series of events which I discussed in Chapters IV. and V. of this book; giving, in chronological order, the rise and decline of the various associations and combinations of men which, during the last sixty years, have striven to reform the social and economic worlds on the lines of the Christian Gospel. When I had done speaking, a young clergyman rose in the hall and said that he was as ready as anyone to honour the Christian Socialists of 1848, the Guild of St Matthew, and the Christian Social Union. "But," he said, "these all have had their day. They have done their work. The needs of the new time demand a new combination. Why didn't the lecturer tell us about 'The Church Socialist League,' which some of us younger men have formed?" My simple and sufficient answer was that I really do not know enough about this latest creation to pronounce an opinion on its merits; but the question illustrated the persistency with which the principle of Association asserts itself. One down, another comes on. This combination falls to pieces, and, out of its ruins, another immediately constructs itself. "United we stand," as the Benefit Societies proclaim on their banners. Men find that, single-handed and in isolation, they are powerless to secure the ends which they desire. So, in obedience to a kind of natural law, they ally themselves with others who have the same ends in view, and work together till some difference as to methods forces them into divergent lines. In the region of Politics, this means Party; and with reference to Party Mr Gladstone once said: "Men should form into knots, and act together till conscience forbids." The tendency to tighten these knots, and thereby to fetter individual freedom, is the bad side of Association; and it has been made much stronger and more rigid in its operation by the evolution of Modern Society.

This is conspicuously the case in political association. For three hundred years English politics were divided into two great camps, which, roughly speaking, stood for Authority and Freedom. It was a clear dichotomy; and, though the two opposite sides were, in successive generations, disguised by various nicknames, still they persistently represented two main and contrariant ideas. But, within the limits of either side, there was room for a great deal of independent action; and independence even went so far as now and then to transfer itself, for the nonce, to the opposite side, reverting in the long run to its natural alliance. To put it in concrete form, the history of English politics records repeated instances of people, and even families, who were mainly for the Court or the Country—the King or the Parliament—the Tories or the Whigs—but who still maintained a rather disturbing independence of Party-ties; and, at some unforeseen conjuncture in politics, would forsake their habitual connexions, and vote this way or that, just as conviction or interest moved them. From this condition of Parties in the country there resulted the Independent Member of Parliament, who wrote "C." or "L." after his name, but formed his own judgment, took his own course, and treated Whips and wire-pullers with the contempt which they deserve. The Independent Member has gone for ever, and he has gone with the condition of things which produced him. The principle of Association as applied to politics has become infinitely more stringent. Constituencies more and more require it of a representative that he should be staunch, through evil report or good report, to the party which he professes. Independence of thought and action is more and more regarded as treason.

But this excessive tightness of Party-bonds tends sometimes to defeat itself. Strong wills and clear intelligences resent bondage; and, if their resentment takes the form of secession, it injures and may even shatter the party. The Peelite Secession of 1845 left the Tory Party permanently poorer in intellect and character; and in more recent years the Liberal Party has undergone similar impoverishment. First the Liberal Unionists and then the Independent Labour Party broke away from the Liberal Party, with which, in the main, they had agreed. In the one case, men resented the enforcement of Home Rule by the use of the Party-machine; in the other, they resented the domination exercised over the party by Capitalists and Manufacturers. In both cases, the principle of Association, strained to bursting-point, resulted in schism. Yet the victory of Independence was not long-lived. The Liberal Unionists found that, if they wished to exist, they must join themselves to allies who on the chief issue of the moment were at one with them, and so they became part of the great Conservative confederation. The Independent Labour Party has been compelled to adopt strict rules of discipline and cohesion; and the various sects and subdivisions into which the cause of Labour is subdivided seem to perceive that, if their cause is to triumph, they must revert to the principle of Association, and weld all who work for one end into one body. The fate of those Unionist Free-Traders who, having broken away from their party on the Fiscal issue, hoped to maintain a separate existence is within the remembrance of us all. Some of them have been forcibly recalled to their old moorings, and some, after a fierce tussle with contending waves, have been cast up on the Liberal shore.

I have spoken so far about Politics, because to Englishmen generally Politics afford the most familiar and intelligible medium for the discussion of principles or general truths. But the same law of Association, with its advantages and its defects, is at work all round us. Trade Unionism affords a salient instance; but, if I were to discuss that theme during the present tension, I should probably involve myself in controversy. Let me turn, then, to matters ecclesiastical, where I am more at home. There we see the "Three Historic Schools of Thought," as they are called, and in them we see the principle of Association actively at work. High Churchmen, Low Churchmen, Broad Churchmen have banded themselves in compact organizations for the maintenance of the truths which they hold; and (as regards at least one of the three parties) for the coercion of their opponents. The very titles under which they have enrolled themselves bear witness to the principle. "The English Church Union," "The Church Association," "The Liberal Churchmen's League," all testify to the value of co-operation; and certainly an isolated clergyman, constrained to dwell with the Mesech of Ritualism or to have his habitation among the tents of a Protestant Kedar, derives support and encouragement from the knowledge that a thousand or so of his fellow-Churchmen are sworn to the same standard, and, at a pinch, will support him in his fight for the principles in which he and they believe. Here is the use of Association; but the abuse is not far off.

A member of a society must either be committed to the policy of those who guide the society, or else must constantly disturb the peace by protesting or resigning. So Association tends to the suppression of free thought, and, when at length conviction compels a man to come out and dissociate himself from those with whom he has acted, the cry of treachery, half-heartedness, or sordid motives is incontinently raised. And, when the man who has established his freedom begins to feel lonely amid his new surroundings, and seeks some fresh form of Association, he is apt to find himself in the position of the Rev. Amos Barton in "Scenes of Clerical Life." "He was like an onion that has been rubbed with spices; the strong original odour was blended into something new and foreign. The Low Church onion still offended refined High Church nostrils, and the new spice was unwelcome to the palate of the genuine onion-eater."

After the Clergyman comes in due course the

Doctor; and, if in any department of human affairs the principle of Association is strong, it is strong in the medical world. An extraordinarily close Trade Unionism is that which binds the medical profession together; and beyond doubt it has had its advantages in protecting doctors against calumny and misrepresentation, improving their social status, and (sometimes) concealing their blunders. But it presses very heavily on individual opinion; and a doctor who runs counter to the unwritten rules of his profession, or refuses to worship discredited idols, or coquets with new theories in medicine, will probably find before long that Association has its disciplinary as well as its protective side. The bare mention of such words as Vivisection, Vaccination, Homœopathy, and Hypnotism will recall some brisk encounters between individual opinion and professional authority.

Even in those "regions mild of calm and serene air," where Philosophy dwells and human passions should have no place, Association is found to operate. Men whose habits of thought tend in the same direction, whose opinions coincide, and who are convinced, like Job's friends, that they "are the people, and wisdom shall die with them," are drawn together by a kind of spiritual affinity; and, though the penalty inflicted on independent thinking is not so visible as that which prevails in political, or ecclesiastical, or medical circles, it still is real and effective. It may take the purely intellectual form of treating the independent thinker as a harmless lunatic, whose errors are to be corrected from above, but who is never to be encountered on equal ground of argument; or it may translate itself into a more material shape.—" Well. I heard Frothingham one night at the Synthetic Society, debating with Haldane about the Pathway to Reality; and I maintain that a man who is absurd enough to quote F. D. Maurice in a serious discussion is quite unfit for preferment."

Here, then, are some of the abuses of Association; its uses are palpable. What is the conclusion of the whole matter? Surely this. In a highly-organized society individual effort working in isolation has little chance of being effective; but it gains enormously in power by Association with some larger force. Every man, then, who wishes to serve his day and generation, should be a member of a Party, and should be willing to sacrifice crotchets to a cause. But when it comes to matters more important than crotchets—to issues of principle, and questions where conscience has a voice—he should stand sternly for the right of private judgment, and be ready to break all Party-bonds sooner than renounce it. " My Party, right or wrong," is a thoroughly unprincipled maxim; and the additional command of the Birmingham Caucus, " Don't vote as you like, but vote as you are told," prepared the way for the political servitude which still oppresses that once-famous town. One of the most impressive passages in "John Inglesant" is that in which the Jesuit exhorts the youth to "choose his part from the instinct of his order," and then to follow it to the end. Commenting on this "sonorous wickedness," Lord Acton said—"It matters not what cause we take up, provided we defend it well—that is Probabilism. It matters not what wrong we do in a good cause—that again is the maxim that the end justifies the means." It was a noble saying of Mr Gladstone when, repudiating certain nicknames which had been attached to his opinions, he told Queen Victoria that to adopt them would be to forfeit "what he cherishes as the first of earthly blessings—his mental freedom." And mental freedom is exactly that which Party tends to destroy.

XXXV

CONVENTION

It was said of old time concerning one who represented Manchester in Parliament that "he talked to his constituents as Manchester people like to be talked to—in the language of clear, manly intelligence, which penetrates through sophisms, ignores commonplaces, and gives to conventional illusions their true value." The intelligence which could do all these things in a political speech must have been of a very unusual cast; for political oratory is, as a general rule, the climate in which sophisms, commonplaces, and "conventional illusions," flourish most abundantly. It will be enough for me if, in the purer air of this meditative chapter, I succeed in giving to one or two "conventional illusions" something like their true value.

The subject of Convention, which I now discuss, is in some measure related to Association, which I discussed last. It might be said that Convention is in the world of thought what Association is in the world of action. Association binds people together in the pursuit of common ends and, to a large extent, in the use of common methods, even where individual judgment might suggest a different line of action.

Convention represents a prevalent opinion or belief, which the individual may question, but which he cannot openly disavow unless he is prepared to confront the universal disapproval of society. Indeed, disregard for Convention is a much more serious matter than rupture with Association; for the world in which Association acts is divided into equal, or almost equal, parts, so that, if you forsake one, you can take refuge with the other; whereas, in the world which Convention dominates, almost everyone is on one side, and the rebel must stand pretty nearly alone.

Convention, like Wordsworth's world, "is too much with us, late and soon." If it does not actually begin at the cradle and end at the hearse, it occupies an enormous share of the intervening space. No Conventions in the world are stronger than those of school, where boys profess to despise virtue and cleverness and industry, though secretly in their little caitiff souls they admire all three; and make idols of hulking athletes (whom they know to be beasts) because it is the right thing to do. An Eton tutor told the Royal Commission in 1862 that the fact that a boy was known to be the best scholar at Eton would not do him any harm, provided he was sufficiently good at games; and the Head Master of another school said that even the best boy in his school would have no influence if he was known not to care about games. Powerful indeed is the Moloch of Athletics, and our Convention is to represent him as being not only powerful but beneficent.

The favourite Convention of Schoolmasters is to profess that the Athletes are the salt of the school. They really must know better, if they have kept their eyes and ears open, and watched their heroes in unguarded hours. But they know that the Athletes are powerful; that they set the tone, and rule the roast; so that a master who gets them over to his side makes his own office much less troublesome and exacting. Hence arises the Convention of the Athlete's virtue, and, to do him justice, no one contemns it more heartily than the Athlete himself.

The Universities are dominated by a Convention of Seriousness. Everyone professes to take everything —religious, political, educational, social, athletic— so desperately seriously. The practice of reporting in the London press the votes on a division at the Oxford Union is a leading instance of this Convention. Of what conceivable importance are the votes of an assembly of which perhaps three members in three hundred will ever have anything to do with politics in later life, and where the most conspicuous leaders will probably have turned their coats before they are thirty? Not long ago the Head of a College said to me: "It is time for me to resign. I can no longer take undergraduates seriously. I can't think their crimes very dreadful or their achievements very glorious." There spoke the revolt of realism against Convention.

Endless, of course, are the Conventions of professional and public life. Convention requires that we should speak with a forced and hollow heartiness of "my learned friend" or "my reverend brother" who is poaching on my practice or seducing my flock. The rival newspaper which is cutting into our circulation is "an esteemed contemporary"; and, when we know that our rival has won the seat by the dirtiest malpractices, we think it our bounden duty to say that the contest has been fought out in a thoroughly honest and gentlemanlike fashion, and that the bitterness of defeat is sweetened by the fact that so many good men (though they were too few) supported us at the poll.

In the region of Taste, Convention reigns almost unchallenged. Nothing, surely, but Convention of a very tough sort can account for the annual display of the Royal Academy, and the places assigned to such pictures as recent portraits of the Duke of Northumberland and King Edward VII. I believe that a great majority of Englishmen care for music just about as much as Miss Jenkyns, "who was not musical, but beat time out of time by way of appearing to be so." Yet the Convention of delighting in operas, concerts, and even "a little music after dinner," is so strongly established that few dare to confess that music is for them only regulated noise. One season when we had the Wagnerian Cycle over here a brutal man asked a lady, who had been enthusing overmuch, if she really cared for Wagner.

She replied, with a look of startled surprise, "Oh! I think one likes Wagner—doesn't one?" Poor soul! She was a born slave of Convention, and was stung by a sudden fear that she might have been admiring a type of music which had gone out of fashion—like a hat.

Matthew Arnold, describing a visit with his children to a ruined abbey, gave this pleasant instance of Conventionalism rebuked: "We entered the precinct, and there were the beautiful ruins, and capitals and fragments of arches lying about the grass, as you see them at such places. We all said how beautiful, etc., etc.; but B., surveying the litter with the greatest contempt, exclaimed at last these words: 'What a nasty, *beastly* place this is!' You have no notion what a comic effect the child and his speech produced." Dear little B.! I knew him well in later years, and it is pleasant to recall as true to his developed character this early detestation of claptrap and humbug.

It is, of course, one of our national Conventions—and perhaps the chiefest—that we are the most honest, the most religious, and the most courageous race in the world. Some, I believe, add that we are the only people who can ride. As to patriotism, it is not only assumed—I hope rightly—that every Englishman is patriotic; but our Convention claims a monopoly of the virtue; and, if any other nation presumes to fight for its home, its property, and its freedom, we call the spirit that prompts it by every other name than Patriotism. And yet once again. It is conventionally assumed that, in some exalted sense not attainable by other races, Englishmen are manly; that their manliness is mixed with gentleness; that they enjoy hardship for themselves, but shrink from inflicting it on others; and that our field-sports are glorious because they train our youth to endure pain and confront danger, and make us, in short, what we are. Over against this Convention of our unrivalled manliness, and of the moral efficacy of field-sports, it may perhaps be instructive to set this quotation from a paper dedicated to the glorification of sport:

"Strict orders by the Master to let the otter go where she liked resulted in *seven hours and ten minutes' sport.* Hounds, as usual, were put to water at Otterton Bridge, drawing up. Along the road hounds dashed across the river and put an otter out of a patch of brambles. The Master saw the otter creeping across on the bottom of the river, and quickly doubled his horn. A glorious scent being on the water enabled hounds to drive the otter up and down at a great pace, *never allowing her a moment's respite.* Just fifty minutes after being found she landed, racing along the cliff, down again through an orchard, up under the hedge, and up the next cliff, to a fox-earth. For fifty-five minutes she kept little Jenny busy, and *not until a tool was used* would she bolt. The digging had the desired effect, and out went our otter, and fell headlong over the cliff to the rocks below. It looked as if our sport was over; but no! with a shake, off went our quarry again, giving us a fine turn below the Rocky Weir. Here in the rough water she kept hounds busy, as from side to side of the pool she went, crossing over the weir head and swimming up the long reach above, then back and over the weir again, hounds being hurled under into the pool below by the rush of water. After a fine turn of an hour, the otter made up over the weir and to the end of the pool, crossing two stickles, and into a 9-inch drain-pipe. Here it looked as if it was the end of all things, as no terrier could go up for the amount of water. The otter *was, however, flooded out,* hounds being taken well away for fear of chopping her as she bolted at the lower end, knocking away the turf, and going down the river. Hounds were called on, when our otter took to the cliffs again, and into still another fox-earth. Paddy, however, evicted her after thirty minutes, the otter racing along the cliff side, and then to water again. *One hour's good sport* in the river followed, when our dodging friend again sought shelter in a huge badger-earth. Hopes of a kill seemed lost, and our large field dwindled. Paddy, however, was game for a tussle underground, and after an hour's work bolted this cunning old otter. This time, however, she got caught by three hounds, and they gave her a pretty good shaking ere she broke away. *The hunt, which had been so fast, now got much slower, as our quarry tired.* She started hide-and-seek measures, going from some weiring to a rabbit-earth. She was shifted repeatedly, until she got into another fox-earth, where *she had to be dug out,* getting killed just before reaching the river. This day must have been the best of the season, scent being of the very best, hounds working well, and also the terriers."

Even the most conventional of sportsmen must admit that in this case the odds were heavily against the otter ; and, if these are the sports in which our young soldiers learn the art of war, it is not surprising that they found more difficulties than they expected in South Africa, even though, as they proudly said before they knew better, " the Boers had forgotten how to shoot."

XXXVI

A FORTRESS OF FREEDOM

WHEN first I came to live in London, a prominent figure in society was Sir Walter Stirling. He was a funny little old gentleman, running about the town in a yellow wig, with an umbrella tucked under his arm. He had lived long, had known everyone, had been everywhere, and had seen everything. On the 23rd of June 1880 I chanced to run across him in Piccadilly. The House of Commons had, only a few hours before, committed Mr Bradlaugh to a farcical imprisonment in the Clock Tower for refusing to withdraw, after the House had refused him leave to swear or affirm. Sir Walter took the situation very seriously, and bubbled over with excitement. "I don't like this at all," he exclaimed. "When I was a Westminster boy I saw Sir Francis Burdett carried a prisoner to the Tower. I saw a riot then, and I'm afraid I shall see a riot again now. That's the house they took him from, and Piccadilly looked like a street in Paris during the French Revolution."

Now, for my own part, I sympathize with Sir John Evans, who held that "there is no fear of God in a riot"; and I should have shared Sir Walter's dismay if Bradlaugh's supporters had stormed the

Clock Tower, silenced Big Ben, and liberated the recalcitrant Member for Northampton. But somehow I felt an assurance that we were safe from civil disturbance, and I gratified my historic sense by gazing on the house—No. 80 Piccadilly—which, just seventy years before, had been, in literal truth, a Fortress of Freedom. Sir Francis Burdett (1770-1844) was a champion of political liberty and a pioneer of Reform, in the dark days of Pitt and Addington and Liverpool. He was a country gentleman of ancient lineage and great estate, who had no axe to grind, no ambition to gratify, no personal object to serve. He cared solely and passionately for Freedom, and on that account the Radical electors of Westminster returned him exultantly to the House of Commons, of which he was for forty years one of the most conspicuous ornaments. I have known men who, as boys, had joined in his triumphal processions, shouting, "Burdett for ever! Universal Suffrage, Triennial Parliaments, and the Ballot," and who used to remark, in pensive age, that, in spite of all their shouting, they had only secured one out of their three objects in the course of a long lifetime.

In 1793 Sir Francis Burdett had married a daughter of Thomas Coutts, the banker, and his marriage determined the site of his "fortress." Mr Coutts lived at the corner of Stratton Street, where it debouches into Piccadilly, and Burdett established himself at the adjacent house, standing in Piccadilly and facing the Green Park, in order that Lady Burdett might be close to her widowed father. Early in the session of 1810 a Radical orator called Gale Jones made a public attack on what he considered the unconstitutional practice of excluding strangers from the debates in the House of Commons, and the House committed him to Newgate for his pains. This rather arbitrary action stirred Burdett to his depths. It was an abuse of the power of the House. It was an invasion of personal liberty. It was a violation of Magna Charta (which to Burdett was always the first and last word in the oracles of Freedom). He denounced the imprisonment with all the resources of his fiery eloquence, and moved for Jones's release. Strong as his speech was, and violently offensive to the ruling powers, it was made safe by the privilege of Parliament; but, scorning the security of an unassailable position, and determined to try conclusions with the enemies of Freedom, Burdett published his speech in "Cobbett's Annual Register." By so doing he courted political martyrdom, and he got what he courted. The House treated his printed speech as a high breach of its undefined but far-reaching "Privilege," and on the 6th of April resolved that Sir Francis Burdett be committed to the Tower. Burdett, who was out of London, immediately returned, established himself in No. 80 Piccadilly, barricaded his doors and windows, and dared the officers of the House of Commons, who were charged with the awkward duty of arresting him, to do their worst. He rested his case on the venerable dogma that "An Englishman's house is his Castle," and called on the civic authorities, as the guardians of popular rights, to defend him against the attacking host. The officers of the House were supported by a strong body of the Life Guards, who cleared a space in front of the house, prevented all access and egress, and kept the mob at bay. But the mob, Burdettites to a man, gave the troops a good deal more trouble than they had bargained for, and the riot which Sir Walter Stirling saw soon broke loose in Piccadilly.

Meanwhile Burdett, secure in his fortress, was cut off from consultation with his political supporters. His right-hand man was a breeches-maker at Charing Cross, called Place; and as Place knew to a nicety the temper of the populace and the strength of Burdett's cause, it was imperatively necessary that he should have access to his chief. On the fourth evening of the siege Burdett's brother came to call Place to a Council of War. They were admitted into Mr Coutts's house in Stratton Street, and thence made their way by cellar-passages, through guarded iron doors (the watchword for the evening being "Place"), into No. 80 Piccadilly. This was a masterpiece of strategy, but the triumph was short-lived. On the following morning the officers of the House, having obtained the sanction of the Law Officers of the Crown, broke down the front door of No. 80, and forced an entry. "They disturbed a hastily-arranged scene, in which Sir Francis was teaching his son to translate Magna Charta, and carried him off in a coach, surrounded by a strong force of cavalry, through a yelling mob, to the Tower."

That touch of the infant Burdett receiving instruction in the barbarous latinity of the Great Charter at the moment of his sire's arrest seems to show that the ever-popular Sir Francis knew the value of histrionic effect; and, indeed, at every stage of his long career, he appealed to the eye, as well as to the ear and the understanding, of the populace which followed him through all vicissitudes. Burdett's residence in the Tower was uneventful. Popular excitement soon died down. He sent pacific messages to his friends outside; and occupied himself with his private and political business as if nothing particular had happened. At the end of two months he was automatically released by the prorogation of Parliament; came away quietly by boat, to the great disappointment of his supporters, who had arranged a tremendous demonstration, and returned in peace to the Fortress of Freedom. On his death, the house in Piccadilly passed to his daughter, Miss Angela Georgina Burdett, so well known in later years as the benevolent Lady Burdett-Coutts. She acquired her second name from the widow of her grandfather, Thomas Coutts, who had married as his second wife the famous actress Harriet Mellon, afterwards Duchess of St Albans. The Duchess made her husband's granddaughter her heir; and thus, by a curious evolution of destiny, the house in Stratton Street and the house in Piccadilly, which, in the days of the siege, had been so hastily connected by surreptitious passages through the cellars, passed into the same ownership, and were made into one dwelling. There Lady Burdett-Coutts resided till her death in 1906. Then those two houses were again disconnected; and No. 80 Piccadilly, having been united to No. 81—once "Watiers's" famous gambling-house and restaurant—has now opened its hospitable doors as "The Royal Thames Yacht Club." The reminiscent epicure in "Sybil," brooding over what once had been and could never be again, exclaimed: "Oh! do not mention Watiers's. You make my mouth water." 'Tis a felicitous combination. The Fortress of Freedom, united to the Temple of Gastronomy, ought to make the most attractive club-house in the world.

XXXVII

THE PRIVY COUNCIL

"THE Lady Free-mason" is a well-known but rather mythical figure. So far as she was historical, she seems to have been Mrs Aldworth, an ancestress of the present Lord Doneraile. At any rate, I have seen a picture of a lady so named, with her finger on her lips and Masonic insignia all about her. But perhaps, after all, she was not so much historical or mythical, as typical. A curiosity which will brave unknown perils sooner than be balked is one of the most endearing features of the feminine character. "The prospect of finding anybody out in anything would have kept Miss Miggs awake under the influence of henbane." The same spirit may have animated the Lady Free-mason, when she bored a hole in the wall (or crept into the clock, for the legend has two versions) in order to gaze unseen on the ceremonies of initiation; and I fancy that I can trace it in a lady-correspondent, who implores me to tell her all about the constitution and doings of "The King's Most Honourable Privy Council." I am dreadfully afraid that what I have to tell will prove a great deal less thrilling than the nocturnal adventures of Simon Tappertit, or the mysteries of Jachin and Boaz. But I can only give what I have, and she who enquires must be merciful if the response seems lacking in interest.

In the dawn of our Constitutional history—some say from the days of Alfred, certainly from the period of Magna Charta—the King was surrounded by a Council which the old books call *Curia Regis*. It consisted of great officers of State, such as the Justiciar, the Chancellor, the Treasurer; and all the business of the Realm, political, fiscal, and judicial, passed through its hands. It was, in brief, the King's Council for all the purposes of Kingship. In process of time the judicial powers of the Council passed to the Judges, who in turn were divided into three Courts—King's Bench, Common Pleas, and Exchequer—which again, after the lapse of six hundred years, were reunited in the "High Court of Justice." In this dispersion of powers the Chancellor acquired a Court and jurisdiction of his own, represented by the "Chancery Division" of to-day. In time the *Curia Regis* "threw off, as branches or offshoots, the Court of Requests, and the more famous Court of Star Chamber"; but retained its ancient jurisdiction as a Court of Justice, in which the King personally presided, for the settlement of cases which had not been specially relegated to the Divisional Courts; and also as a Court of Final Appeal, in which aspect it is now represented by the "Judicial Committee."

By the gradual withdrawal of judicial business,

the *Curia Regis* became a purely administrative and political body, and in the reign of Henry VI. it acquired the title of "The Privy Council," by which it has since been known. Under the Tudors and the Stuarts it was a body of the highest importance; for, while the Parliament legislated and the Courts administered justice, the Privy Council, at which the Sovereign presided in person, transacted, under an oath of the strictest secrecy (which still survives), all the Executive business of the Realm. At first it was an extremely small body, but gradually it increased in numbers. In 1679 it was, on the suggestion of Sir William Temple, fixed at thirty. But this plan soon broke down. Thereupon, as business is most easily transacted and secrets are most securely kept when the number of councillors is small, there gradually arose a practice of choosing out of the Privy Council a small Sub-Council, or Committee, composed of the most important Ministers, and this acquired the popular name (for it is still unknown to the Law) of "The Cabinet." Sir Walter Raleigh had given the title of "Cabinet Council" to a collection of Aphorisms. Bacon, in his essay "Of Counsel," refers to "Cabinet Councils"; and the term is used both by Clarendon and by Pepys. Till the death of Anne the Sovereign presided over the meetings of the Cabinet Council, or "Cabinet," as it came to be called; but George I. knew no English, so his presence would have been rather a hindrance than a help to the despatch of business, and the Cabinet took to meeting without him, as it does at the present day. It is in strictness a Committee of the Privy Council: it is in effect the Board of Directors of the British Empire. It deliberates in secret, but the result of its deliberations is reported to the Sovereign; and, in Mr Gladstone's words, "as the Cabinet stands between the Sovereign and Parliament, so the Prime Minister stands between the Sovereign and the Cabinet." As this inner body, or Cabinet, began to absorb all the vitally important business of the State, the Privy Council lost effective power, and retained little more of its former greatness than the dignity which belongs to an historic title. The Sovereign addresses a member of the Privy Council as his "Trusty and Well-beloved Counsellor." In the Bidding Prayer the people are exhorted to pray for "The Lords of his Majesty's Most Honourable Privy Council, and for the Great Council of the Nation now assembled in Parliament." There is something that tickles the antiquarian palate in this way of treating the Legislature as a kind of supplement and afterthought to the Sovereign's secret council. The Board of Trade, the Board of Education, and the Local Government Board are in theory Committees of the Privy Council, though really it is only the President in each case that matters. Various acts of Sovereignty are required by law to be performed "in Council," and for such purposes a quorum of three Privy Councillors suffices. An "Order in Council" is held by Constitutional writers to be the most authoritative document, short of an Act of Parliament, known to the law. In certain emergencies the Privy Council acts *proprio vigore,* and without the presence of the Sovereign. Thus it has sometimes examined a prisoner charged with a treasonable assault on the Sovereign, though this would now be done at the more homely bar of Bow Street. It issues orders for Special Prayers and alterations in the Prayer-book. It assembles of its own accord on the death of the Sovereign, and gives instructions for the proclamation of his successor. It sits in judgment on the petition of a town or a society for incorporation by Royal Charter; and of course its Judicial Committee is the Supreme Court of Appeal for the King's Dominions beyond Seas, and (though this was due to an oversight in the Act which constituted it) in ecclesiastical causes at home. All these and others which might be named are special and exceptional uses. Of the Privy Council as a whole, and at ordinary times, one can only say that it is an Honour. Formerly there was this distinction between a Privy Councillorship and other honours—such as Peerages, Baronetcies, and Knighthoods—that it was commonly reserved for persons who had performed political and official services. Mr Gladstone held rather tenaciously to this view, and to some extent, though by no means universally, it still obtains.

It follows from what has already been said that a

Cabinet Minister must first be a Privy Councillor. If he has not attained that rank before he enters the Cabinet, he is "sworn of the Privy Council" before the Sovereign entrusts him with the seals of his Department. The Princes of the Blood Royal are born Privy Councillors and are "introduced" into the Council when they come of age. The Archbishops of Canterbury and York and the Bishop of London are always made Privy Councillors, and Archbishop Maclagan is still a Privy Councillor, though he has resigned his See. The Speaker is always made a Privy Councillor, and there are certain offices in the Government, less than the highest, which carry the dignity of the Privy Council with them. Lord Beaconsfield, in "Endymion," made capital fun of an ambitious M.P. who thought that he could form a party of his own, and become Prime Minister; yet, when a change of Government came, "he was only offered a post of little real importance, but which secured to him the dignity of the Privy Council." This he accepted, saying in extenuation of what looked like a rebuff, that "for his part, he had for some time been painfully aware that the influence of the House of Commons in the Constitutional scheme was fast waning, and that the plan of Sir William Temple for the reorganization of the Privy Council, and depositing in it the real authority of the State, was that to which we should be obliged to have recourse." Time has scarcely justified Mr Bertie Tremaine's prediction, and the most rational view of a Privy Councillorship is that it resembles a "Good Conduct Prize," which is bestowed on the boy who has tried for but not obtained the Gold Medal or the Balliol Scholarship.

Here perhaps I may, without immodesty, adduce a personal illustration. I had been for many years a friend, and during the South African War a political supporter, of Sir Henry Campbell-Bannerman, and had rejoiced unfeignedly in his victory over the "Liberal League." But in one respect I saw that his administration was vulnerable. He knew no more of the English Church than I know of the Sandemanians, and his ecclesiastical appointments were disastrous. I told him, plainly and repeatedly, that in these matters he was badly advised, and that he was doing disservice to Liberalism by outraging the convictions of Churchmen. Few Prime Ministers, I think, would have acknowledged such remonstrances in the words which I here append :

"MY DEAR GEORGE,—This is a clear case of coals of fire. You keep blazing away into me and my poor secretaries.

"I want you to authorize me to submit your name for a Privy Councillorship. Will you? and make glad

"Yours

"H. C.-B.

"BELMONT, 29 *Oct.*, '07."

XXXVIII

THE IMPREGNABLE ROCK

In writing about the Tercentenary of the Authorized Version,[1] I am obeying a request from Edinburgh; and, by a natural association of ideas, I borrow my title from an illustrious Scotsman. In the preface to "The Impregnable Rock of Holy Scripture," published in 1890, Mr Gladstone thus justified the words which he had chosen for his title:

"They lead upwards and onwards to the idea that the Scriptures, though assailed by camp, by battery, and by mine, are still nevertheless a house builded upon a rock, and that rock impregnable; . . . that the weapon of offence, which shall impair their efficiency for aiding in the redemption of mankind, has not yet been forged; and that the Sacred Canon, which it took (perhaps) two thousand years, from the accumulations of Moses down to the acceptance of the Apocalypse, to construct, is like to wear out the storms and the sunshine of the world, and all the wayward aberrations of humanity, not merely for a term as long, but until time shall be no more."

If I were writing a treatise instead of an article, I should pause on "The Sacred Canon," and the

[1] 1911.

length of time which elapsed before it was completed. I should point out that the Bible is not a single book, but a collection of books, written by people of different races, languages, and degrees of religious development, in countries widely separated, and at dates far distant from each other. I should point out that there was a Church before there was a Bible, and that the function of deciding which books should be and which should not be finally included in the Canon was the work of the Church—*i.e.* of the enlightened mind of the Christian community. But I am confined within limits too narrow to permit this method of procedure, and I must confine myself to the Bible as it actually exists ; and, for ninety-nine Englishmen out of a hundred, this means the English version dedicated to King James I. "The Authorized Version," as we commonly call it, though the authorization is not clear, has been for these three centuries the standard of English prose. It used to be said that John Bright was the only man who could quote the Bible in the House of Commons without creating a sense of incongruity ; and this was at once a tribute to his character and to his style. The gravity of his life cleared the quotation from any suspicion of irreverence or flippancy : the purity of his own style made a fit and natural setting for the quoted words. Our English Bible is of course in some sense a product of the Renaissance, for it was only the revival of learning in the Western world which made translation possible ; and the fact that men, working with an apparatus of scholarship so limited, should have produced a version so near in sense to the originals, is an intellectual miracle. Of course everyone has felt from his childhood that the New Testament is easier to understand than the Old; and at school we learned that the difference in intelligibility depended on the greater or less accuracy of translation, and that the language of the New Testament was nearer the original than that of the Old Testament. Certainly the mistranslations in the Old Testament sometimes obscured the meaning; it was hardly ever so in the New. Yet by degrees the experts in Biblical scholarship began to hanker for a more exact rendering of both Testaments.

It was by no means a popular demand,—for the great mass of people were content to be edified by what they understood and to leave what was unintelligible on one side. But the question made its way into Parliament; and then Convocation, fearing that the State might take the work into its own hands, recommended a revision of the Authorized Version. A Company of scholars was formed for the purpose, and sat from 1870 to 1884. The Revised Version of the New Testament was issued in 1881; that of the Old Testament in 1884. The principles on which the Revisers acted in the successive stages of their work are set forth in the prefaces to these two versions. The head and front of the Revision was Dr Ellicott, Bishop of Gloucester and Bristol; and towards the end of his days I had an interesting talk with him about his experiences. He was well past eighty, but was still hard at work on the Greek Testament, and was as keen as a boy about what had been the occupation of his life. "I suppose," he said, "that when you read the Revised Version of the New Testament you think you are reading Westcott? Quite a mistake. Westcott would spend hours in balancing the *pros* and *cons* of this reading or that version, and then, when we were forced to settle it by dividing, Westcott would retreat into a corner of the room and refuse to vote."

When the Revision of 1881 appeared, it was discovered, by some with chagrin and by others with relief, that the doctrinal significance of the New Testament had scarcely been affected. Of course the text of the Heavenly Recorders went out; but it had long been known to be a pious fraud, and its loss was more than balanced by the amended version of Titus ii. 13. A better understanding of the significance of Greek tenses wiped off the stain of Predestinarianism from Acts ii. 47. The minute change from *and* to *or* in 1st Cor. xi. 27 gave Scriptural authority to the Roman doctrine of Concomitance. In a good many passages the meaning was made clearer, and some small misleadings, such as "Jesus" for "Joshua" in Romans iv. 8, and "robbery" for "prize" in Phil. ii. 6, were set right. But, broadly speaking, the New Testament remained, as regards its meaning, what it had been before.

As regards its meaning, I say, for in point of language the change was disastrous. The Revisers knew a great deal of Greek, but they knew uncommonly little English. The method of voting on this word or that did not conduce to perfection of style; and the Revision, as soon as it appeared, made it clear to all who read dispassionately that, whatever else had assisted at its birth, the sense of literary beauty had been conspicuously absent.

The first attack on the Revised New Testament was made by J. W. Burgon, Dean of Chichester, in a pungent treatise called "The Revision Revised," and the Dean secured an unexpected ally in Matthew Arnold. Founding himself on Goethe's theory that "the beautiful is a manifestation of secret laws of nature, which, but for its apparition, would have for ever remained hidden from us," Arnold impeached the literary sense of the Revisers in some persuasive passages which may be here condensed. He spoke, not of the "Authorized," but more aptly of the "Established," Version, and of this he said:

"It comes to us from an age of singular power, and has great beauty. This beauty is a source of great power. Use and wont have further added to the power of this beauty by attaching to the old version a thousand sentiments and associations. Altogether, a force of the utmost magnitude has come into being. The Revisers seem to have been insufficiently aware either of the nature of this force or of its importance and value. They too much proceeded either as if they had the recipe, if they broke up the force of beauty and sentiment attaching to the old version, for producing this force afresh themselves, or else as if the force was a matter of no great importance. In either case they are mistaken. The beauty of the old version is 'a manifestation of *secret* laws of nature,' and neither the Revisers, nor any of us, can be sure of finding the recipe, if we destroy this manifestation, for compounding another as good. And, if we think that its beauty does not much matter, than we have nature against us, for a manifestation of beauty is a manifestation of laws of *nature*."

Then, turning to Burgon's criticism, Arnold praises him for having chosen a "Test-passage" by which the literary merits of the old and the new version can be suitably compared. We are to take three verses from the Second Epistle of St Peter as they stand in the old version :

"And beside this, giving all diligence, add to your faith, virtue ; and to virtue, knowledge ; and to knowledge, temperance ; and to temperance, patience ; and to patience, godliness ; and to godliness, brotherly kindness ; and to brotherly kindness, charity."

Against this, says Arnold, let us set the work of the Revisers :

"Yea, and for this very cause adding on your part all diligence, in your faith supply virtue; and in your virtue knowledge; and in your knowledge temperance; and in your temperance patience; and in your patience godliness; and in your godliness love of the brethren; and in your love of the brethren love."

By merely placing these versions side by side, said Arnold, we have done enough to condemn the Revised Version as a substitute for the old version. We see, by a startling example, how it has not the power of beauty and sentiment attaching to the old version, and can never have it. The instinct of self-preservation in humanity will make us retain the old version, which has this power. "If by an act of authority the new version could be made to supersede the old, and the old to go out of use, a blow would be struck at Religion in this country far more dangerous than the hindrances with which it has to contend now—Beer-shops, Dissent, Ritualism, the Salvation Army, and the rest of the long and sad list. The new enemy would be indifference; an ever-growing indifference to a New Testament which failed to delight and move men like the old and to fix its phrases in their memory."

I have put these words in inverted commas because I do not wish to be responsible for that curious list of the hindrances to Religion; but in the literary judgment I entirely concur. The Revisers were led away by a very natural desire to correct all the mistakes of the old version, and to make a version which should be perfectly accurate. When once one is engaged, indeed, in a task like that of the Revisers, the desire to alter is sure to grow upon one as one proceeds, until at last one is capable of forgetting that even "the aorist was made for man, and not man for the aorist," and of waging against the past tenses of the old version an often pedantic war. To have fallen into this course of proceeding is so natural that we must by no means make it a matter of reproach against the Revisers; but it remains none the less true that, only by resisting the impulse to alter, by never forgetting that the object in view was not to make a perfectly accurate translation, but to preserve unimpaired the force of beauty and sentiment residing in the old version, at the same time that one made such corrections as were indeed necessary—only by submitting to these conditions was real success possible to the Revisers.

As it is, they produced a work excellently fitted to help and instruct in reading the New Testament all who do not know Greek—a work which in this way is of invaluable usefulness, and from which every reader probably imports, for his own use, into his New Testament such corrections as seem to him urgently needed. But they did not do that which they were meant to do: they did not give us a version which is just the old version improved and which can take the place of it. " In fact, a second company of Revisers is now needed to go through the recent Revision, and to decide what of it ought to be imported into the Established Version and with what modifications."

In the foregoing chapter I have quoted the more freely from Matthew Arnold, because his strictures on the Revised Version, originally published in a Review, were not reprinted.

XXXIX

THE ORDER OF MERIT

AMONG the minor arts which the modern world has lost is that of inventing graceful and expressive titles for National institutions. For example, in the days when our English speech was forming itself into its majestic sounds and sequences, the Sovereign's troops were commanded by his Earl-Marshal. To-day they are directed by "Military and Civil Members" of an "Army Council." When England first became the Sovereign of the Seas, she thundered her commands through the mouth of a Lord High Admiral; to-day she speaks (and, as we have lately seen, not always wisely) through a "Board." The Court of King's Bench and the Court of Common Pleas were high-sounding titles which told their own tale; now they are merely "Divisions" of a clumsily-named whole. The Court of Star Chamber and the Court of High Commission, however objectionable from the Constitutional point of view, were better-sounding institutions than the Divorce Court and the Bankruptcy Court. Even if we put aside, as alien in their origin, such majestic appellations as the Order of St John of Jerusalem and the Holy Order of the Temple of Zion, still our indigenous Order of the Garter and its Northern analogue, the Order of the Thistle, conveyed by their very sound something of symbolism and romance. Our modern attempt in the same direction is that triumph of commonplace—"The Distinguished Service Order." Scarcely more felicitous is the title of the society about which I write to-day—"The Order of Merit."

To begin with, it is borrowed. An "Order of Merit"—as far as History goes, *the* Order of Merit—was founded by Frederick the Great in 1740; and the name was copied in turn by Hesse Cassel, Baden, Bavaria, Saxony, Oldenburg, Würtemberg, and Belgium. We come in eighth; and surely we might have been first, with some better invention of our own. The Order *of Merit*—I italicize those two words. What, then, are the other Orders? The antithesis between Merit and Demerit is painfully obvious; and Orders which are not "of Merit" would appear to the unsophisticated to be badges of Dishonour. This unhappily-named company was instituted by King Edward VII. in 1902; and, as Dryasdust in a treatise on Orders justly remarks, "it occupies a very anomalous position, conferring no precedence. It is designed as a special distinction for men eminent in any department whatever—war, science, literature, or art—without in itself conferring the honour of Knighthood." It is limited in number to twenty-four, with the addition of some foreigners as Honorary Members; and its badge is a deformed cross of red and blue enamel, with the words, "For

Merit" in letters of gold, encircled by a wreath of laurel.

Though I have spoken disparagingly of the title of the Order, let me speak with all due respect of those who compose it, and more particularly of one whose name will presently appear. Mine is not the lore which enables a writer to appraise the respective merits of soldiers. My own view of war is expressed in the great sermon preached by Sydney Smith on the Accession of Queen Victoria: "Let fools praise Conquerors, and say the Great Napoleon pulled down this Kingdom and destroyed that Army. . . . The atrocities, and horrors, and disgusts of war have never been half enough insisted on by the teachers of the people; but the worst of evils and the greatest of follies have been varnished over with specious names, and the gigantic robbers and murderers of the world have been holden up, for their imitation, to the weak eyes of Youth."

Wordsworth, indeed, taught us that the Happy Warrior,

> "Though doomed to go in company with Pain
> And Fear and Bloodshed—miserable train,—
> Turns his necessity to glorious gain,"

and that,

> "As more exposed to suffering and distress,"

he is "also more alive to tenderness." We will hope, for the honour of England, that the Generals who wear the Order of Merit are "Happy Warriors" in

Wordsworth's sense; and certainly I see among the sailors who wear it the name of one " Mighty Seaman, tender and true," as " pure " as Nelson himself " from taint of craven guile." Still, I must confess that I feel more at home in eulogizing more pacific members of the Order. Lord Lister, by his antiseptic discoveries, has done a good deal more for the happiness of the world than any General who ever drew a sword. Lord Morley, unless I am much mistaken, is the greatest master of English prose now living; and, when the Order was constituted, it contained the not less illustrious name of George Meredith. " Meredith," said Oscar Wilde, " is a prose-Browning—and so is Browning"—thereby giving deadly offence to a vast number of worthy people who honestly believe that " The Ring and the Book " is poetry. To-day no poet is included in the Order of Merit; and, when we think what might have happened, we bless the influence which guided King Edward's hand. But Painting is doubly represented in the Order, and by the inclusion of Mr Holman Hunt due honour was rendered to our highest achievement in spiritual art. It is in accordance with the tendency of modern feeling that Science should be rather over-represented. Administration is honoured in Lord Cromer; Learning in Professor Henry Jackson; and a mixture of the two in Mr Bryce; but the most interesting name of all comes last.

When the List of the Order was originally published, my first exclamation was: "They have forgotten Miss Nightingale!" It is said that the advisers of the Crown believed that the most illustrious woman of her time was dead, and the ignorant error was only tardily repaired. Florence Nightingale was born at Florence in 1820. She was the daughter of a country gentleman who lived on the borders of Hampshire and Wiltshire, and this accident of neighbourhood made her early acquainted with the admirable Sidney Herbert, who lived at Wilton and was Secretary for War during the Crimean campaign. England was horrified by heart-rending accounts of the needless tortures inflicted on our wounded soldiers by unskilled nursing, and in October 1854, Sidney Herbert determined to despatch a body of trained nurses to the Crimea, placing them under the control of a properly authorized Head who should be responsible both to the medical authorities on the spot and to the Imperial Government at home. But who was fit for this all-important command? In a moment of happy inspiration, he bethought himself of his neighbour Miss Florence Nightingale, who had already made a special study of the art and science of nursing, and combined an enthusiastic love of the work with a strong will and a masterful character. "There is but one person in England that I know of who would be capable of organizing and superintending such a scheme"—so wrote Sidney Herbert to Miss Nightingale. "Would you listen to the request to go out and supervise the whole thing ?" The consent was promptly given, and a week later Miss Nightingale was on her way to the Crimea, "as a recognized official, under whose authority all female nurses in the military hospitals were placed, and on whose recommendation alone they were for the future to be admitted." On the 15th of November an eye-witness of her work wrote thus from Scutari: "Her nerve is equal to her good sense; she, with one of the nurses, gave efficient aid at an amputation of the thigh yesterday. She was just as cool as if she had to do it herself." Another wrote: "In one week Florence Nightingale has gained the confidence of all; the doctors do her will, and the Relief Fund has poured its Cornucopia into her lap."

But this was merely a beginning. Before many months were over she had revolutionized the whole system of the Hospitals, and had in effect created the modern conception of Sick Nursing. And she was no mere theorist. She bore her full share in the physical labours of the wards, and she paid the penalty in fifty years of crippled activity and enfeebled health. Her nightly walk, lamp in hand, along four miles of hospital-beds, "not eighteen inches apart," is a vision which has permanently stamped itself upon English memories. Henry Kingsley described it thus, in his fine tale of "Ravenshoe." His hero, Charles Ravenshoe, is wounded in the charge of Balaclava, and slowly returns to life in the hospital at Scutari:

"Till the last, there was one effect of light and shadow which he always lay awake to see—a faint flickering on the walls and roof, which came slowly nearer, till a light was in his eyes. We all know what that was. It has been described twenty times. I can believe the story of the dying man kissing the shadow on the wall. When Miss Nightingale and her lamp are forgotten, it will be time to consider whether one would prefer to turn Turk or Mormon."

In January 1855 Lord Houghton, who had been a friend of Miss Nightingale from her childhood, thus reported the testimony of a visitor to Scutari: "He says that Florence in the Hospital makes quite intelligible to him the saints of the Middle Ages. If the soldiers were told that the roof had opened, and she had gone up palpably to Heaven, they would not be the least surprised. They quite believe she is in several places at once."

In the following autumn Houghton published in *The Times* a poem called "A Monument at Scutari," from which I extract one striking verse:

"Write that, when pride of human skill
Fell prostrate with the weight of care,
And men prayed out for some strong will,
Some reason 'mid the wild despair,
The loving heart of Woman rose
To guide the hand and clear the eye,
Gave help amid the sternest woes,
And saved what man had left to die."

On this Mr Gladstone characteristically wrote: "It did not enter into your work as a poet; but I wish some one of the thousands who in prose justly celebrate Miss Nightingale would say a single word for the man of 'routine' who devised and projected her going—Sidney Herbert."

. . . .

I had written thus far when I heard that the most illustrious member of the Order of Merit had passed to her reward. And, in order that her fame may be transmitted from generation to generation, let us make our childish friends bring a box of ivory letters; and, when they have heard the story of those lamp-lit walks along the wards of Scutari, let them take the letters which make "Florence Nightingale" and rearrange them thus: "Flit on, cheering Angel." Then they will see that an Anagram is not always such a silly thing as it seems to be.

XL

PAIN

"MEANWHILE, a young student of medicine was embarking on that mysterious voyage of discovery which in the end gave him mastery over human pain." Elsewhere I have written those words in connexion with the history of Edinburgh in the earlier part of the nineteenth century, and of course I was referring to Sir James Simpson, who was born on the 7th of June 1811. Here again is an omitted centenary, and here again, as in the case of Mrs Beecher-Stowe, the competitive excitements of last season must be held responsible. Now let me try to make amends.

The 4th of November 1847 was the birthday of chloroform; for on that day Simpson first subjected himself to the power which he had created or invented, and by so doing lifted for ever a great load of anguish from the tortured nerves of a groaning and travailing creation. Beyond doubt Simpson deserves a place—perhaps he has it—in the Positivist's Kalendar of Worthies. Women in particular should make pilgrimages of gratitude to his grave; and everyone who to-day obtains relief through the Röntgen Rays must admire the genius of the man who first realized them as possible.

The invention of anæsthetics was called by a great divine " God's best blessing to a much-blessed age," and I imagine that a huge majority of people would agree with him. Pain—I mean physical pain—is generally regarded as the greatest of evils, and as one of the most perplexing elements in the insoluble problem of the existence of evil. When the advocates of Euthanasia seek a justification for their doctrine, they generally look for it in the unbearableness of pain. Even our great Sir Thomas More, a man as brave as he was devout, represented the Ministers of Religion in his Utopia as exhorting the sufferer to self-deliverance. " When any is taken with a torturing and lingering pain, so that there is no hope either of recovery or end, the priests and magistrates come and exhort them . . . that they should no longer nourish such a rooted distemper, but should choose rather to die, since they cannot live but in much misery." It is to be noted that the pain, which is here held to justify self-destruction, is purely physical. Moral pain, such as the pain of despair or the pain of remorse—even perhaps the pain of shame—is to a finely-touched nature far more terrible than anything which can befall the body; and yet the advocates of Euthanasia seem to hold that this kind of pain must be endured.

> "When all the blandishments from life are gone,
> The coward slinks to death—the brave live on."

The coward slinks to death. This seems a hard

saying, when one tries to picture the moral agony which has so often driven its victims to self-slaughter.

But, putting moral agony on one side and considering only the sensations of the body, one may reasonably ask oneself if physical pain is really the supreme evil which most men think it. *Securus judicat orbis terrarum.* There is a strong presumption that what all mankind thinks is true. No one, I suppose, could say, with any chance of being believed, that he enjoyed pain. Everyone must admit that he dislikes it, and would avoid it by all methods against which "The Everlasting" has not "fixed His canon." And yet I believe that, even as regards the experiences of the body, there are worse things than pain. One of these is the sense of impending suffocation. When the breath of life is at its last gasp, mankind is indeed unmanned. Miss Nightingale used to say that soldiers in the Crimea who, anæsthetics being scarce, would lie without flinching under the surgeon's knife, the moment their breathing became impeded began to crave for help like terrified children. I believe that it is the sense of breathlessness, far more than the agony of the spasm, which makes the horror of *Angina Pectoris*, or "Suffocative Breast-pang," as our forefathers called it. It is the frantic struggle for air which, in a panic-stricken crowd, turns men into beasts, and impels the strong to trample out their way over the bodies of the weak and the fallen. One of the most religious men I ever knew, just recovering from a nearly fatal paroxysm, once said to me: "Don't put off your business, temporal or spiritual, till you are dying of cardiac asthma. You will have quite enough to do in wondering whether you can ever draw another breath in this world."

So much for suffocation. Another evil, worse, to my thinking, than pain, is approaching collapse. It was described by Cardinal Newman in a passage of Dantesque impressiveness:

> "I can no more; for now it comes again,
> That sense of ruin, which is worse than pain—
> That masterful negation and collapse
> Of all that makes me man."

To feel the earth subsiding under one—all the supports and stays of one's physical existence failing—all human assistances slipping away—and oneself, as it were, disembodied and disappearing—that is an experience compared to which the keenest pain is bliss. "Deeper," cried Johnson to the surgeon who was operating on his swollen leg. "Deeper! I want length of life, and you are afraid of giving me pain, which I do not value."

It would be absurd and affected to speak of the charms, or even the merits, of pain. But one may, without offending against rationality, speak of its uses. It is one of the realities of life—perhaps the most unquestionable reality of the physical life—as real in its own domain as Conscience in the moral sphere. And, being thus real itself, it has a singular power of producing reality in those whom it touches.

In our colloquial but excellent phrase, it "brings a man to himself." Pain makes the incessant joker grave, and the incessant boaster modest. Under pain, flippancy gives place to seriousness. Under pain, an assumed character is laid aside, or, rather, drops off of its own accord. Disturbed by pain, a feigned amiability reveals a disagreeable temper; an acted bravery discloses a deep-seated cowardice. Arrogant self-reliance is replaced by a clinging dependence; and, in brief, the man is seen for what he really is. Dickens caught this truth when he described the relations between the fashionable Physician in "Little Dorrit" and his patients. "People said to themselves, whether they were conscious of it or no, 'Here is a man who really has an acquaintance with us as we are, who is admitted to some of us every day with our wigs and paint off, who hears the wanderings of our minds, and sees the undisguised expression of our faces, when both are past our control; we may as well make an approach to reality with him, for the man has got the better of us and is too strong for us.'"

The reality of pain has another effect which is often extremely salutary. It is a cure for nonsensical imaginations. A neurotic undergraduate, overworked and perhaps over-stimulated, begins, as his friends would say, to "see Bogey." He becomes morbidly introspective. He "gets outside himself." Like Kenelm Chillingly, he is "overwhelmed by a consciousness of his own identity." He grows so over-attentive to his own mental processes, so hyper-sensitive to every subjective impression, that his mind becomes useless for any practical purpose, and, when he ought to be grappling with his books, he is wearing himself and his friends to tatters with psychological questionings. All the time he is neglecting his health, and inviting some definite illness which presently catches hold of him. Then, writhing in the grip of rheumatic fever or appendicitis, he "comes to himself" with remarkable speed. Phantasmal metaphysics are all very well in their way, but this pain is a reality which there is no gainsaying. Even an abscess at the root of a tooth will serve to convince a man of his own personality. I myself, I —Tom Smith and no other—am throbbing and shuddering. Bishop Berkeley himself, in like case, would believe in the Reality of Matter. Only just lately I read, in a rather morbid journal of religious experience, this grotesque but instructive passage:

"Just as I was going to bed last night, I scalded my sound foot in attempting to foment the sprained. The pain at first was agonizing and, having no dear wife to sympathize with me, it *individualized* me remarkably."

Such, as I believe, are some of the uses of pain. If I were to enumerate its other uses, as, for example, when it is penally applied in schools and gaols, I should only be inviting controversy. But how about

Anæsthesia? That some, perhaps most, people believe it to be the greatest of earthly boons we have already seen. If we were confronted by a vital operation, I suppose that we should all desire it. But there are a good many people who would infinitely rather undergo a very considerable amount of acute pain. They shrink from the loss of self-control; they dread the notion, for it cannot be called a sense, of utter helplessness; above all they feel, as was once quaintly said to me, that to take an anæsthetic is to go on a long journey, not feeling at all sure that we have got a return-ticket. To lose consciousness, even for a moment, is a suspension of existence which not everyone can contemplate with equanimity.

Of course, I am only theorizing, and that from very imperfect knowledge; doctors could tell one the fact, but my strong impression is that the reluctance to part with consciousness and self-mastery is far more prevalent among men than among women. Women were the most eager to welcome Simpson's great discovery, and by their persistence they overcame the objection strangely raised by a perverted theology against the employment of chloroform in their peculiar need. The readiness of women—not so great, I suppose, now as in former years—to escape from difficulty or distress by the transient anæsthesia of fainting, points in the same direction. One could easily make the observation ridiculous by culling instances, as Macaulay culled them, of fainting-fits in old-fashioned fiction; but it is remarkable that

Mrs Gaskell, of all novelists the most sane and the closest observer of female character, seems to regard this tendency to temporary unconsciousness as a fixed feature of woman's life. Even when the fainting does not happen, the woman longs for it. At one of the most pathetic passages in the wonderful story of "Ruth," we read that "she would have been thankful for the unconsciousness of fainting; for that one little speech of her son's bore so much meaning to her hot, irritable brain."

But I shall probably be told that there are ways of escape from pain besides anæsthetics and fainting-fits. Some will recommend Christian Science, some Faith-healing, some Hypnotic Suggestion, and some the methods prescribed by St James. Here are abundant materials for another chapter, but I am by no means sure that I am the man to write it.

XLI

HEAD MASTERS

"I WANT to know all about Head Masters, *and especially your own.*"

Breathes there the man with soul so dead, who could be insensible to that appeal, with its graceful insinuation that the mind which formed my own must indeed have been a creative marvel? Let Head Masters then supply the theme of our present meditation, and we will begin with a member of the profession who paid Sir Henry Irving and Miss Terry the most remarkable compliment which they ever received. He invited those great artists to give a Shakespeare Recitation before his boys. In making the arrangements, Sir Henry said that the pieces selected would take about two hours in delivery, so he and Miss Terry must ask for a quarter of an hour's interval in the middle. "Oh! yes," replied the Head Master genially, "of course. One couldn't expect the boys to stand two hours of it straight on end." *It!* But, though some Head Masters are thus bereft of humour, others possess it in abundance, and exercise it—not on the boys, for that would be brutal, but on the parents, who are fair game. "You will find," wrote an anxious mother, "that my boy's temperament is such that he requires a peculiar mixture of strength and tenderness." "Dear Madam," replied the Doctor, "you have chosen the right school for your boy. I supply the strength, and the boys do the tenderness." A purse-proud lady of the middle class wrote to a Head Master that she was thinking of placing her son at his school, but, before doing so, she must ask if he was very particular about the social antecedents of the boys whom he admitted. *Reply.* "Dear Madam, as long as your boy behaves decently and his fees are paid regularly, no questions will be asked about his social antecedents."

These cases are perhaps more or less mythical; but when we come to actual names, Dr Arnold of Rugby always seems to tower a head and shoulders above the rest of his kind; but of him enough and to spare has been written by better pens than mine. His son Matthew glorified him in poetry, Dean Stanley in biography, and Tom Hughes in fiction. The terror which he inspired in evil-doers was well expressed by the nickname of "Tiger Tom"; and Dr Bright used to describe, with vivid dramatization, the scene in the Sixth Form Room at Rugby, when the Doctor had been thundering against some puerile iniquity, and, looking suddenly round, caught his eldest son smiling sweetly at the other boys from behind his chair. "Then the black vein which we knew so well came out on his forehead, and he exclaimed, 'You'd better mind what you're doing, Mat,'" in a tone before which superciliousness fled away abashed.

But, great as Arnold was, Rugby men (and I know that among my readers they abound) should never forget his successor, Dr Goulburn, who, seeking an illustration for his sermon from the process of mining, said, "If I descend into the bowels of the earth in a pendulous basket," and who thus instructed his hearers in the art of chaffing: "Let your pleasantry, my younger friends, be as the coruscation of the summer lightning, lambent yet innocuous." Of quite a different type was Arnold's predecessor, Dr Wooll, who, though diminutive in stature, was so formidable in flagellation that he gave a new sense to the proverbial saying, "Much cry and little wool." As all roads lead to Rome, so all stories of flagellant Head Masters lead to Eton and Dr Keate. Mr Gladstone used in moments of paradox to affirm that no man was truly an Etonian who had not been flogged by Keate. The exploits which that modern Orbilius performed in a single night form a chapter in Eton history, as vivid as "L'Histoire d'un Crime." His persistency in flogging a batch of boys who had been sent to him to be prepared for Confirmation, and telling them that they might explain afterwards, was, as they say, worthy of a better cause.

But Eton had no monopoly of these disciplinary honours. I am writing this on Waterloo Day; and the only Waterloo man whom I ever knew personally —the sixth Lord Albemarle—thus describes his

Head Master at Westminster, Dr Page. "'Pageque furore gravis' was the conclusion of an epigram on the staff at Westminster, and the epithet was not ill applied to the Head Master. With a more savage, ill-tempered man I have seldom come in contact. The great Dr Busby used to assert that the rod was the proper instrument for sifting the wheat of learning from the chaff. Dr Page was, so far, of the Busby school, and unfortunately for me I was that description of grain that frequently required this species of winnowing." It is notoriously dangerous for an outsider to meddle with the discipline of Winchester, for, as the victim of the "good and gentle boy" learned to his cost in 1872, it is mysterious and complicated in no common degree. Before now I have incurred Wiccamical correction, so to-day I confine myself to referring my readers to Mr A. F. Leach's "History of Winchester" for a lifelike portrait of Dr Moberly, and the artful way in which, by affecting the airs of the stricken old man, he disguised the severity of impending punishment. I give on my own personal authority —for I have read it in a book of sermons—this remarkable exordium of Dr Ridding, Moberly's successor at Winchester, and afterwards Bishop of Southwell: "I feel a feeling which I feel you all feel." The man who could write that sentence, read it in proof, and pass it for the press was indeed a hero.

The Founder of Harrow School was a man of

remarkable humanity, considering the time in which he lived; for he decreed that "The Schoolmaster shall use no other kind of correction save the rod moderately, except it be a very thin ferula on the hand for a light negligence." But, in dealing with boys, the virtue of clemency may be carried to a point at which it produces lawlessness; and surely that point was reached when Dr Longley, afterwards Archbishop of Canterbury, was Head Master of Harrow. For generations before his time the Harrow boys had played on winter evenings a magnificent game called "Jack o' Lantern," which was a kind of nocturnal Hare-and-Hounds. The Hare, or "Jack," carried a lantern strapped to his waist, and the great object was to entice the Hounds, "through bush, through brier," into some pool or ditch which "Jack" himself had avoided. This game, though capital fun for the boys, was a very bad joke for the farmers, who found their hedges broken down and their poultry-yards not seldom pillaged; so they complained to the Head Master, and "Jack o' Lantern" was forbidden. Still some of the more adventurous spirits used to get out of window after locking-up and pursue their favourite recreation under cover of darkness. One night Dr Longley was walking in his garden, when he saw a rope dangling from the window of a boy's room. He gave a gentle pull, the rope was tugged up, and the Doctor's comely face—even then unruffled—rose to the level of the window. "Longley, by Jove!" was the cry; the rope was dropped, and the Head Master sank gracefully into his laurel-bushes. The crime remains to this day unexpiated.

Dr Longley, leaving Harrow to become Bishop of Ripon, was succeeded by Christopher Wordsworth, afterwards Bishop of Lincoln, under whose administration things went from bad to worse. In 1845 Wordsworth made way for the youthful Vaughan, who beyond most men combined softness of speech with decisiveness of action. Wordsworth left a servant in the Head Master's House to go through the fixtures with the new Head Master. Everything seemed to be in order, except the fan-light over the front door, in which there was a large hole. Very gently Vaughan pointed out the defect, and presumed that it had been overlooked. "Oh! no, sir. That's all right. The young gentlemen always break that light, so the Doctor doesn't have it mended." I fancy that they did not break it very often when it belonged to Dr Vaughan.

Besides being a great Head Master, and raising a school from seventy to four hundred, Vaughan was in many respects one of the most remarkable men I ever knew, and it is a thousand pities that he prohibited, in his will, any attempt to write his Life. I know the reason for that prohibition; and I should not dream of disregarding it, except in the slight and ephemeral form which this chapter affords. Charles John Vaughan (1816-1897) was son of the Vicar of St Martin's, Leicester. He was educated at Rugby, and was a favourite pupil of Arnold. He was a natural-born scholar. By his own request, as he told me, he learned the Greek alphabet on his seventh birthday, and it was said in after life that he " thought in Greek." The exquisite precision, point, and flexibility of his English style were probably due to his early and absolute mastery of the most perfect instrument by which human thought has ever been expressed. He was Senior Classic (bracketed with Lord Lyttelton) and Chancellor's Medallist in 1838, and in due course became Fellow of Trinity. In early life he had destined himself for the Chancery Bar, and his contemporaries regarded him as a certain Lord Chancellor; but other counsels prevailed. He took Holy Orders, became Vicar of his father's church at Leicester, and at the age of twenty-eight was elected Head Master of Harrow. The school, when he came to it, was in ruins; after fifteen years he left it overflowing in numbers and abounding in prosperity. The secret of his success was not obvious on the surface. His acquaintance with literature began and ended with the classics. " He is a good creature, but brutally ignorant," was the characteristic judgment of his school-fellow, Matthew Arnold. He had no gifts of oratory, no florid rhetoric; his utterance was mincing, his manner rather unctuous; his smile much more terrible than his frown; and his most conspicuous endowment—an exquisite gift of personal sarcasm—was calculated to make boys hate rather than love him. Yet, as a matter of fact, he was loved, admired, and revered by boys who were, and young men who had been, his pupils, almost to the point of idolatry. His tact, his humour, his beauty of face, and his almost uncanny insight into boy-nature, must have been leading elements in his power; but perhaps that power can be best appreciated by those who know his "Memorials of Harrow Sundays"—a book of sermons dedicated "to those who, in the former or the present Chapel of Harrow School, within the last fifteen years have listened and worshipped."

Vaughan left Harrow at the end of 1859. He was succeeded by his favourite pupil, Henry Montagu Butler, now Master of Trinity College, Cambridge. There was a time when the initials "H. M. B." were to me far more awe-inspiring than "F.R.S.," more conclusive than "Q.E.D." Lovers of "Tom Brown" will remember the scene, near the end of the book, where Tom, on a fishing-tour with some undergraduate friends, suddenly learns that Dr Arnold is dead. As he strides away, struggling with his emotion, one of his companions says to the other, "I'm afraid that confounded newspaper has spoiled Brown's fun for this trip," and the other replies, "How odd that he should be so fond of his old Master!" "Yet," remarks the author, "they also were both Public School men." This passage relates to the year 1842, and perhaps it is not so odd that men in general were not very fond of the Head Masters who had adorned the previous decade. But the age of Vaughan and Butler and Hornby and Temple and Ridding and Percival and Bradley and Farrar produced a different tone, and it became a sort of fashion —sometimes excessive—to admire one's Head Master, and to credit him with several imaginary graces and virtues, in addition to those which he might justly claim. Thus, if the Head was proverbial for rudeness, the defect was called by his disciples Rugged Honesty; if he had a savage temper, he was said to be a Vigorous Disciplinarian. If he was too ignorant to teach his Sixth Form, or too lazy to write his own letters, he was credited with a remarkable faculty for Organization; and, if he was conspicuously and even laughably ignorant of boy-nature, enthusiasts cried, "What a crystal soul! Like Charity, he can believe no evil." An inborn predisposition towards criticism preserved the present writer from the worst excesses of Pædagogolatry; yet he, too, has felt the spell.

Henry Montagu Butler, youngest son of Dr George Butler, Dean of Peterborough and sometime Head Master of Harrow, was born in 1833. He was educated at Harrow under Dr Vaughan, and, besides being Head of the School and winning every prize and scholarship worth having, made the highest score in the match against Eton at Lord's. He was indeed the Ideal Schoolboy, as Plato might have conceived him, but as he is seldom seen on this terrestrial sphere. At Cambridge he was Scholar of Trinity, Bell University Scholar, and Battie University Scholar; and won the Browne Medal twice, the Camden Medal, the Porson Prize, and the Members' Prize. Cambridge men will know more accurately than I can what these names import; but everyone knows what it meant to be Senior Classic and Fellow of Trinity. And here it may be remarked that, himself a Senior Classic, Dr Butler was married to a Senior Classic by a Senior Classic, with a Senior Classic as Best Man, and is now father of the nearest approach to a Senior Classic that the modern regulations of the Classical Tripos allow. Mr Oscar Browning has recently told us in his Autobiography that Freshmen of his year, looking with reverent curiosity for the famous Montagu Butler, were told that the object of their quest was "a man with happiness running out of every corner of his face"; and truly he had a good deal to make him happy. Recalling him as he was in those distant days, Sir George Trevelyan once told me that no one else seemed so absolutely to "have the ball at his feet." From Cambridge, Montagu Butler went up to London, and acted for two years as Private Secretary to Lord Mount Temple, then Mr W. Cowper and President of the Board of Health. When his chief left office, Butler returned to Cambridge, and determined to seek Holy Orders on the title of his Fellowship; but before he had actually been ordained Dr Vaughan suddenly astonished everyone by resigning the Head Mastership of Harrow. Butler, then only just twenty-six years old, became a candidate for the vacant post, and was elected. He was ordained Deacon and Priest in rapid succession, and entered on his new duties in January 1860. It is to be observed that he did not, as some have since done, take Holy Orders in order to qualify for a Head Mastership; but had resolved to be a clergyman before there was the slightest prospect of Dr Vaughan's retirement.

When I entered Harrow School Dr Butler was still a young man, and looked even younger than he was. One's preconceived notion of a Head Master was something very solemn, venerable, and grim, if not ferocious. Instead of this I saw a nice-looking young man, with a pleasant smile, and the most graceful figure and bearing. Gracefulness was indeed his leading feature. He was graceful in thought and action, graceful in style, graceful, above all, in public speaking. He had an inborn faculty of eloquence, trained by care and practice to a high perfection. Furthermore, he was a most stimulating teacher, prompt to recognize the slightest symptom of literary taste, and generous in encouraging it. He was not indeed much troubled by ideas, or by the deeper problems of life and thought; but he had a natural affinity to all that was graceful in literature, ancient or modern, and a contagious enthusiasm in communicating it. His preaching in the School Chapel was quite admirable, simple yet polished; and the bow drawn at a venture often sped its arrow with singular directness. On social and festive occasions, he had none of that forced and false *bonhomie* which is so terrible to the young, but was as natural and easy as an elder brother. He genuinely enjoyed a joke ; but, instead of those thin tutorial jests which freeze the soul, he gave us things which were really worth remembering out of his capacious store. He had known a surprising number of interesting people ; he had travelled in Europe and Asia ; had ascended Monte Rosa, Mount Parnassus, and Mount Sinai ; could talk " Cricket-shop " like the Captain of the Eleven, and Politics (rather perverse ones) like the Prime Minister. But I should be giving a completely wrong, because one-sided, picture of Montagu Butler if I conveyed the notion that all this amenity, and even playfulness, were the accompaniments of a weak will and a flabby rule. Quite the reverse. He had, I fancy, by nature a passionate temper, which by strong self-mastery he had learnt to control. He was almost unduly tenacious of his authority ; but, when one remembers that several of his colleagues had been Masters at Harrow when he was a boy there, one can realize that some measure of self-assertion was necessary. In dealing with boys he was absolutely fair, but he suffered from what Bishop Wilson calls the " *offendiculum* of scrupulousness." He made too many rules, and was too much inclined to a " Chinese exactness " in enforcing them. Let one little instance suffice. He had a great dislike to the scratching of a quill-pen, and decreed that, when making notes on the lessons in the Sixth Form Room, we were all to use steel pens. One day, rushing up very late to school, I found that I had mislaid my wooden penholder; so I stuck my "magnum bonum" pen on a quill, and duly took my place near the Head Master's chair. Presently he saw the feather of the quill, and, by a natural process of self-deception, imagined that he could hear the detested scratching. "How often," he asked, with some irritation, "have I desired that you would NOT bring that dreadful quill into the room?" "I'm very sorry, sir. I could not find my pen-holder; but I am writing with a steel nib." *Tableau*—and triumph! During my last year at Harrow the townspeople got up some theatricals in order to raise a fund for a Cottage Hospital. Of course it was a great object to secure the attendance of the School, then more than five hundred strong; but Dr Butler very properly made it a condition that the pieces to be acted should be submitted to him before he gave the requisite permission. One of them was *The Palace of Truth*, and, at a critical point in the story, the hero said to the heroine: "Meet me outside the garden gate at nine o'clock to-night." Dr Butler ran his pen through the words, and substituted "at three o'clock this afternoon." Comment, as they say, is needless; but two or three years ago Sir William Gilbert was a guest at Harrow Speeches. In replying for the Visitors he said that it was with peculiar interest that he found himself at

Harrow, for it was the only place in the world where any line of his writing had ever been vetoed as indecorous. The other guests "looked at each other with a wild surmise"; everyone asked his neighbour what in the world was meant; and only one could answer.

But, after all, a meticulous care in the administration of his trust is the most venial fault which can be attributed to a Head Master; and in Dr Butler's case it was more than outbalanced by his splendid munificence, by his passionate love of Harrow, and by a loyal faithfulness in friendship which all the changes and chances in life are powerless to impair.

XLII

"YOUNG ENGLAND"

A FRIEND who has been studying Lord Beaconsfield's Political Novels suggests that I should write a chapter on "Young England"; and I gladly accept the suggestion, for I concur in the opinion that the movement which was called "Young England" and the men who figured in it ought not to be forgotten.

The General Election of 1841 placed the Tories in power and made Sir Robert Peel Prime Minister. Disraeli had entered Parliament in 1837. He described himself as a "humble but fervent follower" of Peel in Opposition; and, conscious of unique gifts and boundless ambition, he naturally expected office in the new administration. We now know that, as a matter of fact, he begged for the post of Secretary to the Admiralty; but Peel turned a deaf ear to his request. Disraeli, disappointed and revengeful, was a dangerous element in the Tory party. "Peel," says Froude, "among his magnificent qualities, had not the art of conciliating the rank-and-file of his supporters. He regarded them too much as his own creatures, entitled to no consideration. Disraeli met with rebuff after rebuff. He saw that for his own theories there was no hope of countenance from his present chief. He formed a small party among the younger Tory members—men of rank and talent, with a high-bred enthusiasm which had been kindled by the Church revival. A party including Lord John Manners, George Smythe, Henry Hope, and Baillie-Cochrane was not to be despised." This was the party which somehow acquired the title of "Young England." The leader, ruler, and inspiring genius of the group—Disraeli himself—was fond of such aphorisms as "It is a holy thing to see a Nation saved by its Youth," and "The Youth of a Nation are the Trustees of Posterity." He himself was now rather a mature youth, having been born in 1804, but his confederates were a good deal younger. Alexander Baillie-Cochrane, afterwards Lord Lamington, was born in 1816; Lord John Manners, afterwards Duke of Rutland, in 1818; and George Smythe, afterwards Lord Strangford, in the same year. With these were associated Peter Borthwick, who was as old as Disraeli himself; and, to a limited extent, Henry Hope, of Deepdene, and Richard Monckton Milnes, afterwards Lord Houghton, who were only four or five years younger. A letter of J. G. Lockhart, editor of *The Quarterly*, written in 1843, gives some amusing glimpses of the new party:

"P. Borthwick was a notorious man in the Scotch newspapers of 1822. B. Disraeli published his 'Vivian Grey'—the only work that has been at all successful—eighteen years ago, I am sure. He must be forty, or close on that. G. Smythe, Lord Strangford's son, very young—the cleverest of the set, I believe. Cochrane is, I suppose, five-and-twenty or thirty—has a good estate in Scotland through his mother. A little *notice* would have made him and Smythe all right. Disraeli and Borthwick are very necessitous, and wanted places, of course."

Even more characteristic is the judgment of Sir James Graham, then Home Secretary, who viewed this insurgent group of young and irresponsible Tories very much as, forty years later, Sir Stafford Northcote and Mr W. H. Smith viewed Lord Randolph Churchill and the "Fourth Party":

"With respect to 'Young England,' the puppets are moved by Disraeli, who is the ablest man among them: I consider him unprincipled and disappointed; and in despair he has tried the effect of bullying. I think with you that they will return to the *crib* after prancing, capering, and snorting; but a crack or two of the whip well applied may hasten and ensure their return. Disraeli alone is mischievous, and with him I have no desire to keep terms. It would be better for the Party if he were driven into the ranks of our open enemies."

Such were the personal elements of "Young England": its political creed may be gathered from the romances of Lord Beaconsfield and the poetry of Lord John Manners. In the first place, it is interesting to observe that, though all the members of "Young England" were members of the House of Commons, they professed very scant respect for the Chamber in which they sate. Though they wisely kept aloof from Jacobitism and the "White Rose," they believed, so far as the belief is possible under the Hanoverian succession, that the Sovereign reigns by Divine Right, and not only reigns but rules. The personal authority of the Sovereign was a leading tenet of "Young England," and the more conspicuously it could be exercised the better they would be pleased. Next in their estimation came the House of Lords. The natural chiefs of England were the Aristocracy, and the owners of the soil were the stable element of the Constitution. Capitalists grew like mushrooms, and disappeared as rapidly; the owners of the land remained. Capital disfigured the beautiful face of "Merrie England" by creating "Hell-holes," like St Helens and Stalybridge. Capital ground the faces of the poor, and degraded human beings into "Hands," who were no better than slaves. And this touched the most creditable point in "Young England's" Creed. Theoretically, at any rate, it stood for the rights and dignity of Labour. The welfare of the great masses of the population was the foundation on which the Throne could be most securely built. An alliance between "The Monarch and the Multitude" was the most promising form of government; for it excluded the Manufacturers, the Middle Classes, and the Whigs who had so long masqueraded as the Friends of the People, and it gave ample scope for the activities of high-born and generous youths. "Young England" was to mediate, as it were, between the highest and the lowest, and to form a kind of connecting link between the Crown and the Peasantry. "Young England," while it adored the memory of "our martyred Charles," and stood for the extremest claims of an untrammelled Prerogative, was all for Good Wages and Short Hours of Work; Sanitary Reform and National Recreation; Public Holidays, May-Poles on Village Greens, Gothic Schools carefully tended by great ladies and Tractarian clergymen; and an undiscriminating liberality in almsgiving, which should drive the detested Poor Law into deserved oblivion.

A leading feature of "Young England" was faith in Religion and the Church. How far this faith was in Disraeli's case a genuine conviction and how far a counsel of expediency it skills not to enquire; but among his disciples it was a strong and abiding passion. It breathed in the chivalrous oratory of Lord John Manners (who founded, in conjunction with Mr Gladstone, the first Sisterhood in the Church of England) and in the graceful verse of Frederick Faber, who was the clerical ally of these political crusaders. Disraeli himself expressed it, with a curious mixture of belief and irony, in "Sybil," where a glorious Church and a devoted priest are the only alleviations to the barbarism of a manufacturing town; and in "Tancred," where a young aristocrat, seeking Divine guidance amid the political perplexities of the time, makes a Pilgrimage to the Holy Sepulchre.

But a creed without Apostles and Evangelists is naught; so in the Parliamentary recess of 1844 the emissaries of "Young England" spread themselves all over the Northern Counties, and, beginning at Manchester, preached this new and strange Gospel to the astonished manufacturers and operatives of Lancashire and Yorkshire.

Monckton Milnes observed these performances of his younger friends, some at least of whose opinions he shared, with a curious note of political jealousy. This is his judgment on "Young England": "It is a good phenomenon in its way, and one of its products—Lord John Manners—a very fine, promising fellow. The worst of them is that they are going about the country talking Education and Liberality, and getting immense honour for the very things for which the Radicals have been called all possible blackguards and Atheists a few years ago."

But, if the public imagination was to be impressed with the doctrines of the "Young Englanders," something more was required than paradoxical speeches in the House of Commons and flashy orations on provincial platforms; so Disraeli, who had already made some name for himself in fiction, resolved to cast the aspirations of "Young England" into the form of Political Novels. The first of these was "Coningsby," in which the hero renounces a political career and forfeits an inheritance (though both come right in the long run) because the modern Conservatism which he is asked to support is glaringly false to the historic traditions of Toryism. "The Crown was to keep its prerogatives, provided they were not exercised; the House of Lords might keep its independence, if it was never asserted; and the Church, if it was regulated by a Commission of Laymen." In this "organized hypocrisy" young Coningsby will have neither part nor lot, and he thus formulates the conditions under which alone he conceives that a Parliamentary career is even tolerable: "Let us see Authority once more honoured; a solemn reverence again the habit of our lives; let us see property acknowledging, as in the days of old, that labour is his twin-brother, and that the essence of all tenure is the performance of duty."

The second of the Political Novels was "Sybil." Its alternative title is "The Two Nations," and these two nations are the Rich and the Poor. The story shows, in effective contrast to the luxury and splendour of the great, the loathsome squalor and wretchedness of a manufacturing town uncommonly like Sheffield; the ignorance and viciousness of the workers; the hardships perpetuated under the new Poor Law; and the dull indifference of the Conservative Government. It justifies—nay, glorifies—the most desperate efforts of Chartism; but it concludes with "a whisper rising in this country that Loyalty is not a phrase, Faith not a delusion, and Popular Liberty something more diffusive and substantial than the profane exercise of the sacred rights of Sovereignty by political classes."

The third book of the Trilogy is "Tancred," at which I have already glanced. "I go," says the hero, just as he is starting for Palestine—"I go to a land that has never been blessed by that fatal drollery called a Representative Government, though Omniscience once deigned to trace out the polity which should rule it." And with that most characteristic sentence we must leave "Young England." The movement came to naught. It was partly laughed out of existence by *Punch* and Thackeray, partly crushed in its unequal encounter with the "Manchester School" and the Ten-Pound Householder. Commercialism, Utilitarianism, Unrestricted Competition, and "The Devil take the hindmost" were the dominant ideas of the Forties. Against these "Young England" made its romantic but ineffectual protest. The Crown, the Church, and the Aristocracy—the three main objects of its worship—all seemed more embarrassed than gratified by the zeal of their devotees; and "Young England" perished, as romantic adventures are apt to perish, in its heroic assault on the impregnable fortress of British Philistinism. So much for the movement; it may be not uninteresting to trace the careers of the Men.

> "How patient of inevitable ill,
> Yet how determinate in their righteous will!"

This was Lord Houghton's description of the English people, at a crisis when their patience had been strained to bursting-point. Towards the year 1845 Englishmen were awakening to the fact that a great part of the "ill" under which they laboured was in no sense "inevitable," but was the direct consequence of laws which made their principal form of food dear and difficult to procure, even when Nature and Providence supplied it with the utmost bounty. The Anti-Corn Law League, working by an admirable organization, and speaking by the mouths of Bright and Cobden, drove the lesson home to the intelligence of their countrymen, well prepared for it by the sharp discipline of physical privation. This agitation had now been in progress for some ten years, and for the moment it seemed to be losing energy. A series of good harvests had rendered the evils of restrictive legislation more endurable, and Sir Robert Peel closed the session of 1845 with an overwhelming majority in both Houses. But—and here I quote from the creator of "Young England" himself—"one fine day in August, Parliament having just been prorogued, an unknown dealer in potatoes wrote to the Secretary of State, and informed him that he had reason to think that a murrain had fallen over the whole of the potato-crops in England, and that if it extended to Ireland the most serious consequences must ensue. This mysterious but universal sickness of a single root changed the history of the world." In more moderate language, it caused the repeal of the Corn Laws.

At the close of 1845 Peel announced his conversion to the policy of Free Trade in corn, and by so doing rent his party in twain. Now Disraeli's time had come. He saw an opportunity of avenging himself on the Leader who, as he thought, had wronged and humiliated him. He placed himself at the head of the disgusted and betrayed Protectionists. He denounced Peel's change of front, and assailed his political character, with the most biting and malignant satire; and, though the Repeal of the Corn Laws was carried on the 25th of June 1846, he contrived on the same day to defeat Peel on a Coercion Bill for Ireland, and by so doing drove him finally from office. Disraeli—the "Alien," the "Adventurer," the "Scrivener's Clerk," for so his enemies described him—became the Leader of the Conservative Party, and the day-dreams of "Young England" were forgotten.

Lord John Manners, by far the most attractive figure in the group—the "Lord Henry Sydney" of "Coningsby"—sate in Parliament, almost without a break, till he succeeded to the Dukedom of Rutland in 1888. Whenever the Tories were in power he had office, and he served in the Cabinet of his old leader, Lord Beaconsfield. He was a facile and graceful debater in Parliament, and, in private life, a most amiable, gracious, and high-bred gentleman. He held to the end the principles which had inspired

"Young England," and was alike in Church and State a cavalier of the type which J. H. Shorthouse loved to depict.

Probably the most brilliant member of "Young England," next to Disraeli, was George Smythe, the "Waldershare" of "Endymion." He was M.P. for Canterbury from 1841 to 1852, and his eloquence on the Hustings was renowned, but he made comparatively little mark in Parliament. His talents lay rather in the direction of literature. He was an active journalist on the Tory side, and a graceful and prolific writer on such topics as "the Grandeur of the Ancient Nobility of England and France; the days of Chivalry, of Catholic Kings and Cavaliers; and the picturesque splendour of ecclesiastical ceremonial." Before very long he parted company with his comrades in "Young England." When the battle of the Corn Laws broke out, he declared himself a Peelite and a Free Trader. In 1846 Peel made him Under Secretary for Foreign Affairs, but the ministry lasted only six months, and, when the Whigs returned to office, Smythe drifted away into a listless obscurity which was only broken by an absurd duel with his opponent after his last contest for Canterbury. He succeeded his father as Lord Strangford in 1855, and died in 1857. "George Smythe was a splendid failure."

Of Alexander Baillie-Cochrane, the "Buckhurst" of "Coningsby," Lockhart mysteriously wrote: "He is a Cochrane . . . but not a bad fellow." He played no part in public life, though he sate in the House of Commons till 1880, when he was raised to the peerage as Lord Lamington by his old leader, Lord Beaconsfield. In his case the "deceitfulness of riches" was probably the secret of inactivity; for he had by birth most of the boons for which men labour, and he was much too comfortable to be ambitious. I regard him as a hospitable, genial, jovial old gentleman, who enjoyed life in all its aspects, and agreeably diversified a career of fashion, society, and sport with incursions into poetry, fiction, and the literature of the Picturesque.

Henry Hope was one of the less conspicuous members of "Young England," but his wealth gave him a special importance. In dedicating "Coningsby" to him, Disraeli said that the book had been "conceived and partly executed amid the glades and galleries of the Deepdene"—a most beautifully wooded place near Dorking, which contained, in Hope's time, a famous collection of statuary, china, and Italian and Dutch painting. It was there that he assembled his confederates of "Young England," and, after solemn confabulation, "urged the expediency of Disraeli's treating in a literary form those views and subjects which were the matter of their frequent conversations." The results were "Coningsby" and "Sybil," and they were not merely books but events. Yet the man who suggested them has no place in history. He sate in Parliament, off and on, from 1830 to 1852, and died in

1863. Of later years he had chiefly occupied himself in architecture, and his memory lives in a farce. Sir George Trevelyan, in "The Ladies in Parliament," thus indicates the line of the Ladies' Procession—

> "Follow that luxurious pavement all along the Dandy's Slope,
> Past the door where Tom and Jerry robbed the door of Mr Hope,"

and adds in a footnote that "a valuable knocker which, with equal taste and public spirit, Mr Hope had placed upon his door in Piccadilly, was some years ago abstracted by the Mohawks of the period."

Peter Borthwick, a Scotsman who had strayed into English politics, sate for Evesham from 1835 to 1847. The extreme obscurity of his earlier career is illuminated only by the fact that he published a book on the Second Advent and a Lecture on Slavery; but he edited *The Morning Post* from 1847 till his death, which occurred in 1852, and will live in history as the father of the late Lord Glenesk and the grandfather, so to say, of *The Morning Post* as we know it and love it to-day.

So, after all said and done, "Young England," which was to have rehabilitated the Crown, revived the Church, and reunited the Aristocracy and the people by what Lord John Manners called

> "the kind pressure of the social chain,"

ended in nothing more romantic than the personal triumph of Benjamin Disraeli. His name must live as long as the Parliamentary history of England is read, but his confederates are already forgotten. In his Premiership of 1874-1880, he translated into fact the fancies of his youth. When he set out as one of the Plenipotentiaries of England to the Congress of Berlin, he was fulfilling the aspirations of "Vivian Grey" and "Contarini Fleming"; and the policy shadowed forth in "Tancred" was realized when he made Queen Victoria Empress of India.

XLIII

A NEW "YOUNG ENGLAND"

"I AM hoping that there is now in process of formation a new 'Young England' party, filled with the same high ideals as Disraeli pictured, but, being guided by the spirit of Democracy, about to become, instead of a dream, a real means of regeneration of the country." We have been taught to consider it a token of national happiness that the old men should dream dreams, and the young men should see visions. I have no means of knowing whether my friend who believes in a new "Young England" belongs to the former or the latter category, but I observe that in his use of the word "Dream" he follows, though perhaps unwittingly, an idiomatic habit which distinguishes it from "Vision." According to him, the enterprise of the original "Young Englanders" was "a dream"; and by that I understand him to mean something unreal, evanescent, and delusive. This is the usual meaning of "Dream," but "Vision" conveys a quite different significance. He who sees "Visions" sees things as they are. He penetrates through the obscuring medium of time and place and sense, and beholds the ideal perfection of which all that is best in human endeavour or performance is merely the reflection or the foreshadowing. This thought belongs alike to ancient and to modern literature, to sacred and to profane. It is the story of Atlantis and of Utopia, of the Gleam and of the Grail. "The Vision is yet for an appointed time; but at the end it shall speak and shall not lie: though it tarry, wait for it; because it will surely come, it will not tarry." Trusting that my friend's view is in truth a "Vision," I propose to take it as my text, and to enquire into the compatibility of the ideals which animated "Young England" with that "spirit of Democracy" which is to guide the new endeavour.

First and foremost, there is the great question of the Crown. As we lately saw, "Young England" was desperately monarchical. The Sovereign was not only to reign, but to rule. Will the new "Young England," in which my friend believes, take this view? and what will Democracy say to it? Next, the House of Lords. "The natural chiefs of England were the Aristocracy, and the owners of the soil were the stable element of the Constitution." But for the last two years we have been told, with every variety of intonation and every degree of emphasis, that the Lords are the hereditary enemies of popular freedom; and that the soil of England belongs, of right, not to the land-owners but to the Nation. And then the House of Commons—"Young England" denounced it as a "fatal drollery," and "the happy device of a ruder age, to which it was admirably adapted."

To-day the organs of Democracy are telling us that it is the sole depository of legitimate power, and that whatever thwarts its sovereign will must be condemned to instant and ignominious extinction. And, yet once more, the Established Church. "Young England" believed, or professed to believe, in the Church with an ardent enthusiasm, and vehemently resented the slightest infringement of even her temporal privileges. To-day Democracy seeks to regulate the Church's discipline and worship by the votes of a secular House of Commons, and proposes to enforce, at the expense and through the instrumentality of the State, a religion to be formulated by County Councils, under the august sanction of the Board of Education.

Now let us turn to the "New Young England party" which my friend believes to be in process of formation, and see how far it is likely to pursue the ideals and tread in the footsteps of its predecessor. First, as regards the Crown. A famous man of the last century said, "I am no more ashamed of having been a Republican than of having been young." I fancy that there are few young Liberals who have not at one time or another dreamed of an ideal policy, in which the highest place should be accessible to the poorest and the humblest, if only he were the most worthy. A vague Republicanism of this kind, ethical and romantic rather than political and practical, was common enough in my youth. Henry Kingsley touched it very happily in "Silcote of

Silcotes": "James and Reginald, after a fortnight's examination of the question, were quite convinced that Hereditary Governors were a mere stop-gap between the feudalism of the past and the democracy of the future. These terrible young gentlemen had come to the conclusion that Queen Victoria was the last crowned head which would be allowed to exist on the Continent of Europe, and that she was only permitted to exist in consequences of her virtues as mother, wife, and woman."

We have seen the decay of the republican spirit in England and the correlative revival of devotion to the Crown. Something no doubt was due to the divinity that hedged Queen Victoria in her late years; something to the personal popularity of King Edward, and something to that growing love of pomp and pageantry which has so conspicuously marked the last quarter of a century. But another cause which has contributed powerfully to the same result is the ever-increasing insolence of Plutocracy. We have seen the mischief which ill-gotten gold can produce, in South Africa, on the Continent, and at home. We have heard the national flag spoken of as a "Commercial Asset," and we have no mind to put the Headship of the State within the reach of financial combinations. A long-descended Crown is a finer thing than a Presidency speculated in, or gambled for, or bought; and, in this respect, we may expect the "New Young England" to follow its predecessor, and perhaps with a more reasoned and discerning loyalty.

The loyalty of "Young England" to the Throne was blended with, and in a fashion sanctified by, devotion to the Church. That devotion has taken a different form. Surely Establishment and Endowment, and Palaces and Patronage, and Purple and Fine Linen, will be recognized by the "New Young England" as degrading idols, rather than objects of reasonable reverence. The only Church with which Democracy can ally itself is a Church that goes out into the highways and hedges, into the slums and the cellars, and the reeking garrets of a population which lives twelve in a room, and there proclaims "the acceptable Year of the Lord"—the simultaneous deliverance from moral and from physical degradation. The ideal Church shines alike on the evil and on the good. She offers the Supernatural to all who choose to come. She invites the outcast and the downtrodden to find within her walls a resting-place, a sanctuary, and a home. In such a Church as this the "New Young England" may find its natural and most efficient ally.

It is when we approach the House of Lords that I seem to see the parting of the ways. Is it conceivable that the "spirit of Democracy" which my friend invokes will dwell at peace with an irresponsible Legislature, whether "standing where it ought not" in virtue of an hereditary claim, or recruited every few months by the modern processes of sale and barter? It is indeed possible that the schemes of Reconstruction which so severely test the patience of Radicalism, may issue in some Millennium where Democracy and Privilege will dwell together in unity. It is possible; but surely the most inveterate optimist will scarcely call it probable.

And, even if we arrive at a solution of the "Constitutional Question," there will remain the vital subject of the land. "Young England" held that "the natural rulers of England were the Aristocracy supported by the people. To the owners of the soil the tenants and labourers looked up, with a feeling of allegiance; and that allegiance might revive into a living principle if the Aristocracy would deserve it by reverting to the habits of their forefathers." This creed was all very well for Lord John Manners, and might in the present day be very suitably and gracefully professed by Lord Rosebery. But somehow I fancy that my correspondent is looking for his "New Young England" in quite another stratum of social geology. Young poets, young journalists, young ministers of religion, young men of business, young mechanics, young artizans, young workers in the furrow or the mine—these and such as these are, as far as my experience goes, the men who make new and forward movements in democratic politics; and what have they in common with the owners of deer-parks and forests, pastures and covers and corn-lands? or with the men who are growing rich in their sleep on the ground-rents of slums in Manchester or Liverpool? Amid the civil convulsions of 1848, which threatened to shake even our island-throne, Matthew Arnold wrote: "The hour of the hereditary Peerage, and Eldest Son-ship, and immense properties has, I am convinced, struck." The end is not yet; but "the New Young England" may live to see, and perhaps to accelerate, it. Some of my readers perhaps will recognize the following quotation:

"I believe in Democracy. I accept it. I will faithfully serve and defend it. I believe in it, because it appears to me the inevitable consequence of what has gone before it. I grant it is an experiment, but it is the only direction society can take that is worth its taking; the only conception of its duty large enough to satisfy its instincts; the only result that is worth an effort or a risk. Every other possible step is backward, and I do not care to repeat the past. . . . Let us be true to our time. If our age is to be beaten, let us die in the ranks. If it is to be victorious, let us be first to lead the column."

XLIV

"CATHOLIC"

THIS chapter is written by request. A friend in the provinces sends me a cutting from his local journal thus describing the church which he attends: "The order of the services is 'High,' and at special seasons—such as Easter—the ceremony is more distinctly and frankly 'Catholic' than any in the district." My friend says, in his covering letter, "Please give us a chapter on the proper use of terms, and show some of us that a church cannot be 'Catholic' only at certain times of the year."

I am well aware that the subject proposed bristles with controversy; but to handle a controversial topic in an uncontroversial manner may be an exercise not unsuitable to the season [1]; so I comply with my friend's request, and put the pregnant word "Catholic" at the head of this chapter. And then, to show that my purpose is entirely pacific, I hasten to add the exceedingly charitable definition of "Catholic Church" which the Church of England gives in the fifty-fourth Canon: "That is, the whole congregation of Christian people dispersed throughout the whole world."

In the year 1895, a zealous priest of the Roman

[1] Written at Easter 1911.

Communion wrote to Mr Gladstone, urging him to seek peace and safety by joining "the Catholic Church." To this well-intended suggestion, Gladstone promptly replied: "It will surprise you to learn my belief that I was born, and have always lived, in the Catholic Church of this country, founded long before St Augustine extended it; and that by leaving it I should commit an act of rashness and a great sin." To the same effect, when he founded St Deiniol's Library at Hawarden, he wrote in the Deed of Foundation: "The Church of England, I am persuaded, will do nothing, in regard to faith and discipline, to compromise or impair her character as the Catholic and Apostolic Church of this country."

Whether this greatest of Anglican laymen was or was not justified in the claim thus boldly arrogated for the communion to which he belonged, is a question highly controversial. I therefore confess no opinion of my own (though I have a strong one), but cite a very different witness to the same effect. In "St Paul and Protestantism," Matthew Arnold wrote: "It has always been the averment of the Church of England, that the change made in her at the Reformation was the very least change which was absolutely necessary; that she merely got rid of Roman corruptions that were immoral and intolerable, and remained the old historic Catholic Church of England still." To put the case in other words, the Catholic Church, in its strictest sense and fullest extension, is the entire body of Christian people all over the world ; and to us in England it is represented by the lesser body known as the English Church. This, indeed, has been the Anglican "averment." It has been challenged, even vehemently, alike by Romans and by Protestant Nonconformists; and the history of that challenge has been the ecclesiastical history of England for close on four centuries.

The Anglican position has been attacked on both sides. The Romans, "bottoming themselves," as John Evelyn says, "on the inerrancy of Peter," say that the English Church, denying the supremacy of the Pope, is no part of the Catholic Church. Here is our answer: "When we look through, or over, the wall of the Western Church, into the precincts of the Eastern, we seem to find a living confutation of this argument. For there a vast body, nearly a fourth of Christendom, has subsisted from the great day of Pentecost to our own day, which not only does not enjoy, but which renounces and condemns, the whole doctrine of Supremacy ; and which, under the old Patriarchal Constitution of the Church, retains the Christian faith entire, by the acknowledgement of Rome herself, which invites, and invites in vain, to her Councils those unyielding Patriarchs of the East." [1]

The Nonconformists admit that the English Church is indeed a part of the Catholic Church, but insist that the " Free Churches " of the land are equally

[1] Gladstone's " Gleanings," vol. i.

parts of the world-wide whole. I have heard a Roman Catholic say: "If you asked a child in the street the way to the Catholic Church, he would direct you to the Roman Church." But the equally true rejoinder is: "If you asked that child for *the* Church, he would direct you to the Church of England." I have never heard a Nonconformist affirm that even the best-instructed infant would direct an enquirer for "The Church" or "The Catholic Church" to the shrines of Wesleyanism or Congregationalism; though, as the amenities of religious intercourse spread downwards, even this may become possible; and, in the meanwhile, the tiny sect of so-called "Irvingites" disdain any other title than that of "Catholic Apostolic Church," though they claim that title in no exclusive sense. "The Catholic Apostolic Church," wrote Newman in "Loss and Gain," "was at that time meeting in Huggermugger Lane," though it has long since emerged into the Gothic glories of Gordon Square.

It is curious that those who have most vehemently protested against the Roman claims have, in days gone by, often conceded the chief of those claims by using the word "Catholic" as a synonym for "Roman Catholic." 1829 is, in popular parlance, the year of "Catholic Emancipation," and in 1851, when what was called "The Papal Aggression" had frightened England out of its senses, a Protestant Bishop, addressing a public meeting, said: "We are assembled here to protest against the Catholic

Faith," whereupon a voice from the back of the hall was heard to ejaculate the Athanasian formula: " Which faith except everyone do keep whole and undefiled, without doubt he shall perish everlastingly."

Amid the strife of tongues, Matthew Arnold took, as always, a healing and persuasive line. " So on the word *Catholic* we will not insist too jealously; but this much, at any rate, must be allowed to the Church of England—that she kept enough of the past to preserve, as far as this nation was concerned, her continuity, and to be still the historic Church of England." For my own part, that satisfies me. I am content to belong to " the historic Church of England," and to believe that, in so belonging, I belong to the Catholic Church.

But it willl be observed that, in the passage which my correspondent reprehends, the epithet *Catholic* is applied to " Ceremony," by which the writer probably meant ceremonial. Whether we interpret *Catholic* in its wider or its narrower sense, this use of it must, I think, be wrong. If Catholic means universal, it is rightly applied to a Society or Church which exists all over the world, and to the faith which that Society professes. But there is no such thing as universal " ceremony " or ceremonial. There is Roman ceremonial, and even that, as liturgiologists know, includes considerable diversity. There is the ceremonial practised by the Holy Orthodox Churches of the East, and this is as different from Roman ceremonial as the climate of Moscow is different from the climate of Capua. There is English ceremonial, which again has a marked type and character of its own ; and there is the ceremonial of Protestantism, which, whether one admires it or not, is at least unlike anything else in the world. Furthermore, "Catholic," as Christians use the word, means not only universal in extension, but immemorial in date ; or, in the words of a famous definition, what has been accepted always, everywhere, and by all. The word has a very definite meaning when attached to belief ; but when applied to ceremonial, it fails. The circumstances of worship in the Upper Chamber, in the Catacombs, and in the Desert were not such as lend themselves to ceremonial ; and few indeed are the Christian rites (outside the Sacraments themselves) which can be traced to the third century. A ceremonial dating from the first days of the Church, and prevailing all over the world, does not exist, and therefore to speak of "the ceremony" of a particular Church at a special season as being "distinctly and frankly Catholic," and more so at one time than another, is a misuse of words. The rule of ceremonial was established by St Paul, in words which have been rendered : "Let all things be done in right, graceful, or becoming figure, and by fore-ordered arrangement." As long as God has held intercourse with man, He has expressed spiritual truths in material forms ; and the Church has always believed that visible beauty is the Vesture of the Divine. She has therefore, in all ages and in all places, striven, as far as her circumstances permitted it, to make her worship beautiful. Her ceremonial has developed with an elastic richness, which in its way resembles the pliant growths and many-coloured raiment of the natural world; and whatever she has of glory and beauty she naturally lavishes on the yearly commemoration of the event, lacking which Christians would be, as St Paul felt, of all men the most to be pitied.

My good friend Mr Birrell, who came rather late in life to the consideration of these subjects, used to say that he could feel the presence of the Mass at Havre, and could feel the absence of it at Cromer; but in recent years he has learned an exacter use of words, and he thus comments on the outward aspect of the Church's worship: "The pious citizen of Antioch, who lent his house for the assembling together of those who were first called Christians, would be much startled could he see and hear the Mass as it is performed to-day either in St Peter's, Rome, or in St Paul's, London."

This is perfectly true; and it would be accepted, not as blame, but as eulogy, by those who are most intimately connected, whether as ministrants or as worshippers, with the rites described. A letter, received since Easter Day, lies ready to my hand:—

"Just at Easter, I feel the heart of St Paul's

beating, and all the many altars shining for us—each of us—to say our Mass. All the rush and flow and glory of the choir, and the trumpet-stops, and the *shout* we give on 'Now above the sky He's KING!' There's nothing like it in all the world. And the great church is flooded with people all day long; and we never stop; and it is all one splendour."

There, if you like, is the true note of "Catholic" worship.

XLV

THE PARSONS' TEAM

HARRY BUMPSTEAD was the pride of Roslyn School. We all know Roslyn as delineated for us by the vivid pen of the late Dean Farrar, but I fancy, from what Bumpstead has told me, that it has changed a good deal since the days of Eric and Owen and Montagu and "holy and happy Edwin Russell." Certainly I cannot imagine my friend Bumpstead being on very intimate terms with any of those worthies. He never was spiteful or calumnious, but, if his opinion had been invited, he would have lumped them together as "ghastly rotters," and then would have dismissed them from his mind. I have said that Bumpstead was the glory of the school. His glory did not consist in intellectual brilliancy, though he had plenty of good sense; nor in his moral character, though that was of the highest. Glory in these latter days belongs to athletics, and Bumpstead was glorious because he played Rugby football better than any contemporary schoolboy. From Roslyn he passed to Bungay College, Oxford (so called from its founder, Benedictus de Boungaye, Bishop, *in partibus*, of Melipotamus). Bungay is a college famous for football, so Bumpstead was welcomed with open arms; played for his college within a week of his matriculation, and covered himself and Bungay with lustre by getting his Blue in his first year. His four years at Oxford were given with lavish prodigality to "Rugger," and, if he spared a few weeks to rowing in the summer Term, it was only because there was no "footer" to play. His name was honoured wherever Football Intelligence was read. "Surveying all the Paladins of that game, which, far more than her Parliament, her literature, or her commerce, has made old England great, we affirm, without fear of contradiction, that the most consummate exponent of the science who now titillates the leather is that typical old 'sport,' Harry Bumpstead, of Bungay."

Thus *The Football News*, and other sporting papers wrote in the same sense, only some of them called the ball "the pill," and others "the sphere"; but this is the classical style of sporting journalese. The prophets proclaimed that "international honours were reserved" for Harry Bumpstead; but, as soon as he took his degree (or "donned the rabbit-skin," as the sporting ones preferred to say), he disappeared from the football world, except in so far as a Saturday afternoon's game at his Theological College gave him the opportunity of astonishing a local team of choirmen and Elementary School-teachers. The mention of a Theological College reminds me that, when it became known that Bumpstead was going to seek Holy Orders, no one was surprised. On the contrary, it seemed the most natural thing in the world. He had been neither a priggish schoolboy nor a Ritualistic undergraduate ; but he had been, in all places and at all stages, so simply good that everyone recognized in him the stuff out of which priests are made. His career as a footballer had been remarkable for thoroughness, pluck, and hard work, and everyone felt certain that the same characteristics would mark his ministry. When the time drew near for ordination he chose the South London Diocese, and in due course found himself established as junior curate in the thriving suburb of Brickville.

He entered on his parochial work with all the zest of an unspoiled nature and a fresh experience. He was a Hercules in body and a Galahad in heart. Every month as it passed showed with increasing clearness that he had realized his true vocation, and found the path of life in which he would be happiest and most useful. His preaching was plain and fresh, and was enforced by the cogent arguments of conduct and character. The sick felt the charm of his strong but gentle presence. The children in the schools romped with him as with an elder brother. The opulent inhabitants of Campidoglio Lodge and Laurustinus Villa competed for the pleasure of giving him his Sunday dinner ; and, if the ladies of Brickville could have had their way, he would never have had his tea at the Clergy-House. The Vicar could scarcely show his face in the street without encountering a chorus of gratitude from the parochial waterproofs. "Oh, Vicar, what a delightful colleague you have found! At last we have got an Assistant Priest after our own hearts. As an old woman in my district said the other day, 'I do declare as that young man is quite an angel in sheep's clothing.'"

Yet, in spite of all this popularity and praise, those who knew Bumpstead well could see that he was not perfectly happy. He was by nature reticent about subjects which lay near his heart, though he would chatter for ever about Queen's Club. He had, in truth, a secret grief; not dyspeptic in origin, as young men's griefs so often are, for he could have digested a football; nor yet romantic, for he was contentedly, and rather contemptuously, heart-whole. No. Bumpstead's grief was pastoral. In seeking Holy Orders he had not destined himself to be merely a comforter of the sick and infirm, a play-fellow of children, or a sitter at rich men's feasts, or the light of suburban tea-tables. All these functions were well enough in their way, all "came within his job"; but he longed very specially to be a "Man's Parson." Manly in every physical and mental fibre, in keen sympathy with all forms of manliness in others, adhering with all his heart to the dogma that he who would put off the Old Man need not put on the Old Woman, he longed to help his fellow-men to that true manliness which means a disciplined body and a self-controlling will. And here was the disappointment. The working men of Brickville, and especially the young men, were absolutely irresponsive to his ministry. They were perfectly civil when he visited them in their homes, offered him tea, talked about the Boat Race and the All Blacks; but on the subject for which he really cared they maintained a stony silence. They never crossed the threshold of the church; and, though they would play billiards all night at the Parochial Club, they gave it a very wide berth when a lecture or a Bible Class was billed. Gradually, for the most flippant Tram-conductor, the most obdurate Road-mender, could not long stand out against Bumpstead's simple and unaffected geniality, the truth leaked out. In the view of these excellent but unenlightened men, religion was all very well for people "getting on in years," for ladies who had nothing else to do, for weak-minded youths, and "sloppy girls," but it had no relation to the daily life of ordinary men; and parsons—well, they were pleasant-spoken gentlemen, and did a lot of good in the schools and when there was illness about, but, in some sense clearly understood though not easy to explain, they were something less than men.

To Bumpstead, who, though absolutely free from the athlete's swelled head, could not but be conscious that he was in every sense a man, this doctrine, so entirely opposed to what he had learnt at Roslyn and Bungay, was a hard saying. In all his leisure hours he pondered it, and often asked himself if there could be any foundation for such a view. Even in the pulpit, when he gazed on the wide expanse of many-coloured millinery, the same thought sometimes obtruded itself; and, if he had not been tightly "tied to the paper," he would certainly have burst out some day with the passionate avowal that the office of a Woman's Preacher was not that to which he had meant to dedicate his life.

One Saturday afternoon Bumpstead was taking his weekly "breather" in the comparatively open country which Brickville has not yet overflowed, when he observed with interest a game of Rugby football—not a common sight in South London. As he watched the game he noticed that some of the players were inhabitants of Brickville, and on inquiry he learned that Brickville possessed a Rugby Football Club, and often found a difficulty in arranging a match owing to the prevalence of the Association game. (At Brickville we do not talk of "Rugger" and "Soccer.") It was one of the decisive moments of life. At last he saw his way. Now or never. "Stung by the splendour of a sudden thought," he lay in wait for the Brickville captain, praised the sportsmanlike comportment of the practising teams, and then launched his insidious proposal. "If I could collect a team of parsons, would your club play us one Saturday afternoon?" "Of course," was the reply, "with pleasure. It would be a little holiday to us, we could do it on our heads"—with other phrases of good-natured disdain. Off went Bumpstead, and in three days had collected a team of his own profession, composed of Internationals, Blues, and men who had played for their colleges. A fortnight later the match came off, amid intense excitement, on the local ground. I append an account of the match transcribed from *The Football News*; and, after the lapse of all these years, there can be no harm in giving the real names of the clerical combatants, only substituting that of Bumpstead for a fictitious "Rev. A. P. Arson":

"This fixture came off on Crackshins Common on Saturday last, when many good men and true—alas! now consigned to oblivion—turned out to show that they hadn't quite forgotten how to play the game. The Parsons, though lacking the services of the Revs. R. H. Cattell and E. M. Baker, had the upper hand throughout, and won easily by three goals (kicked by Howard) and four tries to a penalty goal and a try. The game was full of interest to the spectators, and many a cry of 'Break their necks, and they won't be able to preach on Sunday' was humorously raised by the local supporters. The Parsons, however, were far the more powerful team, and their forward rushes, headed by A. C. Elwes (three tries), R. B. Littlewood, and L. J. Percival (two tries), all of the Oxford University XV., were the feature of the game. The match was played throughout in a most sporting spirit, and the opponents parted with much mutual goodwill. The Parsons' Team was as follows:—Rev. H. Bumpstead (Bungay, Oxford), K. Clarke (Emmanuel, Cambridge), A. J. Thompson (St John's, Cambridge), H. E. Newton (Emmanuel, Cambridge), E. T. Johnson (Queens', Cambridge), H. Holden (Worcester, Oxford), H. H. Winterbottom (Durham University), L. J. Percival (Trinity, Oxford), R. B. Littlewood (Wadham, Oxford), A. C. Carey-Elwes (St John's, Oxford), W. J. Carey (Hertford, Oxford), H. Lee (Keble, Oxford), F. Howard (Keble, Oxford), E. Bryant (Emmanuel, Cambridge), and H. S. Woollcombe (Keble, Oxford)."

So Harry Bumpstead won his match, and a good deal besides. The unquestionable success of St Boniface, Brickville, in attracting and keeping the young men of the parish may, I believe, be referred, at least in part, to the historic encounter which still lives in parochial annals as "The Cloth *v.* The Corduroys."

XLVI

GILBERT ON THE WHITE HORSE[1]

" THE Gilbertines were an order of Canons and Nuns established at Sempringham in Lincolnshire, by Gilbert of that place—in 1131. At the Dissolution there were 25 houses of the Order in England and Wales." I quote from the Ecclesiastical Dictionary of the learned Dr Dryasdust, but my copy is out of date. When a fresh edition appears, it will certainly refer to a revival of the Order, *circ.* 1900, originating, not at Sempringham, but in London, where " Gilbert of that place " gathered round him a company of loving disciples. This Order spread to a great many more than " 25 houses in England and Wales "; and presently its centre shifted from London to Beaconsfield, but the genial Re-founder remained unchanged by change of environment. One of his disciples, finding prose all powerless to express his devotion, declared that this second Gilbert was:

> " The sweetest thing that ever grew
> Beside a cottage door " ;

[1] " Ballad of the White Horse." By G. K. Chesterton. Methuen & Co.

and it was universally admitted that the author of the Sonnet beginning:

> "Stilton, thou should'st be living at this hour"—

was of the lineage of Wordsworth.

But historical analogies should not be unduly pressed, nor parables indefinitely extended. Let me say then, quite plainly, that Mr Gilbert Keith Chesterton, a son of the soil of London, who knows its many-coloured life and has described it enchantingly in prose and verse, has of late betaken himself to pastures new and fresh inspirations. In the first chapter of "Tom Brown" (which is worth all the rest put together) we were taught when we were young to love the Vale of White Horse, with its glorious legends of Ashdown, where Alfred broke the Danish power, and made England a Christian land. "After which crowning mercy, the pious King, that there might never be wanting a sign and a memorial to the country-side, carved out on the northern side of the chalk hill the great Saxon White Horse, that gives its name to the Vale, over which it has looked these thousand years or more."

Mr Chesterton, having deserted London and quartered himself at Beaconsfield, has taken up his pilgrim-staff, and made his way through the beech-clad recesses of the Chilterns, past the spires of Oxford, to the steep slopes of those Berkshire downs, where men still cherish the story of Alfred with his Cakes and his Harp and his conquering Sword. It is in vain for Dryasdust to suggest inglorious doubts : Mr Chesterton brushes him aside with appropriate contempt. " I do not know when or where the story started ; it is enough that it started somewhere and ended with me ; for I only seek to write upon hearsay, as the old balladists did." If hearsay were always as good as this, we should want no history. Mr Chesterton has taken the tale of Alfred, " fighting for the Christian civilization against the heathen nihilism," and has woven it into a ballad worthy of the name. A curiously inept critic has suggested that " Mr Chesterton ought to have been a Troubadour " ; but light, fantastic prettiness and love-making, poised on one toe and playing a guitar, are not the characteristics of Mr Chesterton's ballad. It is a song of fighting ; of impassioned yet disciplined strength ; of deep humility and self-mistrust, and of victorious faith.

The verbal medium through which this is conveyed shows afresh the writer's command over the illimitably rich resources of our English speech ; the glowing, apt, " inevitable " words, which all the time are lying ready to be used, but which most of us are too unskilful to discover. As to form, well, the very idea of a ballad justifies irregularity, and may condone some unwelcome reminiscences of Macaulay's " Lays," and here and there a rhyme which is true only to the eye.

Mr Chesterton rides his metre as one rides an impetuous horse. As we gallop along by his side, we feel the brisk air of the Downs stinging our faces, and the short turf soft under out feet ; and the horses catch the freshness of the hill-tops, and strain between our knees, and every now and then take a strong pull on the bridle, and, unless we can take a stronger pull, will inevitably bolt. But then comes in Mr Chesterton's horsemanship. His mount is as fresh as a four-year-old, and pulls in sheer exuberance—but does not bolt. In other words, he is master of his metre.

In Book I. King Alfred, who has fallen on evil times, seeks comfort, in a vision, from the Mother of God :

> "' When our last bow is broken, Queen,
> And our last javelin cast,
> Under some sad, green, evening sky,
> Holding a ruined cross on high,
> Under warm westland grass to lie,
> Shall we come home at last ? ' "

And the reply is not what he desired.

> "' I tell you naught for your comfort,
> Yea, naught for your desire,
> Save that the sky grows darker yet,
> And the sea rises higher.' "

That verse might serve as an epitome of the whole ballad.

In Book II. Alfred, who has heard in the Voice of the Vision a call to arms, sets out to collect his forces for a more desperate encounter.

"'I am that oft-defeated King,
Whose failure fills the land,
Who fled before the Danes of old,
Who chaffered with the Danes for gold,
Who now upon the Wessex wold
Hardly has feet to stand.'"

Yet, inspired by what the Blessed Mother has told him, he summons all true hearts to his side.

"'For I go gathering Christian men
From sunken paving and ford and fen,
To die in a battle, God knows when,
By God, but I know why.'"

And one of the chiefs makes answer :

"'Where would you meet ? For you must hold
Half Wiltshire and the White Horse wold,
And the Thames bank to Owsenfold
If Wessex goes to war !'

'If each man on the Judgment Day
Meet God on a plain alone,'
Said Alfred, 'I will speak for you
As for myself, and call it true
That you brought all fighting folk you knew
Lined under Egbert's Stone.'"

Book III. discovers Alfred a wandering pilgrim, with an old harp on his arm. The heathen are in the land, and all around are the signs of their habitation.

"The fires of the Great Army
That was made of iron men,
Whose lights of sacrilege and scorn
Ran around England red as morn,
Fires over Glastonbury Thorn—
Fires out on Ely Fen.

King Alfred gazed all sorrowful
  At thistle and mosses grey,
Till a rally of Danes with shield and bill
Rolled drunk over the dome of the hill,
And, hearing of his harp and skill,
  Men dragged him to their play."

And there they sate carousing, and singing their heathenish songs of slaughter and lust and the spoils of conquest.

" Great wine like blood from Burgundy,
  Cloaks like the clouds from Tyre,
And marble like solid moonlight,
  And gold like frozen fire.

Smells that a man might swill in a cup,
  Stones that a man might eat,
And the great smooth women, like ivory,
  That the Turks sell in the street."

And then, on all this debauch of insolent animalism, falls the warning word of the unknown King.

" ' Sirs, I am but a nameless man,
  A rhymester without home,
Yet, since I come of the Wessex clay
  And carry the Cross of Rome,

I will even answer the mighty earl
  That asked of Wessex men
Why they be meek and monkish folk,
And bow to the White Lord's broken yoke ;
  Here is my answer then.

That on you is fallen the shadow,
  And not upon the Name ;
That though we scatter and though we fly,
And you hang over us like the sky,
You are more tired of victory,
  Than we are tired of shame.

That though you hunt the Christian man
Like a hare on the hill-side,
The hare has still more heart to run,
Than you have heart to ride.' "

Book IV. presents the long-loved tale of Alfred and the Cakes—" disputed," says Mr Chesterton, " by grave historians, who were, I think, a little too grave to be judges of it." So here is Alfred in the hut:

" Bright-eyed, but lean and pale ;
And swordless, with his harp and rags,
He seemed a beggar, such as lags
Looking for crusts and ale."

And the woman pitied his poor plight, and bade him mind the cakes, and promised one for his reward ; and he fell to meditating on the miseries of servitude, and wished the woman a happier portion —and so:

" The good food fell upon the ash,
And blackened instantly."

And then the punishment:

" Screaming, the woman caught a cake
Yet burning from the bar,
And struck him suddenly on the face,
Leaving a scarlet scar."

And for one moment the torture awoke the demon of offended pride ; but strong self-mastery beat him down. The woman who struck the blow shall go scot-free, and the insult shall ennoble while it stings.

"'He that hath failed in a little thing
Hath a sign upon the brow;
And the Earls of the Great Army
Have no such seal to show.
This blow that I return not
Ten times will I return
On Kings and Earls of all degree,
And armies wide as empires be
Shall slide like landslips to the sea,
If the red star burn.'"

Books V., VI., and VII. give the ballad of Ethandune:

"Then Alfred, King of England,
Bade blow the horns of war,
And fling the Golden Dragon out,
With crackle and acclaim and shout,
Scrolled and aflame and far."

And in Book VIII. we read the conclusion of the tale, and withal its interpretation:

"In the days of the rest of Alfred,
When all these things were done,
And Wessex lay in a patch of peace,
Like a dog in a patch of sun—

The King sat in his orchard,
Among apples green and red,
With the little book in his bosom,
And the sunshine on his head."

And there he held his Court, and gave the law, and ruled with the strong hand, and punished the wrong-doer, and let his almsgiving flow like a river in flood; and bore himself in all things as a high Christian King.

And, when he began to draw towards his end, he bade his followers keep the Great White Horse scoured and clean, as an everlasting memorial of the great victory of Light over Darkness. Yet, even as he uttered his command, the shadow of a doubt fell upon his soul, and he remembered the Virgin Mother's prophecy that the skies would darken once again for a perilous storm ; and he foresaw that the white symbol would grow dim, and that the once-conquered enemy would lift his hated head once more.

> " I know that weeds shall grow in it
> Faster than men can burn ;
> And, though they scatter now and go,
> In some far century, sad and slow,
> I have a vision, and I know
> The heathen shall return.
>
> . . . .
>
> They shall come mild as monkish clerks,
> With many a scroll and pen ;
> And backward shall ye turn and gaze,
> Desiring one of Alfred's days,
> When pagans still were men.
>
> By this sign ye shall know them,
> The breaking of the sword,
> And Man no more a free knight,
> That loves or hates his lord.
>
> Yea, this shall be the sign of them,
> The sign of the dying fire ;
> And Man made like a half-wit,
> That knows not of his sire.
>
> What though they come with scroll and pen,
> And grave as a shaven clerk,
> By this sign you shall know them,
> That they ruin and make dark ;

By all men bond to Nothing,
Being slaves without a lord,
By one blind idiot-world obeyed,
Too blind to be abhorred.

By terror and the cruel tales
Of curse in bone and kin,
By detail of the sinning,
And denial of the sin ;

By thought a crawling ruin,
By life a leaping mire,
By a broken heart in the breast of the world.
And the end of the world's desire ;

By God and man dishonoured,
By death and life made vain,
Know ye the old barbarian,
The barbarian come again."

There is Mr Chesterton's true message to the age. He sees what our authorized teachers of Religion either fail to see, or, seeing, prefer to ignore. He sees that, masking their true natures under a parade of pseudo-science, " the heathen have come into the inheritance " of Christendom. He detects in their jargon of " lesser breeds," and the rights of " the Blood," and " the survival of the fittest," and the supremacy of brute force, the negation of the Christian Ethic and the dethronement of the Christian Ideal. He sees that the Offence of the Cross has not ceased ; that there is no discharge in the war to which the followers of the Cross are pledged ; and that the eternal duty of the Church is not to court or caress, but to fight and to conquer, the " obscene empires of Mammon and Belial."